I
THE MEANING OF THE FIRST-PERSON TERM

I
The Meaning of the First-Person Term

MAXIMILIAN DE GAYNESFORD

CLARENDON PRESS · OXFORD

OXFORD
UNIVERSITY PRESS

Great Clarendon Street, Oxford OX2 6DP

Oxford University Press is a department of the University of Oxford.
It furthers the University's objective of excellence in research, scholarship,
and education by publishing worldwide in

Oxford New York

Auckland Cape Town Dar es Salaam Hong Kong Karachi
Kuala Lumpur Madrid Melbourne Mexico City Nairobi
New Delhi Shanghai Taipei Toronto

With offices in

Argentina Austria Brazil Chile Czech Republic France Greece
Guatemala Hungary Italy Japan Poland Portugal Singapore
South Korea Switzerland Thailand Turkey Ukraine Vietnam

Oxford is a registered trade mark of Oxford University Press
in the UK and in certain other countries

Published in the United States
by Oxford University Press Inc., New York

© Maximilian de Gaynesford 2006

British Library Cataloguing in Publication Data
Data available

Library of Congress Cataloging in Publication Data

De Gaynesford, Maximilian.
I: the meaning of the first person term/Maximilian de Gaynesford.
p. cm.
1. Grammer, Comparative and general–Person. 2. Personality. 3. Reference
(Linguistics) 4. Reasoning (Psychology) 5. Language and Logic I. Title.
P240. 85. D4 2006
415'. 5–dc22
2005036618

Typeset by SPI Publisher Services, Pondicherry, India
Printed in Great Britain on acid-free paper by
Biddles Ltd., King's Lynn, Norfolk

ISBN 0-19-928782-1   978-0-19-928782-6

1 3 5 7 9 10 8 6 4 2

To the memory of my father
JOHN WILLIAM DE GAYNESFORD
Ung Foy Je Tens

Preface

I is perhaps the most important and the least understood of our everyday (every *minute*) expressions. This is a bizarre situation, a constant source of deep philosophical confusion, and it calls urgently for treatment. This book offers a remedy by giving the meaning of the expression.

The book is written so that the reader may begin with either part. The first reviews what we do not know in order to ask. The second establishes what we need to know in order to answer. So those who need immediate assurance that previous accounts of *I* fail should begin with Part I. Part II is the starting place for those who want to know at once what I propose and why. The book is ordered in this way because previous accounts can be undermined without appeal to the advantages of an alternative; they fail in their own terms.

To grasp the meaning of *I* is to understand the device used to express first-personal thinking. Knowing how such thoughts are expressed is necessary if we are to investigate first-personal thinking itself. That enquiry is not pursued here, though it is one to which the conclusion looks forward. So I have written in large part for those without specialist knowledge in the philosophy of language but who can nevertheless make use of the findings.

Achieving this aim has dictated content and style. The book tries to stimulate rather than assume interest in questions about the meaning of *I*. Narrative is prominent, with a radically different conception of the term emerging from the history of debate. I have drawn constantly and gratefully on the vast literature devoted to the first person, but have resisted the temptation to survey this ever-accumulating body of work. My aim is to be thorough and engaged, not comprehensive.

The book develops, corrects, and supersedes material presented and published since 1994, when I began defending its central claims (de Gaynesford 1996*a*; 1996*b*; 1997*a*; 1997*b*; 1998; 2001; 2002; 2003*a*; 2003*b*). The first drafts of the book formed the basis of successive graduate classes at Reading (1996; 1997), Oxford (1999; 2000; 2002), Bremen (2001), and Berlin (2003). I also benefited from giving individual faculty talks, seminars, colloquia, and conference papers on different aspects of the material over the past decade. I remember particularly useful discussions with audiences at Arizona State University, Auckland, the Freie Universität Berlin, Birmingham, Boulder, Bremen, the University of Kent at Canterbury, the College of William and Mary in Virginia, Liverpool, King's College London, Old Dominion University, Oxford, Pittsburgh, Portland, Reading, the University of Southern California, and Virginia Commonwealth University.

Many individuals read parts of the text at various stages of its development and gave me helpful criticism: Peter Bieri, John Bishop, Karin Boxer, Robert Brandom, Bill Brewer, John Campbell, Quassim Cassam, Sara Coulon, John Cotting-ham, Sean Crawford, Jonathan Dancy, Martin Davies, Simon Glendinning, Hanjo Glock, Lisa Grimes, Peter Hacker, Jim Higginbotham, Brad Hooker, John Hyman, Frederick Kroon, Gerald Lang, John McDowell, Elinor Mason, Eugene Mills, Georg Mohr, Stephen Mulhall, Lucy O'Brien, David Oderberg, Michael O'Rourke, Derek Parfit, John Preston, Brett Price, Michael Proudfoot, Michael Rosen, Adrianne Rubin, Kenneth Safir, Galen Strawson, Peter Strawson, Christine Swanton, Stephen Williams, and anonymous readers of the Press.

The final draft was written in 2003–4 while I was on leave from the College of William and Mary as an Alexander von Humboldt research fellow. I thank both institutions for support, John Hyman for encouragement, and the editors of the Press, Rupert Cousens and Peter Momtchiloff, for guidance. I have made use of material from my 'Corporeal Objects and the Interdependence of Action and Perception' (*Ratio* (2002), 335–53) and 'Is *I* Guaranteed to Refer?' (*Pacific Philosophical Quarterly* (2003), 138–56) by permission of Blackwell Publishing, and from my 'On Referring to Oneself' (*Theoria* (2004), 121–61) by permission of Stiftelsen Bokförlaget Thales.

I would like to record my deep gratitude to former students and colleagues at Lincoln College Oxford, and particularly Michael Rosen, for setting me on this career in so ideally happy and richly instructive a way.

M. de G.

28 January 2006
Williamsburg, Virginia

let me now sum up, after this digression, there is I, yes, I feel it, I confess, I give in, there is I, it's essential, it's preferable, I wouldn't have said so, I won't always say so, so let me hasten to take advantage of being now obliged to say, in a manner of speaking, that there is I

(Samuel Beckett, *L'Innomable*, 1952)

Contents

Introduction

Gottlob Frege declared that *I* 'gives rise to some questions'. Those with an ear for his artful style will hear in this offhand phrase calculated hints of the dismay in Wittgenstein's cry: 'The I, the I is what is deeply mysterious!' Bertrand Russell once tried to let the air out of the debate, saying that *I* is a term 'which we all know how to use, and which must therefore have some easily accessible meaning'. But the underlying stridency of tone hints at the affectation in this tranquil pose. And Russell had reason to be a trifle desperate, being about to offer his third solution in as many years. He would eventually admit that misconceptions about the meaning of *I* are 'very hard to avoid, but very fatal if they are not avoided'.[1]

Viewed generously, Russell's more optimistic remark can be regarded as the awkward embellishment of a plain and helpful truth. Our universal expertise with the use of a term demands that an adequate explanation of its meaning look to that fluency. Those very strands of shared familiarity, if heeded, can help supply such an account. Taking the advice, this book focuses on our common usage, on things 'which we all know', in an attempt to explain the meaning of *I* as plainly as possible.

'Why bother?' someone might ask. There would be little point if the meaning of *I* were something obvious and commonly agreed on by philosophers of language and linguists. But it is not. Frege's serene tone should not mislead. It is the studied cool of someone who would say of Late Capitalism that it 'gives rise to some questions'. In the case of *I*, the most troublesome are those on which we shall focus. What is the logical character of the term? What does it contribute to the inferential properties of the sentences in which it occurs? How does it refer? What puts us in a position to express thoughts with it? How are we able to communicate thoughts with it?

Of course, such questions could safely be ignored if the issues were of no moment beyond the professional wrangling of certain experts. But they are not. First-personal thinking is not well understood because we have deeply misunderstood its expression using *I*. And it is important we should appreciate both. This was clear even before Descartes's *Cogito ergo sum* inaugurated our philosophical

---

[1] Frege (1918: 24). Wittgenstein (1916: 80). Russell (1914: 164; 163). For the three views, see Russell (1910: 212; 1912: 27–8; 1914: 165).

era by demonstrating the magnitude of these issues in the clearest possible fashion: that from the expression of thoughts using *I* all our knowledge of the world might derive.

Since the Early Modern period, much great and significant work in philosophy has depended on assumptions and conjectures about the meaning of *I*. Descartes had better be right to regard *I* as a referring term and as an expression whose uses are logically guaranteed against reference-failure. Otherwise his meditator obtains no release whatsoever from the depths of his methodological doubt. Hume had better be justified in assuming that one can express thoughts using *I* without identifying what is being referred to. Only so can he derive the distinctive feature of his epistemology: that we have no idea corresponding to the self. Kant had better be right that *I* is capable of serving as a completely empty term in the phrase *I think*, one without referential or ascriptive significance. Otherwise his *Transcendental Deduction* cannot account for the possibility of experience. A major motivation for this book is seeing which such views are correct, which assumptions are justified, which conjectures stand up to scrutiny.

To clarify parameters at the outset: this book focuses on the meaning of *I* rather than on the thoughts it expresses. The two subjects are intimately related, as I have noted. Indeed the book will argue that first-personal thinking will remain confused and opaque until we appreciate the fact that it is expressed by a term deeply akin to *You* and *He/She*. But it is possible to divide labour. A sound understanding of the meaning of *I* will remove major obstacles hindering investigation of first-personal thinking. That is why I have thought the problem worth addressing, and it is why readers outside the philosophy of language might want to work through the argument to the results. We need knowledge of the kind to be provided here, knowledge of expressions, if we are to investigate what I have not supplied: knowledge of the thoughts expressed.

To say that this book is about the meaning of *I* is convenient shorthand. 'The meaning' of an expression stands here for its logical character, inferential role, referential function, expressive use, and communicative role. And '*I*' is short for all and only expressions used to formulate first-personal reference in any language.

The latter phrase may seem circular, but it is not. For first-person reference need not use *I*, and *I* need not be used for first-person reference. On the one hand, then, this book is not *only* about use of the word *I*. It is also about its formal variants, like *Me*, *Mine*, and *My*; about words whose occurrence in sentences substitutes for *I*, like the arch use of *One* in 'Thank you Jeeves; one will have supper now'; and about whatever terms are used for expressing first-personal reference in languages other than English, whether they be separate words like *je*, *ich*, and *ego*, or contained in verbal inflections like *cogito* and *sum*, or embedded in compounds. On the other hand, this book is not about *every* use of *I*. For *I* and its formal variants in various languages have eccentric uses which do not express first-personal reference. So a speaker who has some identifying property might, for example, use *I* as a *general* term, one that stands for all those with that same property. This is the case when a mother-in-law says, 'I am conventionally a figure of fun,' confident that her audience will take her to be embracing all mothers-in-law. If this is indeed a use of *I*, rather than a homonym, it is certainly not the expression of first-personal reference. For such reference is expressed using a *singular* term. Hence it is not dealt with here. (There are superficially similar cases of which we should be wary, such as the condemned prisoner's utterance 'I am traditionally allowed to order whatever I like for my last meal.'[2] Here, the speaker is intuitively to be heard as using the singular term *I* rather than its general cognate. For unlike the mother-in-law case, the salient reference is to a single person and not the category to which the person belongs: 'It is I who ought to be allowed to order whatever I like; for I am a condemned prisoner; and condemned prisoners are traditionally given this privilege.')

There are various advantages to focusing on first-person reference rather than on whatever reference *I* expresses. These advantages will be felt when the findings of this enquiry into expression are applied in subsequent work to the thoughts expressed. For it has become customary to speak of '*I*-thoughts' in such a way as to narrow investigations to those thoughts which are actually expressed by the term.[3] Such talk will be avoided here. This is partly because it is potentially misleading: it smudges the distinction between the thoughts expressed by *I* and their expression using *I*. It is also unduly restrictive. Consider our use of *One* as an example. Sometimes it is synonymous with *We* of some implied category like social class, as in 'One holds one's knife like *this*.' But it can also stand for *I*. Thus Tennyson's wife was evidently expressing a first-personal thought when she asked to be called 'Emily Lady Tennyson' after his death, rather than 'the Dowager Lady Tennyson', noting that 'there seems to be in it a feeling that one is still his wife as one feels that one is'.[4] Moreover, we can imagine terms used to express first-personal thinking that are quite unlike the English *I* in belonging to a severely restricted class of users. It seems that Japanese emperors reserved to themselves exclusive use of one such expression. Our interest is in what is common to these terms. So our findings will be relevant to thoughts expressed in all these different ways.

The key to understanding *I* is that it is the same kind of expression as the other singular personal pronouns, *You* and *He/She*. That is the central claim of the book.

It might seem mildly astonishing that this was ever in doubt, let alone conventionally denied. Yet the dramatic isolation of *I* is one of the very few positions which can claim near-unanimous support among philosophers. So the claims advanced by this book encounter resistance all along the way, together with forms of opposition whose attractiveness needs to be understood. Overcoming resistance is not a bad thing. All mill and no grist would make philosophy a dull job. Moreover, as Aristotle encourages: 'We should not only state the true view, but also explain the false view, since an explanation of that promotes confidence. For

---

[2] Nunberg (1993).   [3] For example, Evans (1982: 205–66); Bermúdez (1998: *passim*).
[4] Martin (1980: 583).

when we have an apparently reasonable explanation of why a false view appears true, that makes us more confident of the true view.'⁵ But the aims and objectives of the book are positive throughout. The book examines the standard positions on *I* in order to discover what truths they contain. It then draws on this resource to explore in turn each facet of the meaning of *I*.

The strategy of Part I is as follows:

(*a*) to dissolve three especially active myths about *I*: *Rule Theory, Independence,* and *The Guarantee*;

(*b*) and thus to dislodge a conception of the term that is now as good as universal, beneath the usual surface variance: *Purism*;

(*c*) so as to establish a presumption in favour of a sharply diverging account: *I* is a *Deictic Term*.

The three myths have a particularly strong grip on philosophical imagination. This is so for various reasons, but chiefly because the myths echo that common craving to find *I* simple and undemanding to which we heard Russell give voice:

Rule Theory eases: a 'simple rule' is sufficient to give the meaning of *I* and to determine the reference of any use of the term.

Independence calms: there is no need to identify what is being referred to when expressing thoughts using *I*.

The Guarantee releases: all uses of *I* are trouble-free, since the meaning of the term secures each against the possibility of failing to refer.

These myths answer all aspects of the basic question: 'How does *I* refer?' And they do so with remarkable concision: to the user, directly, and always successfully. Reciprocal endorsement strengthens their appeal. Together, they portray *I* as a *Pure Indexical*, freed of the features and requirements which greatly complicate other referring expressions. Hence the name for the overall position: *Purism*. It is no surprise that this stance is rendered soundproof to piecemeal criticism.

Purism has deeply confused us in matters relating to the first person, with particularly disastrous effects on our understanding of thoughts expressible using *I*. The only strategy with a remote chance of challenging it is one that tackles the myths supporting it, both individually and collectively. Given the interconnections between them, the removal of one prop weakens the others and helps undermine the overall conception. So that is how I shall proceed in the opening part of the book, first establishing the historical significance of the three doctrines in an introductory overview and explaining what is attractive about them. Then, in the three chapters that follow, I shall examine each doctrine in turn, starting with the newest myth (*Rule Theory*) and digging down to the most entrenched (*The Guarantee*).

---

⁵ Aristotle, *Nicomachean Ethics*, VII. 14 (1985: 205).

So the first part of the book challenges false notions about *I*. But it is more accurate to describe its aims positively, as exposing a different conception of *I*. For that is what the disintegration of *Purism* gives way to. One can tackle without advancing and advance without tackling. But there are occasions on which to do one just is to do the other. And in this present case also, the negative task is simply the positive in reverse angle. *Purism* and its myths fail for the very reasons that advance a different conception of *I*. So the first part of the book does not simply open the door to an alternative; it pushes us through it.

The positive account of the meaning of *I* takes centre stage in the second half of the book. *I* is indeed an *Indexical*, but of the *Impure* variety. More precisely, *I* is a *Deictic Term* like *You* and *He/She*, an expression whose reference depends on making individuals salient. The exclusion of *I* from this group is precisely what *Purism* requires. For it would be simply absurd to say of *You* or *He/She* that a simple rule determines their reference, or that their use involves no identification, or that they are logically secured against failure to refer. And if the myths mislead us into thinking that *I* is different from *You* and *He/She* in these fundamental respects, we will naturally assume that *I* is just fundamentally different from these terms. But the myths are myths and *I* a *Deictic Term*.

The strategy of Part II is as follows:

(*a*) to investigate and discover what is deictic about the meaning of terms— what is deictic about their logical character, inferential role, referential function, expressive use, and communicative role;
(*b*) and thus to show that *I* is deictic in each such aspect of its meaning;
(*c*) so as to establish the positive account: that *I* is a *Deictic Term*.

As we shall find, uses of *I* refer to an individual salient in the extra-sentential context. That is what is deictic about its *logical character*. If sentences containing *I* are to entail or be entailed by other sentences, they must refer to an individual salient in the extra-sentential context. That is what is deictic about its *inferential role*. It is the *referential function* of *I*, as a singular term, to achieve determinacy of reference, and it fulfils this task in the deictic manner: by making individuals salient relative to the utterance. What is deictic about *I*'s *expressive use* and *communicative role* follows from what is deictic about its referential function. If the term is to express thoughts, its reference must at least be discriminable to the reference-maker and to the audience. And an individual must be made salient to them if this is to be achieved. So *I* is a *Deictic Term*, through and through.

This book has a certain focus, which is necessary if it is to clarify questions and obtain results. Certain constraints define that focus. It will avert misunderstanding later on to mention them here.

First, this is an enquiry into the meaning of *I*, and hence primarily in the philosophy of language. So its focus is not on the thoughts expressed by *I*, but on the logical form and inferential role of that expression, the referential function underpinning it, and the expressive and communicative uses made possible by it.

The nature of the thoughts thus expressed is a topic set squarely in the philosophy of mind, and one for which the findings of this book can only prepare. But these preparations are illuminating as well as necessary. The conclusion will give several examples of this.

Second, features of *Here* and *Now* are mentioned where relevant but the book does not concentrate on elucidating these terms. This may seem surprising since standard discussions tend to emphasize supposed links between *Here*, *Now*, and *I*. But then it is natural for the standard view to carry on in this way since it assumes all three terms are grouped together as *Pure Indexicals*. This book, however, shows that *I* belongs to the group of *Deictic Terms*. So it is with bona fide examples of such terms—expressions like *You*, *He/She*, and *This/That*—that connections with *I* are to be stressed instead. It may well be that the standard view is thoroughly wrong, and that *Here/Now* are no more *Pure Indexicals* than *I* is. But showing this would distract from the present goal: elucidating *I*.

Under the same constraint of maintaining focus, the book will mention but not elucidate so-called 'mixed demonstratives'. These words are a sub-category of *Deictic Terms*. They combine a simple demonstrative term (e.g. *This*) with a sortal (e.g. *Horse*) to form a compound referring expression (*This Horse*). The complex sets of logical and semantic features peculiar to this group are not sufficiently relevant to our enquiry. For the expression we are interested in (*I*), and the expressions to which it is most closely conjoined (*You*; *He/She*), are neither themselves mixed demonstratives nor simple terms able to combine with sortals to form such demonstratives.[6] Some forms of personal pronouns have the appearance of mixed terms. *My Horse* (*Your Horse*; *His/Her Horse*) are examples. But this superficial resemblance does not reflect structural form. 'My horse' is a genitival expression equivalent to 'The horse of me', for instance. But 'That horse' is simply a referring expression and not equivalent to 'The horse of that'.

Fourth, a viable account of *I* requires attending to both semantic and epistemic questions. But it is necessary to describe the relations between the two without confusing them. The three myths of *Purism* do confuse semantic and epistemic features, as we shall see. One purpose of the discussion in Part I is to disentangle them, which requires looking into both. That is not a problem for my discussion, of course, but for the myths themselves. It is one more reason to be rid of them. Part II is designed specifically to avoid further confusion. So it addresses the semantic questions first (what is the logical character of the term; how does it fulfil its referential function?) and only then answers the epistemological questions (what is the expressive and communicative role of the term; how is one to know which individual a use refers to?).

To distinguish semantic and epistemic questions in this way is not to deny that evidence relevant to one is useful in elucidating the other. This usefulness is

---

[6] *Pace* Corazza (2002); see below, Ch. 6.

obvious in one direction: knowing which individual an *I*-use refers to requires awareness of its referential function. But it is also apparent in the other direction, even if semantics is more basic than epistemology. For just as melody can tell us about sound, even though the latter is basic to the former, so semantic features of *I* are partly elucidated by their implications for other features of the term, some of which are epistemic. This approach is legitimate wherever we stand on the priority question. So it is not an issue we need resolve. Constraints of focus tell us that what we do not need to resolve, we need *not* to resolve. So we shall be agnostic about priority.

Finally, some advance warning about details of definition and style. When I talk of the 'expressive use' of *I* in what follows, I mean this in its straightforward sense: its use to express thoughts. So no contrast with 'descriptive use' or any other technical sense is intended. And 'use' means *genuine* use: the competent employment of an expression in an utterance which means something by sincere, reflective, competent, and truthful interlocutors who are also trusting (i.e. they take their partners to be sincere, reflective, competent, and truthful).

Terms like *I* have a referential function, so I shall say. They are referring terms, they refer. Perhaps, strictly speaking, it is the *user* of such terms who refers and who has a referential function, not the term itself. Then 'referring term' would be used as a transferred epithet, but no less validly for that. For we are content to say that one's heart is sick for love when, strictly speaking, it is oneself that is sick. So we may continue in this loose talk, if that is what it is, unless and until there is sufficient philosophical reason to mark the distinction.

Italics are used when attention is drawn to the distinction between the mention and use of terms. The practice lapses where such emphasis would be merely pedantic or distracting. An analytic table of contents is provided as an appendix. Sections in the main text are numbered so that readers may use the analytic table to navigate themselves through the arguments. Recurrent terms of art are listed in a second appendix for ease of reference. Some are neutral definitions which we are under licence to introduce. Others denote substantive positions for which we shall argue.

PART I

QUESTIONS ABOUT THE MEANING OF *I*

1

Historical Background

§ 1.   When we ask about *I* and the thinking it expresses, we are commonly told that the topic is straightforward: a simple rule gives all that needs to be said, '*I* refers to the speaker or writer.'[1] If we complain that this ignores signing and typing, that it wrongly attributes reference to the expression itself rather than its uses (which one thing is such that *it* is '*the* referent of *I*'?), and that it is inapplicable to sessions of sweet silent thought, we may be offered something more discriminating: for example,

The term *I* is governed by a simple rule: any use of *I* refers to whoever produced it. To characterise the meaning of the term, this is all that is needed.[2]

Like a clock-face, this plain front hides a mass of intricate workings whose construction and design represent substantial achievements. For there are very few other referring expressions of which it might plausibly be said that their meaning is given by a simple rule. Indeed, *Now* and *Here* may exhaust the group. So the prevailing view presupposes an apparatus, a background system made up out of logical distinctions between different kinds of referring expression, together with the principles justifying them.

Such systematicity as we now have began to be introduced in the nineteenth and twentieth centuries. Previously, it seemed possible to effect considerable progress in philosophy without the mechanism to which the current standard conception appeals. When Descartes, for example, made the proposition 'I am thinking, therefore I exist' the first principle of his philosophy, describing it as 'so firm and secure that all the most extravagant suppositions of the sceptics were not capable of overthrowing it', he did not trouble to say what *I* means, how it may be used to express what kinds of thoughts, what kind of referring expression it is, or indeed whether it should be considered a referring expression at all.[3]

This insouciance would have been acceptable had Descartes's principle been cogent and foundational no matter how these questions are to be answered. But this is evidently not the case. For he assumes that *I* refers to a self, and his second step is precisely to infer something about that self. If 'I am thinking' is true, then that to which *I* refers must be a thinking thing. But suppose that, as some profess

---

[1] e.g. Kaplan (1989: 505).   [2] Campbell (1994: 73).   [3] *Descartes* (1984: i. 127)

to believe, *I* merely *appears* to be a referring expression, like the expletive use of *It* in 'It is raining' which (unlike the referring use in 'It is a rain-drop') does not purport to pick anything out. Then 'I am thinking' only really means something like 'there's thinking going on', and there is no self to draw conclusions about. The crucial step from Descartes's first principle to every other is missing.

The absence of apparatus for specifying the meaning of *I* caused confusion to ramify exponentially in the course of the next century. For Descartes's casualness permits several interpretations of his first principle, and each such reading triggers different objections to the Cartesian programme, each of which in turn admits of different interpretations. The sets of 'Objections' by Antoine Arnauld (the Fourth) and Pierre Gassendi (the Fifth), when coupled with Descartes's 'Replies', are examples of this deadly ramification. But perhaps the best instance springs from Lichtenberg's addition to the debate. For at least three (mutually inconsistent) readings of his well-known anti-Cartesian remark are now prominent in philosophy:

'It thinks'; that is what one should say, like 'it is raining'. To say *Cogito* is already saying too much—if one translates it as 'I think'.[4]

On the first interpretation, Lichtenberg is claiming that *I* is a referring expression, one that picks out a substantial self, a 'somewhat'. He is protesting that *Cogito* adds one thought too many to those available to the Cartesian meditator. Given what this person has just methodically doubted away in the First Meditation, he is not entitled to assert anything about states of affairs involving a substantial self in the Second. A very different reading makes Lichtenberg assert that *I* is an expletive, or at least that the sentence 'I am thinking' is parallel in grammar and synonymous with the expletive sentences 'It is thought' or 'There's thinking going on'. He is then protesting against translating *Cogito* as 'I am thinking' because until *I* is recognized for what it is, no more a referring expression than the expletive use of *There* or *It*, philosophers (like Descartes himself) will continue to assume that it refers and look for its referent. According to the third interpretation, Lichtenberg accepts that *I* is a grammatical subject and that it does not function as an expletive. He is protesting that this feature of *I* is not sufficient of itself to justify the claim that the term stands for or identifies anything at all, let alone a substantial self. The justification for postulating a substantial self to which *I* refers may be forthcoming. But, *pace* Descartes, not from the mere fact that *I* is used as a grammatical subject.[5]

The point is that, without contextual apparatus for making the relevant concepts distinct and sharp, Lichtenberg's remark is simply not robust enough

---

[4] 1796: 412.

[5] For the first interpretation, see Williams (1978: 95); for the second, see Wittgenstein (1933: 100–1) and Katz (1990: 169); for the third, see Shoemaker (1963: 10) and Parfit (1984: 224–5).

to sustain any one interpretation. All are valid readings, which is as good as saying that none are.

TO WHAT DOES *I* REFER?

§ 2.   Nevertheless some specificity attaches to the writings of earlier authors, if only because they argued about what kinds of thing *I* refers to, and a crucial task for any adequate account is to address precisely this question. By noting the various answers provided by foremost writers, we gain clues as to how they regarded the meaning of *I,* and thus retrospectively discover whatever precision and order lie implicit in their views.

Descartes evidently assumed that *I* cannot but be a referring expression, at least in the broad sense that its uses stand for or pick out some particular object (the self). He argued that what its uses single out are particular substances on the grounds that thoughts are acts, uses of *I* refer to the subject of the thoughts they express, and 'the subject of any act can be understood only in terms of a substance'.[6] To claim that *I* refers to substances is not very precise since he acknowledged that many kinds of item belong to the class of substances, including God and matter. We can only make sense of his precision on this point if we equip him with a further assumption about *I*: that by the very meaning of the term, any use of *I* is guaranteed to have something, and the right something, to refer to. This is the doctrine we have called *The Guarantee*. This assumption enabled Descartes to narrow the field considerably. As he makes clear in the Second and Sixth Meditations, uses of *I* must refer to a substance that is entirely distinct from the body and other material objects, simple, indivisible, indestructible, immortal, and numerically identical through time.

Locke and Berkeley also assumed that uses of *I* single out objects by referring to them. But both complicate the way in which this occurs, demanding a more intricate role for *I* and thus a more complex notion of its meaning. It is Locke's linguistic sensitivity and choice of referent that complicate. With Berkeley, it is his choice of means.

Locke evidently thought that (due perhaps to superficial misunderstandings) *I* occasionally refers to 'the Man only', by which he means, roughly speaking, the human being one is. On most occasions, Locke uses the term to refer to what he calls a *Person*, a thinking item in which ideas are interrelated but which is neither a human being nor any other substance. It is something *annexed* to a substance. So Locke cannot be fitted into, and thus wrecks, William James's oft-repeated classification of historical theories of the self as *Substantialist, Associationist,* and *Transcendentalist.*[7] *I* must be a peculiar term if we are to suppose its meaning

---

[6] Descartes (1984: ii. 124).
[7] Locke (1689: ii. xxvii. 20 ff., pp. 335–6). James (1891: 324–5; 325–52).

sufficiently flexible to fulfil both referring tasks Locke assigns it and to pick out the kind of item he identifies as its referent.

Berkeley demands that *I* be viewed as a term which one can use to single oneself out, not by some simple means like perceiving oneself, but only by reflecting on one's agency. This might be acceptable if our agency is understood to include the usual abilities to manipulate our environment. But he limits the extent of our agency severely, allowing us little more than the ability to will ideas into existence by the imagination.[8] If we are to suppose *I* competent to single out a referent in these straitened circumstances, then again, it must be a most unusual term. But no explanation of its peculiarities is forthcoming from these writers, nor could it be without the proper apparatus.

§ 3.   Hume rejected all such views, arguing that the referent of uses of *I* cannot be 'something simple and continued . . . and individual'. If it were, it would have to be observable as such when one introspects. But he professes himself unable to reason with anyone who supposes that might occur. When *he* introspects, he observes only perceptions.[9]

Hume makes at least two assumptions about *I* and its capabilities here. First, it must be a term which one can use to express thoughts about an item (oneself) without the need to identify what is being referred to. This is the *Independence* doctrine. It tells us what must be true of *I* if it is to have an expressive use. That is, if the term is to be used to say something of the individual one is thinking about. These are cases where the individual needs to know that the individual spoken about is the same as the individual thought about. According to the doctrine, in using *I*, one can know that the individual thought of is the same as the individual spoken about without having to make an identity judgement.

Hume's second assumption is that *I* must be capable of referring to whatever unites a particular series of perceptions, determining them precisely as mine. And what is that? Relations of causation and resemblance cannot serve if, as he supposed, they provide no real connections themselves. There must be some prior explanation of how a set of experiences comes to be a set, of how discrete entities can be observed as causing and resembling each other in the first place. His inability to find a solution to this problem notoriously caused his own hopes to vanish. But there is a deeper set of questions that would have survived discovery of such a solution. What kind of referring term must *I* be, what meaning must it have, that it fulfil the task set for it: to refer independently of identification, and to stand for logical constructions made up out of causal connections between different perceptions?

Kant diverges more radically, focusing his attention on the use of *I* in the phrase *I Think*, which he considered 'the sole text' from which rational psychology develops its wisdom. This *I* which thinks is not to be considered as 'in the world' but rather as a phenomenal item, for it cannot be intuited or conceived

---

[8] Berkeley (1734*a*: 115–17; 1734*b*: 112–13).   [9] Hume (1739: 252, 633; 252).

as either a material object with a spatio-temporal location, or a merely spatio-temporal object, or even a purely temporal one. But upon its existence depends the possibility of self-ascribing experiences, itself a precondition of experience under any conception which we can make intelligible to ourselves. What most clearly sets Kant apart, however, is his realization that taking any such position demands giving an account of that term, *I*, which expresses it. Called on to supply such an account, however, he can only really say what kind of term *I* is *not*. Its use depends on neither an intuition nor a concept, and it does not 'distinguish a particular object'.[10] Such are the obstacles arising.

It has been suggested that in his analysis of this use of *I*, Kant espoused the *Independence* doctrine: that there is no need to identify what *I* refers to in order to express thoughts using the term.[11] This is at least to suppose that the use of *I* in *I Think* refers. Yet he steadfastly denies that *I* fulfils the task required of a referring expression: to say which one thing is being spoken about. It may be said to 'represent' [*vorstellen*] or 'designate' [*bezeichnen*], but only 'a thing of indeterminate signification', 'the mere form of consciousness'. It is, indeed, 'a completely empty expression'.[12] Is the use of *I* in *I Think* then to be regarded as blank (having no function at all), or mere vocalization (a function outside structured language, like a grunt), or an expletive (like the semantically redundant 'it' in 'it is raining'), or eliminable (contributing nothing that could not be expressed fully by other terms)? He leaves us with little clue.

The fundamental problem, which this last quandary reflects most graphically, is now familiar. Without some background organizing conception, we cannot license the assertion that *I* is or is not a referring expression. For without it, we are not able to specify with suitable precision what it is to be, or indeed *not* to be, such a thing. Nor can we license the assertion that *I* is the kind of term which could support any of the positions on offer. For without such apparatus, we have not begun to determine what kinds of term there are and into which category *I* properly falls.

IS *I* A NAME?

§ 4. It is because the now standard view conforms to an apparatus determining these issues that its simplicity may be said to hide immense philosophical effort. Two steps were crucial for progress.

The first was to explain the distinction between terms that are genuine singular referring expressions and those that are not, though they may appear to be. Compare two utterances, one of which contains a genuine singular referring

---

[10] Kant (1787: A341–405; B399–432; A96–130; B129–69; A382; A 346).

[11] Strawson (1966: 165–9); Brook (1994); McDowell (1994: Lecture V).

[12] Kant (1787: A382; B407; A103; A382; A 436).

expression ('Abelard is hot') and one which does not ('It is raining'). Whether or not the first utterance is true depends on how it is with some particular. Namely, the one indicated by the meaning of the subject-term (in this case, a particular person). The second utterance contains no expression whose meaning indicates a particular, and it does not need to contain such a term to be true or false. So, in a move that is prominent and fruitful in Frege, a genuine singular referring expression comes to be characterized as a linguistic counter whose meaning indicates which one particular thing is relevant to the truth-value of the sentence containing it. Uses of such terms help determine the meaning of sentences in which they are embedded by pointing out what one thing, if the whole utterance is to be true, the predicate must be true *of.* It is an expression we use to indicate (and in communication to anticipate questions about) what, who, or which one individual we are thinking of or speaking about. Unlike plural expressions, uses of such terms take singular verb forms.

I seems to conform to this model. Suppose both you and I say 'I am hot' but in fact I am cold (perhaps I am lying) and you alone are hot. Then one utterance of that same sentence is true and the other false. So the truth-value of each utterance depends on how it is with a particular individual. Namely, or so it seems plausible to say, the one indicated by the meaning of *I*. When used to issue such statements, then, sentences embedding *I* alter in truth-value depending on how it is with this indicated individual. Indeed, any statements of the form 'I am F' are true only when, but whenever, the one so indicated is *F.*

We can be misled by the grammatical name 'First Person Plural' into supposing that *I* is not necessarily a singular term. How can it be if it has this plural form? Grammarians sometimes assume that *I/We* are two forms of the same term that differ only in number. For example, when they describe *I/We* as morphologically unrelated number forms, in contrast to the typical regular formation of noun plurals—e.g. *boat/boats.*[13] But if *We* were indeed the plural form of *I*, then sentences of the form 'We are *F*' would mean 'I and I and I . . . are *F*' when evidently they mean that I and at least one other are *F* (typically people one would otherwise refer to as *You* or *He/She*). The speaker with the appearance of a man possessed by demons in Mark's Gospel who explained, 'My name is legion for we are many,' was using *We* to speak of what, at the time of utterance, he took to be himself and each other devil associated with him, not for more than one 'himself'. I and I and I do not amount to We but I, just as Abelard and Abelard and Abelard do not amount to more than Abelard. *I* no more has a plural form than does *Silver* or the number *One*. We are not just routinely fortunate when we correctly attend to exactly one individual on hearing the first person used. Perhaps no one ever seriously asserted that, qua plural of *I*, *We* can be analysed as 'I and I and I . . . ' The point is still worth making. For that is how *We* would have to be analysed if the term were indeed the 'First Person Plural', the plural form of *I*.

[13] e.g. Greenbaum et al. (1990: 108–15).

Most theorists have been persuaded by these and like considerations that *I* is a genuine singular referring term. The evidence certainly seems sufficient to make this the 'default position'. By this, I mean the stance we would need to be argued out of rather than into; the position whose truth we are entitled to assume, unless and until there is sufficient counter-evidence to suppose otherwise. But the doctrines of *Independence* and *The Guarantee* present counter-evidence. The details will occupy us later, but the challenge can be expressed immediately to capture its intuitive appeal. Genuine singular terms single out the items to which they refer. So if *I* were such a term, one would have to identify that item to which it refers in order to express thoughts using it. Moreover, failing to single out that item from all other and like things would be a risk one would have to overcome. But, according to the doctrines, one's expressive use of *I* requires no such identification and courts no such failure. So there is a puzzle here awaiting those who try to combine the claim that *I* refers with adoption of the doctrines. Since this group includes those who advocate what it is now conventional to say about *I*'s meaning, a resolution for what is otherwise a deep inconsistency is urgently required.

Strawson's comment that '*I* can be used without criteria of subject-identity and yet refer to a subject because, even in such a use, the links with those criteria are not severed' has convinced some that a simple resolution exists.[14] The idea seems to be that, no matter what I may or may not have to do when using *I*, *other people* still have to identify the item to which my use refers, and *other people* still have to overcome the risk of failing to do so. This is certainly compatible with the doctrines, which make no mention of others. It is less obviously congruent with what we plausibly require of a genuine singular term. For the fact that other people must try to identify the referent of my use of *I* if they want to understand it is in danger of seeming curiously irrelevant. It is not, after all, necessary that other people understand my use of *I* if I am nevertheless to use it. And if what I use *is* a genuine referring expression, then the problem is not resolved. How *can* what I use be a genuine referring expression if my use does not depend on successful identification of its referent? Moreover Strawson's manoeuvre confuses semantic with pragmatic issues. It may be true that uses of *I* have a referring role even if they are used without criteria of subject-identity in virtue of the fact that their audience applies empirical criteria of personal identity precisely to single out a referent. But this is an appeal to what an audience requires to understand a speaker's utterance, i.e. to issues of communication, of pragmatics. Whereas it is evidently a semantic issue whether or not uses of *I* have a referring role.

Wittgenstein is often said to have denied that *I* is a referring term. Since his interventions in debate on the meaning of *I* will play a significant role in what follows, it is worth establishing certain historical and interpretative points immediately.

---

[14] Strawson (1966: 165); see also (1959: 99–100).

Commentators who find anti-referentialism in the early Wittgenstein focus their argument on one aspect of the *Tractatus* project: the apparent attempt systematically to reduce every occurrence of 'I believe that p' to the assertion of 'p'.[15] This is to argue from redundancy to anti-referentialism. For if *I* can be eliminated in this way, so it is said, it must surely be redundant. Now the very definition of 'referring term' requires that a linguistic counter of this sort have a set of tasks to carry out: to single out individuals, forestall questions about which individual is in question, and so on. So if *I* is a referring term, it cannot be redundant. But if this were Wittgenstein's argument, it would hardly be persuasive. What is true for the logical analysis of present-tense belief-sentences need not hold for the analysis of non-belief-sentences, nor even for belief-sentences in other tenses. And it is notoriously difficult to see how his 'I Vp' → p' schema (where V holds place for a verb) may be used to reduce sentences like 'I made a promise.' In short, the fact that *I* may be eliminable from a small sub-set of cases does not show it is redundant overall. Moreover, there is ample evidence that the early Wittgenstein regarded *I* as neither eliminable nor redundant. He continued to employ the term throughout the *Tractatus*, in both pronominal and substantive uses, and with particular reference to the 'metaphysical subject', an entity described in Kantian-Schopenhauerian terms as presupposed by the existence of the world. His purpose in analysing certain present-tense uses of *I* was certainly destructive, but of views about what *I* referred *to*, not of the view that *I* referred. He was rejecting the claim that *I* refers to a simple, enduring, empirically encounterable self.[16]

Many commentators have claimed that Wittgenstein held anti-referentialist views in various different forms and for various different reasons as his later views developed. But his strongest assertions commit him to nothing stronger than an ignorance theory. This is true not just of his published claims ('*I* does not name [*benennt*] a person'), but of his unpublished thoughts also ('*I* does not designate [*bezeichnet*] a person'). In brief: *I* may or may not refer. If it does refer, it is unclear what it refers *to*, though certainly not to a person.[17]

So why has the later Wittgenstein been misrepresented as an anti-referentialist? One explanation may be that those most closely associated with his programme themselves moved from an ignorance theory to anti-referentialism. Though differences of nuance separate these philosophers, all seem to have found this background thought compelling: it is so wholly unclear what *I* might refer to, surely it cannot refer at all. So Peter Geach has claimed that there is nothing for which *I* stands. And Elizabeth Anscombe has argued that *I* is 'neither a name nor another kind of expression whose logical role is to make a reference, *at all*'.[18]

---

[15] Wittgenstein (1916: 118; 1921: §5. 542; §5. 5421).

[16] Wittgenstein (1921: §5. 542; §5. 5421; §5. 63; §5. 632; 1916: 79–80). For the contrary view, see Hacker (1993: 213–14) and Glock and Hacker (1996: 160).

[17] Wittgenstein (1958: §410; 1936: 228). *Bezeichnet* is misleadingly translated 'refer to' by Glock and Hacker (1996: 95), who identify him as anti-referentialist.

[18] Geach (1957: 23–4). Anscombe (1975: 154). See also Malcolm (1979) and Kenny (1989: 88).

Another explanation may be that Wittgenstein himself is being mildly ironic. Perhaps his remarks are really to be interpreted as anti-referentialist. For it has generally been assumed that persons are the best candidates as referents for *I*. So if the term does not refer to a person, what else could it refer to? The question would expect the answer 'nothing', of course. But its rhetorical force is considerably weakened by the availability of at least one venerable answer. A Lockean might reply, 'If not to a person, then *I* refers to a human being.' For on their view, first, human beings and persons are not identical. And, second, usage provides evidence that we can use *I* to single out the human being *rather than* the associated person.

§ 5.   So we have an account of what a singular referring expression is, one that gives us reason, prima facie, to include *I* in the class. The second crucial step towards making *I*'s meaning and role tractable was to explain distinctions between different kinds of referring expression. This meant appreciating the subtly different conditions and means by which various kinds of expression fulfil the referring task—names; pronouns; descriptions; demonstratives; indexicals; and so on.

The grammatical characterization of *I* as a personal pronoun may cause one to suppose that it replaces or substitutes for proper names, and consequently should be grouped with them. Though tempting, the inference is hardly compelling, since personal pronouns also go proxy for whole noun phrases (as in: 'The Parisian philosopher asked his young student whether *she* liked *him*'). Nevertheless, it is reasonable to hypothesize that, within the class of referring expressions, *I* belongs to the class of names. Mill and Frege certainly described it as such, though it should be admitted that in their hands the classification is not much sharper than 'referring expression'. For the former specifically included in the set common and abstract nouns, descriptions, and adjectives, while the latter included any expression whose logical and semantic role it is to stand for a given object.[19]

Frege's view of names is considerably sharpened by his notion of 'sense'. He argued that such terms are to be associated not just with the object denoted, but with the sensitivity of a rational subject's capacity for recognizing that object. Definite descriptions, demonstratives, and indexical expressions can be made to fall under the category of names, so conceived, with varying degrees of plausibility. *I* is a name, but of a special sort, at least in certain of its uses: it is the name which reflects the 'particular and primitive way' in which 'everyone is presented to himself' and 'to no one else'. These particular uses are characteristically employed privately, in soliloquy. Frege argues that the public and communicative use of *I* is associated with a wholly different sense.[20]

If *I is* a name, it must be proper rather than common, for it refers to individuals rather than kinds of individuals (like *City*, *Vegetable*, *Planet*). It is more akin to personal proper names like *Abelard* or *Heloise* than those proper names requiring an article (*The Reichstag*, *The Mediterranean*). But it was soon noted that there are significant differences between *I* and personal proper names. Every person can use

[19] Mill (1843: I); Frege (1891; 1892*a*: 42–53).   [20] Frege (1892*b*; 1918: 24–6).

I and refer to himself, while only those called *Abelard* can use that name and refer to themselves. Every person who uses *I* can only refer to himself, while only those called *Abelard* can use that name and only refer to themselves. Every person who knows which proper name is at issue when someone says 'Abelard' can know which particular person is referred to without knowing certain facts about the context—e.g. who is speaking. No person who knows which singular term is at issue when someone says 'I' knows which particular person is referred to without knowing such facts. And whereas the context of proper names may be used to disambiguate which name is at issue (e.g. Abelard *of Paris* or Abelard *Jones*), the context of *I* is only ever used to determine which object the expression refers to.[21]

As is often noted, there is deep significance to these features of *I*: they give the term a unique role in manifesting self-reflexive self-consciousness.[22] One may have a private name for oneself, *NN*. But this name will be unlike *I* in that no one else need even have a private name, let alone the name *NN*. Conversely, one has a public name by which one may archly refer to oneself. Abelard himself might say, 'I see Abelard has spilt the wine again.' But this name will be unlike *I* in that it may be used to refer to others also. Moreover, one cannot say, 'I am the *F* who is *G*' ('I am the fool who is spilling the wine'), without recognizing the direct bearing of the information conveyed by the statement on *oneself*. Not so with any name. Abelard may forget, for whatever reason, that his name is *Abelard* and therefore that the name refers to him. He may then say, 'Abelard is the fool who is spilling the wine,' without entertaining as a possibility what simply could not fail to occur to him had he said, 'I am the fool who is spilling the wine'—i.e. that the information he is broadcasting is precisely information about *himself*.[23]

These features of *I* give it the character of a device with varying referents. Such terms are often called 'one-off' or 'unrepeatable' devices in the literature. This is misleading because it suggests that the same individual could only once be the referent of uses of *I, You, He/She* and so on. In fact, of course, the same individual may be the referent of different uses of these terms regularly enough. The point is just that of no one individual is it true that it is *invariably* the referent. (Compare: bad weather in England is not constant. But nor is it a one-off, being regular enough. It is, rather, *variable*.) So I shall call such terms 'variant devices'. The contrast is with proper names, like *Abelard*. Adopting for now the usual convenient simplifying fiction that there is a single such name with which a single individual was baptized, *Abelard* invariably refers to the same individual. *I*, on the other hand, is without a constant referent. In this respect, it is like *You, He/She*,

---

[21] For one way to draw this distinction between pre-semantic and semantic uses of context, see Perry (1997: 593).

[22] Perry (1979).

[23] The gradual recognition and delineation of these features can be traced through Frege (1918: 24–6); Russell (1912: 27–8; 1914: 164–5); McTaggart (1927: 62–86); Strawson (1950); Shoemaker (1963); Castañeda (1966; 1968). Recent appreciation of their full significance is due particularly to Anscombe (1975); Perry (1979); Kripke (1972); and Kaplan (1989).

This, *That*, *Now*, and *Here*. These terms may pick out the same person or time or place regularly enough. But there is no single person, object, time, or place such that *it* is the referent *whenever* one of these terms are used.

These features distance *I* from proper names and associate it with the other singular personal pronouns. This dissociation may be recognized in different ways. So Saul Kripke explicitly regards *I* as a rigid designator, for example. But he does not claim that it is a proper name.[24] And there is good reason to reject such a view within his theory of reference. For what counts as reference-relevant context in this causal theory, and the role such context plays, differ markedly as between *I* and proper names like *Abelard*. The reference-relevant context of a proper name within an agent's idiolect is the causal history which links it to an original dubbing. Thus reliance on testimony replaces Fregean recognitional sensitivity in this part of the theory. By contrast, the context of *I* is its possible occasions of use. Moreover, as noted above, such context is not necessary to disambiguate which term is at issue when *I* is used, unlike proper names such as *Abelard*.

In brief: if *I is* a name, that must be so either in the very general sense that all singular referring terms are, or in some very specific sense that personal proper names like *Abelard* are not.

Russell at one time seized the possibility afforded by the second disjunct, classifying *I* as a *logically proper* name. McTaggart later advanced a similar position with considerable force.[25] Both rely on a background dualism: whatever 'things' (as opposed to truths) we can know and refer to, we must either know and refer to 'by acquaintance' or 'by description'. They argued that it is 'by acquaintance' that we know and refer to the self using *I*. This is to suppose that we are directly (non-inferentially) aware of the self in perception, that the self is 'before the mind', and that its existence is logically guaranteed. The self is a simple for which *I* stands. And to be adequate to stand for such a thing in the referring way, *I* must be a logically proper name. That is to say, in particular, a simple symbol, resistant to logical analysis, whose successful reference is logically guaranteed.

So the notion that *I* is a logically proper name requires one familiar doctrine, *The Guarantee*. But it flouts another, *Independence*. For it makes expressing oneself using the term depend on being acquainted with the item to which it refers. And that is a form of identification. So Russell soon renounced the notion, arguing for the only alternative consistent with his background dualism: that *I* is a descriptive term.

IS *I* A DESCRIPTIVE TERM?

§ 6. The claim that *I* is a descriptive term answers one question and raises another. For it tells us what kind of expression *I* is, but we want to know what uses

---

[24] Kripke (1972: 10 n. 2).   [25] Russell (1912: 27–8); McTaggart (1927: 62–86).

of the term mean. And in the case of descriptive terms (unlike proper names, probably), that requires saying what description *means the same as* the term in question. Evidently *I* cannot be an *in*definite descriptive term—an expression to be understood in terms of the existential quantifier ('there is *at least* one thing which ... '). For on each occasion of use it refers uniquely ('there is *exactly* one thing which ... '). So if *I* is a descriptive term, we must ask 'what definite description, the ϕ, is such that it means the same as—is synonymous with—any use of *I*?' And it is this aspect of descriptivism about *I* that has attracted most attention. Russell suggested 'the subject of the present experience' and Reichenbach 'the person who utters this token'.[26] The basic position continues to appeal though the suggested descriptions change. So Peacocke offers 'The subject who has *these* conscious states' as a candidate. Parfit suggests '*this* subject of experience' instead. And, in response to perceived difficulties with these descriptions, Rovane has worked up the more complex candidate: 'the set of rationally related intentional episodes of which *this* one is a member'.[27]

The suggested descriptions change consistently because each has consistently proved unsatisfactory. So consider only the most recent descriptivist option: Rovane's alleged solution to the problems raised by earlier attempts. What is wrong with her position is that the description she offers as a candidate falls foul of several basic requirements for the analysis of any singular referring expression: it is either circular or solipsistic, and falsifies the motivational role of the term in question.

The first set of considerations relates to the distinction between one's own states and states that are not one's own. Solipsism is a bad thing, as is generally recognized. And avoiding solipsism requires (minimally) that one have a use for this distinction. Now Rovane's description offers us such a use, but at a price she herself cannot afford. For it leaves nothing but reference to *myself* with which to distinguish what makes certain states *these* and not *those* (they fall under the category of states that are *mine*, directly experienced by *me*, and so on), or to legitimize combining two or more states as part of the set (it is because *that* state is also *mine* that it is part of the set of which *this* is a member). And if the candidate-description must make ineliminable use of *I* in this way, it cannot *give* the meaning of *I*. The description must instead *assume* it. Thus Rovane's candidate-description puts her position in a constructive dilemma. Either it is solipsistic (and thus immediately problematic), or it incorporates the very expression it is meant to analyse, escaping solipsism only by reneging on its appointed task.

The second set of difficulties with this most recent attempt at a viable descriptivism relates to the fact that, as many have noted, *I* has a crucial motivational role. It makes no sense to suppose that agents might know 'I am *F*' (where, in Perry's well-known examples, *F* stands for 'spilling sugar'; 'late for a meeting';

---

[26] Russell (1914: 163–9); Reichenbach (1947: 284).
[27] Peacocke (1983: 109–51). Parfit (1984: 252). Rovane (1998: 214).

'approached by a bear') without their recognizing the crucial bearing of that information on themselves. And this first-personal feat of self-conscious self-reference, by which the agent recognizes the subject and object of an intentional episode as identical, partly explains the way they are regularly motivated to do what they do. Now if Rovane's candidate-description genuinely gives the meaning of *I*, it should at least preserve these crucial features of the term. But evidently it does not. For one might be in a position to know that the set of rationally related intentional episodes of which *this* one is a member is F without doing something about it, precisely because one does not know that this set is *oneself.*

Moving from this particular case to general descriptivist strategy in giving the meaning of *I*, it is notable that each proposed description contains a particularizing element: *Present*; *This*; *These*. This is just as well since descriptions without such elements—'pure' descriptions, like *The Subject* or *The Speaker*—fail to track uses of *I* in crucial respects. When I use *I*, I always refer to myself and never to you. When you use the very same term, you always refer to yourself and never to me. But I routinely use pure descriptions like *The Subject* or *The Speaker* to refer to you or to me just as you do. Unlike *I*, these pure descriptions need not refer to any one person rather than another on an occasion of use. They refer instead to some general property characteristically instantiated by satisfiers of the description—subjects, speakers, and so on. So it is by adding particularizing elements that descriptivists hope to capture these aspects of *I* with their candidate-descriptions. The underlying point here reflects a general claim (due ultimately to Russell): demonstrative or indexical reference as a whole is irreducible to descriptive reference.[28]

§ 7. McTaggart and others helped formulate a well-known objection to descriptivism based around the following observation: it is possible for a subject to know that '*the* φ is F' to be true for any description φ without knowing what is the case, that '*I* am F'. And if this is so, then *I* cannot be synonymous with any definite description *the* φ.[29] The observation can be illustrated with Russell's candidate-description: 'the subject of the present experience'. You might be on a fairground ride and, seeing one of your group's reflected faces, know that 'the subject of the present experience is terrified', while not knowing (perhaps sincerely denying) that you are terrified and that it is your face you have seen.

There are manoeuvres that a Russellian can make in response and counter-moves to these. Moreover, the candidate-descriptions of other descriptivists like Reichenbach need to be tackled differently. But it is sufficient that the outlines of anti-descriptivist strategy be broadly clear to appreciate one crucial point. Either these strategies are hostage to fortune, or some underpinning reason exists for regarding uses of *I* as irreducible to descriptions. For at present, if we are

[28] Russell (1905). See Evans (1982: 51–60; 143–204).

[29] McTaggart (1927: 63–75). See also Castañeda (1966; 1968: 160–6); Perry (1979: 167–8); Evans (1982: 206–7).

persuaded of the truth of the observation, it is because all the cases we can think of exemplify it and none are counter-examples. And without some reason that would explain *why* this is so, we cannot say in advance that *no* candidate-description will ever be found that proves a counter-instance.

The obvious solution is to appeal to the doctrines of *Independence* and *The Guarantee*. They would serve as such underpinning reasons if they hold for *I* and do not hold for any candidate-description. And this is precisely the move made by theorists. This suited McTaggart, of course, who regarded *I* as a logically proper name and hence was already primed to suppose that its reference was logically guaranteed. Similarly, Castañeda argued that *The Guarantee* governs our use of *I* to refer to ourselves and does not regulate the use of descriptions. So the use of *I* must be 'ontologically prior' to any descriptive self-reference. Hence the meaning of *I* must be irreducible to any description.[30] This would explain why McTaggart's original observation turns out to be true for any case we have thought of in the past or might dream up in the future.

IS *I* A *(PURE) INDEXICAL?*

§ 8. The fact that *I* differs from proper names and descriptive terms is now commonly explained by first distinguishing such expressions from the group of so-called 'indexical' terms, and then assigning *I* to that group. What virtue is there in this programme?

The first step we may accept for the sake of argument and maintaining focus. Some question it. But the fact that they do is of much less interest than the reasons they offer for doing so. For these reasons will become a point of focus in Part II. Some claim we should regard proper names as indexical expressions because they are terms which depend for their literal content upon extra-semantic features of the contexts in which they are uttered.[31] As we shall find, this profoundly misrepresents what it is to be an indexical expression. Logical character and inferential role reveal that the literal content of an indexical is fully dependent on intra-semantic features of the contexts in which it is uttered. That is how we should understand the function of devices like demonstration, for example, which make the referent of a particular use count as such by being salient.

With regard to the overall programme, we have certainly noticed signal differences between *I* and proper names like *Abelard*, and between *I* and definite descriptions like *The Subject of the Present Experience*. But that is the negative point. We need to know whether these differences should lead one positively to

---

[30] McTaggart (1927: 63–75). Castañeda (1968: 160–1). See also Perry (1979: 167–8) who appeals in addition to a third doctrine, *Rule Theory*, which we shall examine below.

[31] See Pelczar and Rainsbury (1998: particularly 293).

identify *I* as an indexical. And in particular, we need to know what an indexical expression *is*, what makes a term count as such.

Indexicals are often defined as context-sensitive expressions. But what meaningful expression is not? No matter how one thinks words get their meaning—by stipulation; shared experience; convention; application to the way the world is; and so on—they are thus sensitive to *something* counting as their context. It follows that there must be some particular characteristic sense in which referring expressions that count as indexicals may be said to be 'sensitive to context'. Some identify that sense, when pressed, by saying that the reference of indexical terms *shifts with* context, or is *identified via* context, or is *determined by* context. But proper names (*Abelard*) and definite descriptions (*The Author of the* Logic) satisfy these definitions. We might disagree about how some item counts as the unique referent of these kinds of term. For example: being the individual presented under a certain mode; baptized on a certain occasion; or uniquely satisfying a certain cluster of descriptions or conventions. But the fact that *something* must play this role on each occasion means that the reference of these kinds of term shifts with, is identified via, and is determined by, *something* that counts as context—on whatever view we take of what context is, be it the situation in which the statement is made, or the situation in which it is evaluated.[32]

In brief: we might be prepared to define indexicality in such a way that proper names and descriptive terms are included. But the price would be high: we could no longer appeal to indexicality to explain what is special about *I*, what distinguishes it from other kinds of term. And that, recall, was our original purpose.

§ 9.   The solution proposed for problems of this sort turns on the claim that indexicals are terms associated with rules. Their reference is governed by them. But the familiar objection returns. For rules can be supplied that govern descriptive terms also (e.g. 'Any use of *the author of the* Logic refers to x if and only if x is the author of the *Logic*'), just as we can regulate the use of proper names (e.g. 'Any use of *Abelard* refers to x if and only if x is Abelard'). So there must be some particular characteristic sense in which the reference of referring expressions that count as indexicals may be said to be 'governed by rules'.

Rules give the meaning of indexical expressions and determine the reference of their uses in relation to context (their situation of use). Descriptive terms and proper names may be associated with rules, but the *meaning* of neither is a rule. For the former it is a synonym, as we have seen, and for the latter, plausibly, it is the referent. David Kaplan and others who have articulated this response regard such rule-governance as the essence of indexicality. It is not simply that rules give the meaning and determine the reference of indexicals in context. If some term is an indexical, then a rule is *sufficient* to give its meaning, and that rule is *sufficient* to determine its reference. *Now* and *Here* are examples in their central uses. (Cases

---

[32] See Kaplan (1989: 494).

like that in which one points to a map and says *Here* are treated as eccentric.) So expressions like *He/She*, *This (F)* and *That (F)* which behave rather like indexicals—they are variant devices whose reference shifts from context to context—are not '*Pure* Indexicals'. For their reference is determined not simply by the rule which gives their meaning, but also by associated demonstration—a gesture or something of the sort. These *Im*pure Indexicals are often called 'Demonstratives' or 'Deictic Terms'.[33]

So the history of debate brings us to this question: 'what sort of indexical *is* I?' If the distinction between *Pure* Indexicals and *Impure* Indexicals (henceforth *Deictic Terms*) is even roughly in order, to which group does *I* belong? Answering this question is the central task of the essay. On its solution depends the nature of *I* and of the thoughts it expresses—and hence, amongst much else (if Descartes or Kant are correct), the possibility of all our knowledge.

§ 10. *I* is a *Pure* Indexical. A rule in context is sufficient to give the meaning and determine the reference of the term. This has been the prevailing view for some time. Deep differences of approach and position may otherwise divide philosophers. But about this doctrine—call it *Rule Theory*—there is an impressive uniformity. No dissent is apparent in the community here.[34]

So Sydney Shoemaker claims that *I* is 'a referring expression whose meaning is given by the rule that it refers to the person who uses it'. According to Barwise and Perry, 'whenever it is used by a speaker of English, [*I*] stands for, or designates, that person. We think that this is all there is to know about the meaning of *I* in English and that it serves as a paradigm rule for meaning.' For Christopher Peacocke, 'the reference rule for *I* fully determines its meaning in English'. John Campbell claims: 'The term *I* is governed by a simple rule: any token of *I* refers to whoever produced it. To characterise the meaning of the term, this is all that is needed.' For Kaplan, *I* is the term it is precisely because it is governed by a rule: '*I* refers to the speaker or writer.' In context, the rule is sufficient to determine reference for all tokens of *I*.[35]

Kaplan introduces a small complication: two supplementary rules are required, one to govern indexicality, and the other direct reference. But the caveat is irrelevant to the overall claim. For these additional rules are simply required to determine the way in which *the* rule is to be interpreted: *the* rule is the rule it is because of them. So the supplementary rules operate in an anterior way: they do not determine the reference of tokens of *I* alongside *the* rule. *The* rule, once established, is sufficient for this role. Thus Kaplan is in wholehearted agreement

---

[33] See Kaplan (1989: 489–92).

[34] For advocacy in addition to that mentioned below in the text, see Nozick (1981: 78); Rovane (1987: 147); Mellor (1988: 79); Strawson (1994: 210); O'Brien (1995*a*); Perry (1997: 598). Bermúdez (1998: 9); Soames (2002: 103). Reichenbach evidently thought *I* was a descriptive term *and* one the reference of whose uses is sufficiently determined by the rule (1947: 284).

[35] Shoemaker (1968: 91). Barwise and Perry (1981: 670). Peacocke (1983: 133–9). Campbell (1994: 73). Kaplan (1989: 493; 505; 520).

with the prevailing view. A simple rule is sufficient to give the meaning and determine the reference of *I*. Indeed, he is largely responsible for making it the current orthodoxy.

Unity on this issue is made that much more striking when we recognize the complete disunity about related matters. Even those who deny that *I* is a referring term, and consequently do not regard the rule as having a reference to determine, nevertheless regard the rule as giving the meaning of the term.[36] But it would be wrong to treat *Rule Theory* as a unique unifier. For the armistice extends to embrace both *Independence* and *The Guarantee*.[37] What explains this extension of the truce is the fact that the three doctrines are logically related. Supporters of the doctrines often appeal to the existence and nature of these relations for the mutual support they afford.

Thus Strawson, taking the example of someone thinking 'I am feeling terrible', writes:

Anyone who is capable of formulating such a thought will have mastered the ordinary practice of personal reference by the use of personal pronouns; and it is a rule of that practice that the first personal pronoun refers, on each occasion of its use, to whoever then uses it. So the fact that we have, in the case imagined, a user, is sufficient to guarantee the reference, and the correct reference for the use.[38]

And Campbell makes the point in the other direction in a characteristically understated way: 'when we leave this rule behind, the datum that reference-failure is impossible is hard to understand.'[39]

Why should these theorists suppose the doctrines offer each other such strong mutual support? Suppose that uses of *I* are sufficiently determined in context by the rule that it refers on each such occasion to whoever uses it, and it is guaranteed that there is exactly one user for every use. Then it seems that every use must be guaranteed to have a referent (the user), and that every use must express a thought *about* someone *by* that same someone (i.e. the user) without their needing to identify the one as the other. The endorsement is reciprocated, for if *The Guarantee* and *Independence* are true, then the rule must be sufficient in context to determine the reference of uses of *I*. For suppose *Rule Theory* were false and *I* a *Deictic Term* like *He/She*, its reference dependent on an associated demonstration.

---

[36] For example, Anscombe (1975: 154).

[37] For endorsement of *Independence* (often discussed under 'immunity to error through misidentification'), see in particular Woods (1968); Shoemaker (1968; 1986); Anscombe (1975); Evans (1982: esp. 179–91; 215–20); Rovane (1987; 1993); Brewer (1992; 1995); Campbell (1994: esp. 121–34); O'Brien (1995*a* and *b*); Cassam (1995); Bermúdez (1998: esp. 6–12); Wittgenstein (1969: 63–70) is a special case as we shall see. For endorsement of *The Guarantee*, see in particular Castañeda (1968: 160–1); Anscombe (1975: 149 and 151–2); Peacocke (1983: 175–9); Shoemaker (1986: 126–7); Rovane (1987: 151–5); Kaplan (1989: 509); Hacker (1993: 223); Strawson (1994: 210–11); Campbell (1994: 125); McDowell (1998); Bermúdez (1998: esp. 9).

[38] Strawson (1994: 210).

[39] Campbell (1994: 125). See also Bermúdez (1998: 9).

Independence would fail because it would be necessary to identify whichever someone the thought is *about* (i.e. the demonstrated one) with that someone whom the thought is expressed *by* (i.e. the user). And since it is not guaranteed that such a demonstration will accompany each use anyway, *The Guarantee* also would fail.

A crucial effect of the corroboration these three doctrines offer each other is to make the gulf between *I* and the other singular personal pronouns (*You* and *He/ She*) unbridgeable. The distinction was originally drawn by reference to *Rule Theory*. It is true of *I* and not of these other terms that its reference is sufficiently determined in context by a simple rule. But *Rule Theory* brings in its train two doctrines which constitute two more ways of marking the cleavage which consolidates the divide and makes it comprehensive. For the reference of *You* and *He/ She* is not logically guaranteed, and their use to express thoughts is not independent of identification. Hence, if these doctrines are correct, in every relevant way *I* is marked out by its meaning as radically different.

The triumph of *Rule Theory* should not surprise. In saying what kind of term *I is*, it also gives an explanation of why *I* is not the kind of term we have decided it is *not*—a proper name, for example, or a descriptive term. But there is something more peculiarly satisfying about *Rule Theory*. It is the recently acquired centrepiece of a comprehensive position to which we have seen debate about the first person long tending. For *Rule Theory* satisfies a need that had become increasingly stark: to justify two doctrines which dominated that history but which lacked both grounding and explanation. *Rule Theory* validates *The Guarantee* and *Independence*, and acquires validation by so doing. It seems appropriate to label the comprehensive position at whose heart these doctrines lie *Purism*. For, together, they set out an appealing conception of *I* as purified of the demanding features and requirements which make other terms so complicated. A 'simple rule' gives its meaning. No identification is necessary in the central cases. Each use is logically secured against failure.

So the history of debate has brought us to *Purism*, with its component doctrines strongly bound to each other by ties of reciprocal endorsement. The question remains, however, whether any of the doctrines in this mutual support group deserves our support. And one nagging anomaly looms up like Banquo's ghost, unsettling the triumph with reminders of a suppressed past. Regarding an expression simultaneously as a genuine referring term and as either logically guaranteed against reference-failure or independent of identification is a trick we have yet to master. Unless and until we do, *Purism* remains an unstable position and its three components call for careful examination.

2

Questions of Reference

§ 11. We are after the meaning of *I*. To give the meaning of any referring expression is not one task but several. We can ask about what uses of the expression refer to, or about how those uses express thoughts, or about what words would be synonymous with the expression, or about what determines reference, and so on. At one or another occasion in the historical debate, as we have seen, one or another of these issues has been privileged. So Descartes and his immediate successors tried to illuminate the whole subject (and much else) with answers to the first question. Hume made the second serve in this way. Russell and his descendant descriptivists tried to make the third of critical importance. And it is an answer to the fourth which *Rule Theory* offers, thus generating the currently standard position. A 'simple rule' in context determines the reference of any use of *I*. Since it is to this position that history has brought us, it is with this answer to the fourth question that we should begin investigating.

There are almost as many candidates for *the* 'simple rule' as there are explicit proponents of *Rule Theory*. This is the first fact that should strike us. It is distinctly troubling given that the meaning of *I* is supposed to rest on this one rule. Minor variations at any such hinge-point must expand into ever more significant differences when we move away from that point. Oddly enough, however, this divergence seems to have bothered advocates of the doctrine not at all. A sample of candidate-rules will include: 'whenever *[I]* is used by a speaker of English, it stands for, or designates, that person'; '*[I]* means the person using it'; '*[I]* refers to the person who uses it'; 'the first personal pronoun refers, on each occasion of its use, to whoever then uses it'; '*I* refers to whoever uses it'; 'Any utterance of *I* refers to its producer'; '[Uses of *I*] refer to those who produce them'; 'Any token of *I* refers to whoever produced it'; '*I* refers to the speaker'; '*I* refers to the speaker or writer'; '*I* refers ... to the speaker as presented in the context of utterance'; 'In any utterance containing *I*, the pronoun refers to the person who makes that utterance'.[1] The variations and differences may seem slight at first (as we shall see, they are actually

---

[1] Respectively, Barwise and Perry (1981: 670); Russell (1956: 164); Shoemaker (1968: 91); Strawson (1994: 210); O'Brien (1995*a*: 237); Peacocke (1983: 135); Mellor (1988: 83); Campbell (1994: 73); Rovane (1987: 147); Kaplan (1989: 505); Brinck (1997: ix); Larson and Segal (1995: 215).

quite significant). But one point should be immediately appreciable. If the rule itself is simple, it is evidently much less simple to specify quite what it is.

Rule Theory exercises an extraordinary hold over philosophical imagination. Only very rarely do authors feel the need to present arguments in its support. It is commonly sustained instead by bare assertion or by brief appeals to plausibility.[2] The simplicity of the theory, when compared with various alternatives, is often taken to be sufficiently compelling evidence in its favour. Since current literature offers so few arguments in favour of *Rule Theory*, it is tempting to look for some predisposition or other to explain adoption of the doctrine. Here, David Kaplan's advocacy stands out to his advantage. For he offers reasons for thinking that no other theory of the meaning of *I could* be preferable. And he does so within a powerful general account, *Direct Reference*, capable of distinguishing clearly between types of indexicals. So I shall often take him as spokesman for the doctrine.

There are, of course, differences between Kaplan's own advocacy of *Rule Theory* and that of others. But my arguments aim to make these differences relatively superficial. Some Kaplanian *Rule Theorists* formulate the 'simple rule' differently, for example.[3] But since no simple rule is sufficient to determine the reference of every use of *I*, as I shall show, this difference is of minimal interest. Some depart more significantly from Kaplan, but are still vulnerable to the arguments set out below. Consider François Recanati's position as a case in point.[4] His views on the use of *I* and on egocentricity in general can be distinguished into three categories. Some are versions of Kaplan's own views and will be met in this chapter. So, for example, Recanati holds that *Rule Theory* is correct, and that the 'simple rule' determining the reference of any use of *I* is that '*I* refers to the person who utters this token'. Views in the second category are wholly non-Kaplanian. They concern the *Independence* doctrine. This material shows the marked influence of Gareth Evans on self-identification and is vulnerable to the same criticisms set out in the next chapter. The third category of views are those that concern the nature of the thoughts expressible by *I*. Like many other *Rule Theorists*, Recanati builds his position on the meaning of *I* around such views. He is particularly interested in the constant association between such thoughts and egocentric conceptions of oneself, as well as the psychological modes of presentation 'directly expressed' by indexicals in general. Here it is worth recalling what constraints govern the focus of this book. Our attention has been and will remain concentrated on the meaning of *I*. The nature of the thoughts expressible by *I* is a deeply significant issue, but it is not ours. It is one to which the conclusion looks forward.

---

[2] For example, Shoemaker (1968: 91); Barwise and Perry (1981: 670); Peacocke (1983: 137); Bach (1987: 176); Bermúdez (1998: 9).

[3] See Predelli (1998*a* and *b*); Corazza et al. (2002).

[4] See Recanati (1993: 87–91); Gareth Evans (1982: ch. 7).

Three difficulties with *Rule Theory* should be noted immediately. The first concerns the fit between *Rule Theory* and its background account on the Kaplanian model: *Direct Reference*. Some understand by *Direct Reference* the claim that certain linguistic expressions refer without any mediating entities like the 'meaning' of the expression or the 'concept' it expresses.[5] But advocates of *Rule Theory* cannot apply this claim to their account of *I*. For they regard the reference of *I* as mediated by the definition which convention associates with the expression. Others take *Direct Reference* to be the view that there is nothing more to the 'meaning' or semantic value of certain expressions than their referents.[6] Kaplan himself understands 'directly referring expressions' to be those whose linguistic rules provide directly that the referent in all possible circumstances is determined as the actual referent.[7] This claim is compatible with *Rule Theory* (and it is precisely this claim which I shall deny). But confusion arises here also. For at one point Kaplan maintains that 'The character of an expression ... determines the content of the expression in every context.' While at another point he argues that 'The meaning of *I* is given by the rules' for its use, explicitly rendering 'meaning' here as character. And these rules are described as 'providing a way of determining the actual referent'. Does character then determine *both* content *and* referent?—if so, the definition of 'character' is insufficient. Or are content and referent to be identified?—a claim that may be suggested at one point but remains unsupported.[8]

A second difficulty with *Rule Theory* is that it claims the rule expresses all there is to know about determining the reference of uses of *I*. It is not just *a* fact, but *the* fact about this matter. Now this claim should be responsive to various background constraints on language-use and -interpretation. How can it be that determining the reference of a token-sign just is to recognize its rule-governed use? A minimal condition would appear to be the clearly established functioning of well-defined contextual features surrounding a candidate-term. And an explication of what would thus be required for certain referring terms has yet to be accomplished. It will be anything but simple.

A third difficulty is that, in treating *I* as a term whose meaning is fully given by a rule, *Rule Theory* cannot accommodate other determinants of that meaning. And it may seem that some significance should be accorded to the determining role of other features (the intentions of the speaker, for example).

I shall set objections of this sort aside. They either assume *Rule Theory* is broadly true and worry about its explication, or assume the theory is false for reasons that have to do with specific theories of meaning. But if the arguments which follow are correct, *Rule Theory* should be wholly rejected. And this follows for reasons that run deep and appeal widely.

[5] e.g. Devitt (1989: 206–40). [6] e.g. Burge (1992: 26).
[7] Kaplan (1989: 493). [8] Kaplan (1989: 505; 520–1; 493; 500–1).

WHAT IS *RULE THEORY*?

§ 12.   It will be convenient to introduce a small number of special terms. This is partly to perspicuously represent *Rule Theory* and ease constant reference. But it is mainly to prevent the semantic theories we shall be considering from converting terminology into ideology without argument. The special terms introduced here disambiguate descriptions of semantic attributes and thus block attempts to conflate features whose identification should be argued for. So, for example, Frege's single term 'sense' is regularly used by sympathizers and critics alike to stand for what are in fact two different semantic attributes (distinguished here as 'content' and 'determinant'). Similarly, the single term 'referent' has been used to blur the distinction between two different semantic features (here called 'content' and 'referent'); this is particularly apparent in discussion of Kripke's distinction between 'fixing a referent' and 'supplying a synonym'. Finally, advocates of Kaplan's programme have regularly used the single term 'character' to cover semantic attributes occurring at two quite distinct levels of description (here called 'determinant' and 'definition'); this is tantamount to confusing genus with species.[9]

(*a*) Referent

The *Referent* is whatever the referring expression refers to on an occasion of use.

(*b*) Content

When Russell said that *I* means the same as *the subject of the present experience*, he was telling us what in his view any use of *I* contributes to the meaning of the whole sentence in which it occurs.[10] This is what we shall call the *Content* of a referring expression. If he is right, *I* and 'the subject of the present experience' must have the same content. And consequently sentences like 'I am happy' and 'The subject of the present experience is happy' must be synonymous, identical in their propositional constituents.

(*c*) Determinant

The *Determinant* of a referring expression is an umbrella term for whatever determines (fixes) the reference of its uses. 'Determine' is ambiguous on a crucial point. To avoid confusion, I say that something 'determines' reference if it plays a part in so doing, and 'sufficiently determines' if it is all that is needed to do so.

---

[9] Frege (1892*b*; 1918: 24–6). Kripke (1972: 55–60). Kaplan (1989: 500–7).
[10] 1914: 163–9.

When *Rule Theorists* claim that the meaning of *I* is exhaustively given by a simple rule in context, for example, they are telling us what in their view is the sufficient determinant of *I*.

Various features count as possible determinants of a referring expression:

Determinant (i): context

The *Context* of a referring expression is its possible occasions of use. For example, the occasion of its utterance. It is sometimes important, as Kaplan has pointed out, to distinguish between these occasions and possible occasions of *evaluation* or *interpretation*. The latter come into their own in certain less central cases, such as the answering machine paradox (discussed below): deferred utterances in whose production recording devices play a part.[11] Kaplan himself notes the difficulties with such cases.

The function of context in determining reference is clearer when we have noted another determinant:

Determinant (ii): definition

The *Definition* of a referring expression is its linguistic meaning, something that we would expect to find in an adequate dictionary entry for the term. Governed by linguistic convention, it may be identified with the rules governing use of the expression. So the simple rule in context which *Rule Theorists* claim as the sufficient determinant of *I* is one such definition. Suppose that the simple rule is as Kaplan formulates it: 'I refers to the speaker or writer.'[12] This rule can then be applied in some situation where a use of *I* is spoken or written so as to determine a particular individual within that context—the speaker or writer—as its referent. Kaplan offers another example of a definition when claiming that *He* refers to the male at whom I am now pointing.[13]

Definition is not to be equated either with Kaplan's term 'character' or Putnam's term 'stereotype'.[14] Focusing on the precise problems at issue requires that we distinguish between two questions: how the reference of *I* is determined (which is relevant), and how its content is determined (which is not relevant). Since Kaplan specifically defines 'character' as 'that which determines the content in varying contexts', use of the term would confuse the issue. Definitions have certain features in common with 'stereotypes'. Both help determine reference and need not be sufficient to do so. But there is a major difference. Stereotypes are specified as such by their pragmatic function in speaker reference. They facilitate communication by helping other members of a given community to 'fix on' the referent. Definitions, on the other hand, are bona fide semantic functors and

---

[11] Kaplan (1989: 491 n. 12). See also Sidelle (1991); Predelli (1998*a* and *b*); Corazza et al. (2002).
[12] 1989: 505.   [13] Kaplan (1989: 518).   [14] Kaplan (1989: 505); Putnam (1975).

relate to word meaning. They form part of the determinants of referring expressions and express what all competent users of the language know about those expressions, explicitly or implicitly.

Determinant (iii): demonstration

An example of *Demonstration* is the pointing necessary to determine the reference of *He*. Kaplan generalizes, saying demonstration is 'typically, though not invariably, a (visual) presentation of a local object discriminated by a pointing'.[15]

This definition gives rise to many more questions than it answers, as we shall see. Kaplan himself issues the caveat 'typically' because he accepts that 'demonstrations may also be opportune and require no special action on the speaker's part, as when someone shouts "Stop that man" while only one man is rushing toward the door'.[16] (It is irrelevant that he later denied semantic significance to demonstration; what distinguishes true demonstratives is *that* they are associated with demonstration not *how*.) But we can proceed for the time being on a rough approximation. Paradigmatic of demonstration in Kaplan's discussion is the ostensive gesture accompanying use of a visual demonstrative whose task it is to help determine the reference of that use.[17]

With this terminology in place, it is now possible to enter the following caveat. I shall be focused on *Rule Theory* in what follows, and hence almost exclusively on the determinant of *I*—and not, for example, on its possible contents or referents. So what I say will leave me legitimately agnostic on at least two crucial further questions: how, precisely, content and determinant are related (it may or may not be the case, for example, that content is simply a function of what an expression refers to), and what, precisely, content is to be identified with (it may be the referent; or some favoured way of thinking about the referent; or the functional or conceptual role of an expression in the user's psychology; or some possible-world intension associated with its use; or some other option). Also, my use of terms neither forces me to address, nor prejudices, the issue of whether or not theories of reference exist independently of, and additional to, theories of content.[18]

§ 13.   In Kaplan's view, and using his terminology, all indexicals have it in common that 'the referent is dependent on the context of use and that the meaning of the word provides a rule which determines the referent in terms of certain aspects of the context'. Those that are 'pure' require no further determinant, since 'The linguistic rules which govern *their* use fully determine the referent for each context.' Those that are not pure, 'true demonstratives', require something else to determine their referents: an associated demonstration.[19]

---

[15] Kaplan (1989: 490).   [16] Kaplan (1989: n. 9).
[17] As Kaplan's commentators are surely right to interpret him; see Reimer (1991: 177).
[18] See Perry (1977); Evans (1985: 294).   [19] Kaplan (1989: 490; 491; 492).

Using the terms introduced above, these claims may be translated so as to offer a more precise formulation of *Rule Theory*:

(PI1) If *R* is a singular referring expression whose referents are dependent on context, whose meaning is a rule-like definition, and whose definition-in-context is a determinant, then *R* is an Indexical Term.

(PI2) If *R* is an Indexical Term whose definition-in-context is sufficient determinant, then *R* is a *Pure Indexical*.

(PI3) If *R* is an Indexical Term whose definition-in-context is not sufficient determinant and which requires demonstration as a determinant, then *R* is an *Impure Indexical* (*Deictic Term*).

Rule Theory can now be defined more precisely as that position which claims the following extensions for these definition-sets *(PI1)–(PI3)*. *I*, *Here*, and *Now* are *Pure Indexicals*. *You*, *He/She*, and *This/That* are *Deictic Terms*.

With specific regard to *I*, the following implications are worth picking out:

(*a*) The meaning of *I* is its definition;

(*b*) The definition of *I* is the 'simple rule';

(*c*) The 'simple rule' in context is sufficient determinant of *I*.

I shall argue that *Rule Theory* is wholly false. Others have criticized aspects of the doctrine, and in particular Kaplan's version of it. There are various ways in which the arguments to be offered here will differ radically from earlier criticism. It may be helpful to note immediately the five most significant ways in which this is so.

(i) The arguments to be offered here differ in nature from earlier criticism of *Rule Theory*. As will become clear, they are grounded in appeal to logical features revealed by the behaviour of terms in inference. Earlier criticism has focused on more superficial semantic questions, such as whether or not demonstrations are needed to secure reference. For example, John Perry bases his resistance to the way Kaplan describes the extension of the class of paradigm indexicals on the grounds that one indexical (*Here*) has uses which require gestures if their reference is to be fixed.[20]

(ii) The arguments show that there *is* no distinction between *I* and demonstratives. Earlier criticism has merely questioned where the distinction lies. For all Perry's disagreement with Kaplan's account, for example, he nevertheless considers *I* a paradigm *Pure Indexical*, regards Kaplan's view as 'neatly capturing' what determines the reference of *I* (a matter of character and context), advocates *Rule Theory*, and agrees with Kaplan's formulation of the *Simple Rule* (in terms of an

---

[20] Perry (1997: 596).

utterer or speaker). His worries about Kaplan concern two questions which are not relevant to my subject: whether *Here* and *Now* are also paradigm indexicals (on the grounds that, unlike *I*, they appear to have intentional elements), and whether Kaplan's account of indexical *content* is correct.[21]

(iii) The arguments conclude by rejecting *Rule Theory* altogether. Earlier criticism has merely tried to improve it. For example, the discussion of deferred utterances has persuaded some that the *Simple Rule* should be formulated in terms of a broader technical notion of 'the agent' rather than the utterer/speaker.[22] Whereas I argue that the meaning of *I cannot* be given by a rule, no matter how formulated.

(iv) The arguments offer a deep explanation of why, even though it is quite false, *Rule Theory* has exercised so complete a hold over discussion of the meaning of *I*. Earlier criticism has accepted this domination as a given and as it should be. Part of the explanation is that something like a simple rule is indeed operative in relation to *I*; it is just that its role is quite the converse of that assigned to it by *Rule Theory*. But the real key to the domination of *Rule Theory* lies in the deep mutual support network provided by *Purism*. No viable form of *Rule Theory* can accommodate the rejection of *Independence* and *The Guarantee*. If every use of *I* is guaranteed to have a user and the reference of each such use is sufficiently determined on that user (*Rule Theory*), then each such use must have a referent (*The Guarantee*). If it is *as* the one using *I* to express thoughts that the one using *I* is referred to and the reference of each such use is sufficiently determined on that user (*Rule Theory*), then there can be no need for the user to identify that referent (*Independence*).

(v) The arguments draw positive and systematic conclusions from the failure of *Rule Theory*. They do not merely undermine Kaplan's *Pure Indexical/*true demonstrative distinction or suggest narrow ameliorations. Since *I* is a *Deictic Term* in each aspect of its meaning, superficial modification of the sort others have suggested would be quite useless. Earlier criticism has affected single aspects alone, and usually only the referential function or expressive use of *I*. What is required is a complete revision of our prevailing view, one that touches on all aspects of the meaning of *I*: its logical character, inferential role, referential function, expressive use, and communicative role.

WHAT IS THE SIMPLE RULE?

§ 14.　Even from its outline, it is clear that *Rule Theory* stands and falls with the particular 'simple rule' proposed. If we are to have any good reason to believe the

---

[21] Perry (1997: 596–8).

[22] See Sidelle (1991); Predelli (1998*a* and *b*); Corazza et al. (2002). The discussion was prompted by Kaplan himself; see his (1989: n.12).

doctrine, then we must at least understand what the 'simple rule' is, what it means, and what it determines. These are minor requirements, after all. What else but a sound grasp of these matters could have stimulated the current optimistic consensus in the first place?

But specifying the simple rule has evidently turned out to be a less than simple matter. Current literature offers a budget, as we have seen. The candidates differ from each other in quite important ways. So whatever agreement exists on the crucial question of what the 'simple rule' *is*, it seems markedly superficial. Recall the list:

1. 'whenever *[I]* is used by a speaker of English, it stands for, or designates, that person' (Barwise; Perry)
2. '*[I]* means the person using it' (Russell)
3. '*[I]* refers to the person who uses it' (Shoemaker)
4. 'the first personal pronoun refers, on each occasion of its use, to whoever then uses it' (Strawson)
5. '*I* refers to whoever uses it' (O'Brien)
6. 'Any utterance of *I* refers to its producer' (Peacocke)
7. '[Uses of *I*] refer to those who produce them' (Mellor)
8. 'Any token of *I* refers to whoever produced it' (Campbell)
9. '*I* refers to the speaker' (Rovane)
10. '*I* refers to the speaker or writer' (Kaplan)
11. '*I* refers ... to the speaker as presented in the context of utterance' (Brinck)
12. 'In any utterance containing *I*, the pronoun refers to the person who makes that utterance' (Larson; Segal)

(1)–(8) have general application, whereas (9)–(12) restrict themselves to speech, writing, or utterance in general. It is, presumably, a desirable feature of an account of the meaning of *I* that it should deal with all the kinds of case arising. So the 'simple rule' would have to apply not only to *I*-uses that are written or spoken, but to those that are, for example, typed or presented in sign-language. And it would have to cover not only those that are uttered, but, for example, those entertained in silent thought.

All but (7)–(8) give the impression of attributing reference to the term *I* rather than to uses of that term. It seems evidently wrong to attribute reference to the term. Which one thing is such that *it* is '*the* referent of *I*'?

(1)–(2) leave open what (3)–(11) take for granted: that *I* refers. This is a venerable dispute that should presumably be settled by argument, not assumed.

(4)–(11) imply what (1)–(3) and (11) exclude: the referent of *I* may not be a person. (Though the use of 'whoever', as opposed to 'whatever', in (3)–(4) and (6)–(7) leaves things unclear. Does it suggest that these rules are also designed to exclude non-persons?) It matters what kinds of thing are determinable as referents of uses of *I*, since parrots, games- and video-machines, infants, mentally impaired or sensorily deprived adults, angels, corporations, nations, and so on may all count as responsible for some one use of *I*. Are *they* what is referred to *by* that use?

(1)–(5) formulate the crucial relation between term and referent as one of use. In (6)–(8), it is a relation of production. Either has the advantage over (9)–(12): formulating the simple rule in terms of the speaker/writer/utterer is hopeless, since the speaker/writer/utterer may not be the one referred to—for example, if the referent has appropriate control of another's speaking/writing/uttering.[23]

It would be easier to determine what the 'simple rule' must mean if we were able to distinguish clearly between *Pure Indexicals* like *I* and other terms. But when we press this question, similar doubts and disagreements arise. For if definitions *(PI1)–(PI3)* are to function adequately to distinguish different types of indexical, then some good reason had better be found to exclude demonstration from the definition-in-context of any term. Otherwise it could be said of those terms which *do* require demonstration that they are *Pure Indexicals* after all. For then *their* definition-in-content would be sufficient to determine reference.

This is no easy matter, and Kaplan himself seems to fall into the trap when he offers this as the definition of a bona fide *Deictic Term*: '*He* refers to the male at whom I am now pointing.'[24] The formulation indicates how we can express the reference-determining role of demonstration in relation to uses of *He/She* by merely combining its definition with its context—i.e. (roughly speaking) the definition of *He* is represented by a function whose value at each context is the male demonstrated by the agent (speaker) of the context. Similar demonstration-invoking definitions could be specified for *That*, *This*, and other *Deictic Terms*. The linguistic conventions constituting the meaning of these terms consist of (more or less) complex rules specifying the referent of a given occurrence of the word (to recall Kaplan's own description of *Pure Indexicals*).[25] And what makes it the case that some one individual is picked out by some one use of such words is that it is the individual picked out by some one piece of associated demonstration.

There is another way of putting the point: demonstration may be incorporated into Kaplan's two-sided approach to *Pure Indexicals*. Consider two utterances: Abelard says: 'That is a rabbit,' and Bernard says: 'That is a rabbit.' These utterances have something in common—being utterances of the same sentence. Similarly, the word *That* has a single meaning that is shared by these utterances of it: its linguistic meaning, fixed by linguistic convention, which specifies the role of demonstration, shared by all utterances of the expression. There is another respect, however, in which these utterances differ. Suppose they differ in reference since Abelard meant one rabbit and Bernard another. This is explained by appeal

---

[23] See Peacocke (1983); O'Brien (1995*a*).   [24] 1989: 518.
[25] Kaplan (1989: 523; see also 505; 520–1; 524; 568; 577–8).

to the particular demonstration-in-context that the speakers used. Fluffy and Bobtail are picked out by Abelard and Bernard respectively by uttering the same sentence because it was Fluffy that was demonstrated by Abelard, and Bobtail that was demonstrated by Bernard.

This is a problem that arises because of difficult questions that surround the *role* of demonstration. But its *nature* also needs clarifying. To say that demonstration is 'typically, though not invariably, a (visual) presentation of a local object discriminated by a pointing', for example, raises various queries.[26] Does Kaplan's phrase mean that demonstration is the pointing or the presentation made salient by the pointing? In other words, is demonstration an action, or a contextual feature *indicated* by an action? Kaplan himself uses the term in both ways (compare the quoted phrase, which strongly suggests that demonstration is a presentation, with other passages).[27] His commentators tend just to attribute the former view to him, which is odd, since his 'standard form for demonstration' evidently entails the latter.[28]

If the demonstration is the pointing, must it be an ostensive bodily gesture, or can it include non-bodily signs? Must it be the *speaker's* action, or an action under the control of the speaker—could it be the action of another agent? If the demonstration is the (visual) presentation, to whom must it be present—would it be sufficient if the speaker alone saw it, or must the immediate audience see? If speakers refer to something that is (or could be) visually present to others, but not to the immediate audience, does that count as demonstration? Is demonstration to be thought of as a gesture or the situation in which a term is used, a whole of which gestures merely form a part? Kaplan himself does not resolve these issues. This is deeply unfortunate since *Rule Theory* gives a crucial role to demonstration: it helps create the divide between *I* and other singular personal pronouns.

WHAT DOES THE SIMPLE RULE MEAN?

§ 15.   Apparent consensus about the meaning of the 'simple rule' also turns out to be just that.

Some, who agree that the 'simple rule' gives the meaning of *I*, nevertheless deny that it is a reference rule, on the grounds that *I* is not a referring term (e.g. Anscombe).

Some give the 'simple rule' general application, while others think it applies only to the particular cases of speech, writing, or 'utterance' (e.g. Kaplan; Rovane).

Some leave the class of potential referents open while others restrict it to persons (e.g. Barwise and Perry; Shoemaker; Larson and Segal).

---

[26] Kaplan (1989: 490).   [27] Kaplan (1989: 526, 529).
[28] Kaplan (1989: 526); Braun (1996: 146).

Some think the 'simple rule' gives the *content* of I as well as its definition (e.g. Reichenbach). Others, who agree that the reference of I is sufficiently determined by a simple rule, explicitly deny that the 'simple rule' gives its content (Kaplan).

Some think the simple rule explains why I is immune to certain kinds of misidentification, and that this immunity in turn provides *the* key to explaining I. Or, at least, that we cannot understand I without explaining this immunity (e.g. Evans; Brinck). Others think this immunity claim is not obviously comprehensible, let alone well grounded.

Some formulate the 'simple rule' in terms of production (e.g. Peacocke; Mellor; Campbell); others in terms of use (Barwise and Perry; Russell; Shoemaker; Strawson; O'Brien).

Moreover, the 'simple rule' is ambiguous in all its formulations and in ways that have a direct bearing on significant issues. For example, consider the 'simple rule' that 'Uses of I refer to those who use them.' The various levels of ambiguity are most clearly visible when this rule is presented in logical form. So, taking Ix for 'x is a use of I', Uxy for 'x uses y', and Rxy for 'x refers to y' in the domain of singular referring terms and their possible referents, the 'simple rule' is ambiguous between:

(i) $\forall x[Ix \rightarrow \exists y[Uyx \wedge Rxy]\,]$

(ii) $\forall x\, \forall y[\,[Ix \wedge Uyx] \rightarrow Rxy]$

(iii) $\forall x\, \forall y[\,[\,[Ix \wedge Uyx \wedge \exists z\,[Rxz]\,] \rightarrow z = y]\,]$.

On this point alone, the generous spread of meanings consistent with the 'simple rule' is evident. Does it imply that (i) for every use of I there is a user to whom it will successfully refer? Or, more weakly, that (ii) for every use of I which has a user, the use will successfully refer to the user? Or, at its weakest, that (iii) for every use of I which has a user and which succeeds in referring, it will be to the user that the use refers? The first interpretation expresses a strong version of *The Guarantee* while it would not contradict the third to negate even the weakest version of that doctrine.

The domain of the 'simple rule' is not sufficiently specified (when it is specified at all). *Rule Theorists* who seek to rectify this logically unacceptable situation court severe internal dissension. For, as we have seen, some theorists claim that any use of I refers to whichever *person* is appropriately associated with it (e.g. Barwise and Perry; Russell; Shoemaker; Larson and Segal). This implies that non-persons are either incapable of producing/using tokens of I, or that they are not the referents of such tokens as they do produce/use. Other theorists consider that non-persons refer first-personally.[29] Both basic positions fragment in dealing with hard cases.

---

[29] See Woods (1968: 569); Mellor (1988).

The 'simple rule' only implies that, if a use of *I* refers, there is at least one individual that is its referent. *I*, on the other hand, is a singular referring expression. If a use of the term refers, there must be at least and at most (i.e. *exactly*) one individual that is its referent. This gap between term and determinant has unfortunate consequences. For example, the 'simple rule' might equally be said to give the meaning of *We*, determining its reference in context. This is as good as saying that it gives the meaning of neither. For as we have seen, *We* is a plural term lacking first-person form.

WHAT DOES THE SIMPLE RULE DETERMINE?

§ 16.   There is no clear consensus amongst *Rule Theorists* about what gets determined as the referent of uses of *I*. It is too restrictive to specify the 'simple rule' in terms of speakers and writers, as we have seen. The alternative is to determine 'the user' or 'the producer' as referent. But which? For these descriptions are not synonyms. They overlap, undeniably. But they do not map onto each other without remainder. (It is never redundant to say 'Abelard produces a use of *I*' or 'Abelard uses a production of *I*' whereas 'Abelard produces a production of *I*' and 'Abelard uses a use of *I*' usually are redundancies.) So they will always permit cases in which there is a producer and a user but the one is not identical with the other.

For example, you might produce the statement 'I admit to committing this crime' on my behalf (writing it if I am illiterate; speaking it if I am mute) which I then use to make my confession to the authorities. The referent of this use of *I* is evidently me, its user and not you, its producer. Suppose under the pressure of such cases the 'simple rule' is reformulated in terms of use. That option is similarly embarrassed by cases of the opposite sort. Suppose I am the executor of your will and thus sole user of the signed requests you have produced legitimizing various necessary funerary arrangements—'I wish that my body be given to science.' Here, the referent is the producer and not (at least straightforwardly) the user. It is no use modifying the 'simple rule' so that it becomes the inclusively disjunctive 'Any use of *I* refers to whoever produced *or* used it.' For the disjunction we need to capture is exclusive. This is partly because, as the cases above show, on some occasions the referent is the producer and precisely *not* the user. On other occasions, the reverse is true. But it is mainly because, if the 'simple rule' is to be adequate to determining reference, it must say *which thing* is referred to by a use of *I*, and an inclusive disjunction will not achieve this where producers and users differ.

The issue just raised assumes a deeper issue has been resolved. Asking 'User or producer: *which* is determined as the referent of uses of *I*?' assumes that at least we know which item is determined as its user or producer. But almost any number of things have equally valid claims to being counted as 'producing' or 'using' *I* on any occasion. Is it the individual body, or person or human being? The set of lips, tongue, or teeth? The combination of vocal cords, velum, or lungs? The particular neurophysiology (brain-stem, cortices, synapses, autonomic centres, etc.) or musculature? The pen, brush, or printer? The microphone, speaker-system, or answer-phone? The spokesperson, speech-writer, adviser, collaborator, ghost-writer, medium, or mouthpiece? Some aggregate, part, or time-slice of any or all of these? For any one use of *I*, there may be innumerable producers. Conversely, there may be a single producer for innumerable uses. For example, the sign-writer who paints 'Phone Oxford 1212 if you wish to complain about me' on a van that might be used by any member of some firm to elicit comments about their own abilities. (In this case, more troublingly, there is any number of uses of *I*, but *none* appear to refer, at least straightforwardly, to their producer.)

§ 17.   There may be special senses of 'producer' or 'user' that would give invariably accurate statements of the reference of any use of *I* when incorporated in the 'simple rule'. But it would be no simple matter to specify them. And in renouncing simplicity, the whole project loses most of its appeal. Consider an obvious constraint: if it is correct to take the 'simple rule' as fixing the reference of any *I*-use, a use of a singular term, it must uniquely determine a single candidate for each use. One would have to avoid conceiving 'the producer' or 'user' too narrowly or too broadly. Conceive it too narrowly, and the referent of one's *I*-uses would be those enumerated above: one's brain, vocal chords, mouth, tongue, teeth, pen, brush, printer, microphone, etc. Conceived too broadly, and all those who contribute in any way to an *I*-use's production become its referents. The possibility of reference-splitting is intolerable in a singular term.

One would need to stipulate in precisely what relevant sense someone who is the referent of an *I*-use, but who merely signs a pre-written document containing it, or who thinks it, is its 'producer' or 'user'. It would be necessary to specify, for example, in what relevant sense someone who is not the referent of an *I*-use, but whose vocal apparatus is used to utter it, is *not* its 'producer' or 'user'. Moreover, one would need to establish in what sense there is just one 'producer' or 'user' of an *I*-use when two or more items would count as such in the ordinary sense. For example, where producing or using an *I*-use involves a person and a voice-box, or a person and a microphone.

§ 18.   Imprecision about the definition of 'producer' and 'user' results in inaccuracy in determining the referent of *I* in context. Only an underlying rule could solve this problem, it seems. One which identified what should and what should not count as a 'who' and as a producer of a use of *I*. John Campbell accepts the need to complicate matters in this way, suggesting that:

production of a token in the sense we need has to do with one's being causally related to the token in such a way that it can be used to communicate or express knowledge that one has.[30]

----

[30] Campbell (1994: 111).

But if my vocal chords were so played around with that I had no control over them and I were being used, literally, as a mouthpiece in producing the statement 'I am a speaker for the People's Front', I would be causally related to that token in such a way that it is being used *precisely* to communicate knowledge that I have. I do indeed know that I am a speaker for the People's Front. But there is little inclination to suppose that the token of *I* refers to *me* in this case. If I exercise no control over my speech, it surely refers to the person *using* me.

There are other kinds of rule one might add. Clearly, the mere sound associated with the term *I* cannot count as a use of the type picking out its producers: the sound may have been produced by the wind in the willows. So we might stipulate an underlying rule to ensure that *I* refers to the *person* who produced it (following Barwise and Perry; Russell; Shoemaker; Larson and Segal). And we might similarly ensure that 'produce' on this occasion means 'whoever's vocal chords produced this very use'. But then a person would still count as the referent of a use of *I* even if he had been used, literally, as a mouthpiece or ghost-writer by another (as Aaron was 'for the God inspiring him'[31]). This strikes a false note. It could be rectified if we say the person producing means 'the person with whom the information expressed in sentences containing this very use originates'. But then, if I say 'I am a Capricorn', I am actually referring to the fortune-teller who told me so. Again, this could be rectified if the person producing means 'the person with whom the beliefs, desires, and intentions being expressed in the sentence containing this very use originates'. But that description could fit any number of people in any normal utterance: who can say with whom ultimately originates the beliefs or desires expressed when I say 'I believe in democracy'?

The problems are compounded when we consider indirect or fictional contexts. For if *Rule Theory* is correct, then presumably the 'simple rule' must be sufficient to give the meaning of *I*-uses here also. But suppose I produce an utterance: 'John said "I will be in Oxford tomorrow." ' Then the referent of *this I*-use is evidently not its producer but John. Or suppose I quote President Kennedy's statement: 'Ich bin ein Berliner.' Is the referent of that use myself who thinks the line, or Kennedy who spoke it, or the speech-writer who wrote it, or the political adviser whose own rough thoughts were vividly expressed by it? Would uses of *I* lack a unique referent (and thus fail of reference) if no one could precisely be determined as their unique producer? The 'simple rule', *pace Rule Theory*, is not obviously sufficient to deal with such cases. Some argue that fiction is a special case that will always require special treatment. This response appeals to a sensible general practice. But it does little to deflect the objection in this particular case. For the character of the problems arising is identical. Suppose Shakespeare produces a line for his character Hamlet: 'I have that within which passeth show.' Is the referent of that very use the actor who speaks the line, or the character, Hamlet, whose thoughts it is meant to represent, or Shakespeare who wrote the line, or none of these? Would

---

[31] *Exodus*, 4: 16.

this use lack a unique referent (and thus fail of reference) if it turned out that *Hamlet* was a composite work, written in part by Beaumont and in part by Fletcher?

To be clear: it remains to be seen whether any reference-rule for *I* can succeed in distinguishing genuine referents from *mere* producers, users, etc. on all occasions of its use while remaining simple, i.e. without complications and epicycles. Given the indeterminacy of *Rule Theory*, it would be impossible to construct a knock-down argument showing that no such rule could be found. But suppose we do discover a simple rule which does accurately describe the reference of any use of *I*. The question is what we would actually have achieved. Certainly not that *Rule Theory* is true. For that, we would have to have shown that this rule *determines* the reference of *I*, not simply that it *describes* it. And the most plausible explanation of why any rule x accurately describes some practice y is that it is y which determines x, decides that it constitutes an accurate representation of y, etc. So it is unclear why one would be motivated to look for such a rule. We may be lured on by the notion that the vaunted complexities of the first person would evaporate to leave a simple rule that is sufficient wholly to characterize it. But that puts the cart before the horse. We have no good reason as yet to believe this evaporation possible in our present position, the position in which we have *yet* to arrive at something resembling a viable formulation of the rule. We may not even believe it *afterwards* if, as should be obvious from what we know of other referring expressions, the meaning of terms encompasses more than their reference-rules.

WHAT IS THE CONTEXT?

§ 19.   When specified sufficiently carefully, *Rule Theory* states that the 'simple rule' is sufficient determinant *in context*. But those advocates who deal with this aspect of the theory are not agreed on what that context is.[32] And there is good reason to be unsure. Compare the definition given above,

(C$_1$) The context of the use

with an alternative

(C$_2$)   The context in which the user intends the use to be interpreted.

Unfortunately, (C$_1$) and (C$_2$) differ radically and there is something to be said for each that cannot be said for both. To see why, consider a case raised by Kaplan in discussion with Donnellan and known familiarly in recent literature as *(Sidelle's) Answering Machine Paradox*.[33]

---

[32] Compare Kaplan (1989: 494) and Millikan (1993: 266).
[33] See Kaplan (1989: 491); Sidelle (1991); Predelli (1998*a* and *b*); Corazza et al. (2002).

Suppose I record the message 'I am not here now' on my answer-phone with the usual intention: that uses be activated and interpreted only when the statement is true (i.e. when I am absent). The main problem here is a puzzle specifically for *Rule Theorists*. How can we account for the fact that the problematic sentence is true consistently with the view that *I*, *Now*, and *Here* are *Pure Indexicals* whose meaning is given by simple rules? But the difficulties ramify to disturb notions of context also. For if the machine produces the message 'I am not here now' when I am indeed absent, then the utterance comes out false if the reference of the *I*-use is determined by (C_1) and true if determined by (C_2). Thus (C_1) or (C_2) are inconsistent with each other and a *Rule Theorist* must decide between them.

If we are not *Rule Theorists*, however, we need not decide. And this is just as well, since we should commit ourselves to neither. For neither is regularly consistent with what we know to be true of *I*. In the case just described, for example, (C_2) evidently obtains the correct result. But suppose before I go under the surgeon's knife I leave a reassuring message for you to receive on arriving home later on, saying, 'I have been operated on successfully.' In this case, determining the reference of *I* by (C_1) obtains the correct result. The statement is false, not true as (C_2) would have it (the time I *intended* it to be interpreted does not play a part here).

Indeed, if we are not *Rule Theorists*, there is no paradox for us to resolve. An utterer always exists at the time and place of utterance. So if we adopt Kaplan's version of *Rule Theory* (the meaning of *I*, *Now*, and *Here* is given by the simple rules that their uses refer respectively to the utterer, time, and place of utterance), the sentence 'I am not here now' can never be true. Hence all participants in the debate have used the paradox to force a revision *within Rule Theory*: i.e. to find a better version of the simple rule. But suppose we decide *Rule Theory* cannot meet the explanatory demands on an adequate account of first-personal reference using *I* (the demands of logical character, inferential role, referential function, expressive use, and communicative role) and hence reject it, root and branch. Then there is no paradox and no need to engage in the debate on how to revise the simple rule. We need not deny that it might be possible to concoct carefully qualified versions of the rule that would cope with the paradox. We need only deny that such measures would explain the meaning of *I*.

Notwithstanding considerable recent debate on the issues arising, it is still wholly unclear what conclusion a *Rule Theorist* should draw from the answering machine paradox. This tells us something about the way the debate is set up. The situation it aims to account for is an instance of a special, limiting case, the so-called 'deferred utterance'. And this case is itself only poorly understood—too poorly to provide sufficient reason for inferring *that* the *Simple Rule* must adapt, let alone *how*. So it is not surprising that the debate has resisted any move towards resolution. Indeed, given such possibilities of wide divergence at the foundations, we would expect even the diagnoses of what needs to be resolved to vary widely. And this is precisely what we find.

Kaplan, for example, evidently assumes the problem is caused by indeterminacy about the reference of *Now*. If he is right, it is not the simple rule for *I* we need to revise, but our account of temporal indexicality. His critics assume otherwise, insisting that we revise the rule for *I*. And again, as we would expect given such deep background indeterminacy, this response varies widely. Kaplan had identified the referent of any *I*-use with the agent of the context, understanding 'agent' in turn as the speaker or utterer. Later in his career, he emphasized the role of the speaker's directing intentions. This has prompted some critics of his earlier views to insist that we understand 'agent' itself in a more technical sense as something determined by intention (e.g. Predelli). Other critics have turned in another direction, pursuing Recanati's recommendation that we emphasize convention as that which 'determines the linguistic mode of presentation associated with *I*'. They have argued that 'agent' should be understood as a technical term determined by convention (e.g. Corazza).[34]

Whether or not these revisions resolve the answering machine paradox created by *Rule Theory* depends on whether they are independently viable. But the 'intention'-option falls foul of a point that must be stressed against Kaplan's own later views, as we shall see: intentions are neither sufficient nor necessary to determine reference. The 'convention'-option depends on the claim that 'for any use of the personal indexical, the contextual parameter of the agent is contextually given—given by the social or conventional setting in which the utterance takes place'.[35] But this suggestion is merely a restatement of the problem, not a solution to it. For it does not tell us what reference is *determined on* in any given case (if not the utterer in deferred utterances, for example), but merely what plays a part in so *determining* reference. Hence the usual difficulties arise. Perhaps we should regard the referent of the use as its agent 'in the technical sense', where the latter counts as such by convention. But which item *is* it that convention tells us is the agent in any of the hard cases (in deferred utterances, for example)?

In short, we should say the same about the answering machine paradox as about puzzles raised by fiction and conniving usage. There is at least as much reason to think that we should hold our theory of *I* steady (be it based around a simple rule or not) and explain anomalous cases by what is peculiar to deferred utterances in general, as there is to pretend we have a stable account of deferrals in general and fine-tune our account of *I* to cope with anomalies. Sidelle is surely correct when he remarks that it is a 'general theory of deferred utterances' that the paradox calls for, a theory we wholly lack.[36]

§ 20.   Suppose *Rule Theorists* were agreed on the notion of context within which the 'simple rule' sufficiently determines *I*-uses. Might that resolve some of the issues stated above? Some have sought greater precision for the 'simple rule' by

---

[34] Predelli (1998*a* and *b*). See (Kaplan 1989: 582); Recanati (1993: 87); Corazza et al. (2002).
[35] Corazza et al. (2002: 11).
[36] Kaplan (1989: 491); Predelli (1998*a* and *b*); Perry (1997: 596–8); Sidelle (1991: 538).

using another rule to specify the right sense of 'producer' or 'user'. But might we obtain the same result by leaving these senses vague and instead limiting the possible candidates by appeal to context?

Consider this proposal, which makes *Rule Theory* explicit at the relevant points: 'Any use of *I* refers to whoever is its user in the context of use'. 'Context' needs glossing if this proposal is to be helpful. Compare the claim that 'add 2' is a rule (function) sufficiently determining the value of any number when applied to its context. 'Context' may mean any—perhaps *every*—thing whose existence is acknowledged by our ontology, whether it be past, present or future, concrete or abstract, universal or particular; propositions, sets, numbers, events, relations, properties, or states of affairs; bodies material or immaterial. So we do not expect to learn about the rule 'add 2' unless we know *what* parts of context it applies to, and of that part, *which*—i.e. it applies to numbers, and, of those, to that which is given on some occasion.

The proposal invites ambiguity on precisely this point. Expressed in logical form, where *Ix* is '*x* is a use of *I*' and *Dxy* is '*x* determines *y*' in the domain of singular referring terms, the ambiguity is between

   (i) $\forall x[Ix \rightarrow \forall y \ [Dyx]\,]$
   (ii) $\exists x \ \forall y \ [Iy \rightarrow Dxy]$
   (iii) $\forall x \ [Ix \rightarrow \exists y \ [Dyx]\,]$

It may be read as entailing that the reference of every *I*-use is determined by everything (i.e. (i)). But 'everything' includes this very proposal, so its influence is subsumed. Thus the proposal cannot explain why two *I*-uses might have different referents even though they occur simultaneously—for then what determines them (i.e. everything) is the same. If we read the proposal differently as entailing that there is some one thing such that, in addition to the proposal, it determines every *I*-use (i.e. (ii)), the same problem arises. How, then, can two *I*-uses have different referents? We might read the proposal very differently: that, for every *I*-use, there can be found some one thing that determines it (i.e. (iii)). This reading might seem plausible: *if* for every *I*-use, there is one thing that might be said to combine with the proposal to determine its reference—i.e. its producer or user on some occasion. But on many occasions, as we have found, there is no one thing such that it is *the* producer or user of an *I*-use. We wanted to appeal to the supposedly straitening notion of context to make 'producer' and 'user' precise, not to have them straiten that notion. So this is clearly no solution.

WHAT ROLE DOES THE SIMPLE RULE HAVE?

§ 21. All in all, the significant differences of opinion amongst theorists and the fact that we know neither what the 'simple rule' is, nor what it means, nor what it determines, count against the bluff notion that there is a compelling and obvious truth about *I*, and that *Rule Theory* represents it. And yet there is an overwhelming sense that something like the 'simple rule' is operative in the use of *I*. How can this be? It is not very mysterious if we recognize the likeness between saying 'any use of *I* in English refers to whoever uses it' and 'any driver in England drives on the left'. The latter claim is true enough so long as we do not try to claim that it is sufficient wholly to account for car-use in England.

No one would ever dream of exalting the rule for cars in this way—and for very good reason, given that

(*a*) There are areas which the rule does not cover (e.g. what to do when stationary).

(*b*) There are areas in which this rule applies but is insufficient (we need to add what to keep left *of* in any circumstances; what to keep *right* of; etc.).

(*c*) There are occasions on which this rule should not be applied (e.g. when directed by the police to the right).

(*d*) There are occasions on which this rule cannot be applied (e.g. when driving along a one-way street).

The point is that we have just the same good reasons to avoid exalting the 'simple rule' for *I*.

(*a*) The 'simple rule' does not cover what uses of *I* contribute to the overall meaning of sentences, how we are able to make, communicate and understand those sentences, what kind of judgements those sentences express, how we are put in a position to make or comprehend them, how *I* operates in fictional and indirect contexts, and so on.

(*b*) The 'simple rule' is insufficient; we need to add the domain, specify a determinate sense for 'user' and 'producer', determine what kinds of thing count as possible referents, and so on.

(*c*) The 'simple rule' should not be applied on occasions when the referent is the user rather than the producer, or vice versa (e.g. the sign-writing case).

(*d*) The 'simple rule' cannot be applied on occasions when the referent is neither the producer nor the user (e.g. when merely thinking *I*).

The rule 'any driver in England drives on the left' could not be regarded as sufficient to account for car-use in England. If anyone tried to make it do so, the difficulties would be familiar to us, being the same as those that condemn any attempt to perform the same trick with the 'simple rule' for *I*. To carry out such a task, the rule would have to be understood in some very complex way so that we would not be able to say any longer exactly what that rule is, what it means, or what it determines. And yet the rule is perfectly plain and in good order when left to its usual role. The same is true of the 'simple rule' for *I*. Being vague, accommodating, expressible in subtly different ways, and so on, are positive aspects of both rules. But only so long as the rules are not exalted to account for everything about *I*-use or car-use. For then a restrictive and specificatory power is demanded which is quite lacking in either rule. If we do not impose this impossible task on the 'simple rule', there is no problem with it.

By promoting the 'simple rule' beyond its abilities, *Rule Theory* prevents it carrying out tasks for which it *is* well suited. So consider this principal instance. When we use a referring term, we are often called on to back it up. Suppose I say, 'That is worth reading,' and you say, '*What* is?' I can reply with sentences like 'The book on the table' or 'This book [pointing]'. I might also say, 'The item I meant,' or 'The item that was contextually salient on the occasion of use.' None of these sentences are false. But the first two are helpful to you and the second two are not. This is because the first group give you other means of identifying the item referred to while the second group merely give the determinants of the original term. If I tried to pack you off with one of the latter sentences, you might reply, 'I *know* what *That* means; I needed an identity statement, not a dictionary.' The 'simple rule' does not give us the determinant of *I*, as we have discovered. But if it fails in that role, it can nevertheless be helpful as an answer to '*Who* is?' questions. When I evade the police but they see the sign 'Phone Oxford 1212 if you wish to complain about me' painted on my van, it is helpful for them to know that the answer to the question '*Who* can be complained about by phoning this number?' is 'the user', rather than the sign-writer who produced it. If I intend to use your statement 'I wish that my body be given to science' to legitimize funerary arrangements, I will make it clear to the appropriate authorities when they ask *who* wishes this (the signature may be illegible) that it is 'the producer', rather than me, its user.

§ 22.   So an explanation is called for. If no one would ever say 'All you need to know about car-driving in England is "drive on the left" ', except as a joke, why has *Rule Theory* been taken so seriously? There is a clue in what Campbell takes for compelling evidence: the 'simple rule' gives 'an invariably accurate statement of the reference of any token of *I*'.[37] The observation is true, by and large (as we have just appreciated). And it is indeed tempting to think that, if so, then *Rule Theory* must be true. That would explain why the doctrine commands widespread acceptance.

The mistake is well hidden. Part of the problem is that the observation could be true for *two* reasons, and only one supports *Rule Theory*. The issue parallels the *Euthyphro* problem. For if the doctrine is true, then the 'simple rule' determines some individual as the referent of an *I*-use because they are its recognized user-producer. But the 'simple rule' would *also* give an accurate statement of that reference even if *Rule Theory* were false and the reverse was the case: that some individual is determined as the user-producer of an *I*-use because they are its recognized referent. So the inference is invalid. The other part of the problem is

---

[37] Campbell (1994: 110).

that, in so far as the observation is true, it is true for the second reason. For what the second reason requires we can satisfy: by and large we know how to recognize which one thing is the referent of *I* on any occasion of use. Not so with the first reason. We do *not* know how to recognize which one thing is *the* user or producer on any such occasion, and this has been extensively illustrated.

The point can be expressed in another way. We might reason as follows: '*x* is the referent of statement *S*; given the simple rule, the referent of *S* is its user-producer; so *x* must be the user-producer of *S*.' Here, the appropriate sense of 'producer' or 'user' relevant to the 'simple rule' is determined by the reference, it does not determine it. If a rule determines reference, then it should be a function sufficient of itself to provide a value for any use when applied to its context. Now the 'simple rule' is clearly insufficient for this task, in large part because we lack a precise and consistent sense of 'producer' or 'user'. But once we know what that value is on some occasion, it is possible by and large to find an appropriate sense in which that value may be described as 'the producer or the user of that occasion'. And that sense may then be used by the 'simple rule' to state accurately the reference of that *I*-use.

So this is the most plausible way to explain why *Rule Theory* is false but attractive: it claims merit for an ability that it does not confer. By appeal to the 'simple rule' and its use of *I*, we can account for the meaning of 'user-producer'. *Rule Theory* cannot claim the credit, though it seems to have done so in the confusion, because it is set the opposite task: to account for the meaning of *I* by appeal to the 'simple rule' and its use of 'user-producer'.

3

Questions of Expression

§ 23.   *Rule Theory* is a dead end, and so, perhaps, is the composite position at whose heart it lies, *Purism*. Something like the 'simple rule' is operative, but it does not give the meaning of *I* nor sufficiently determine its uses in context. So where does the trail lead now? We should retrace our steps and recall why it seemed advantageous to adopt the doctrine in the first place.

Rule Theory appeared capable of explaining why *I* is not what we discovered it is not—a proper name, for example, or descriptive term. But the main reason why *Purism* won out over its rivals in the historical debate was that it had at its core a doctrine which could also perform a major positive task: validate two more venerable doctrines nestling in the same fold. For every use of *I* must have a referent (the user) if it is sufficient for each that it have a user, and there is no need for the one expressing thoughts by using the term to identify who those thoughts are about—one need only know one is the user to know one is the referent (the same applies if the 'simple rule' is phrased in terms of production rather than use). So *Rule Theory* provided a deep explanation for *Independence* (one can use *I* to express thoughts without having to identify what is being referred to) and *The Guarantee* (one's use of *I* is logically secured against failure to refer). These connections suggest one course of action: to attempt a similar feat by creating an alternative to *Rule Theory* that vouches for these other two doctrines. But we are forewarned now about the whole *Purism* project. So we would do better to ascertain first that these doctrines are worth vouching for.

We may begin with *Independence*, which differs in a complementary way from *Rule Theory* and *The Guarantee*. The two latter doctrines account for aspects of the meaning of *I* by answering the question 'What must be true of *I* if its uses are to refer?' *Independence* covers further ground by telling us something of the expressive use of *I*. It addresses the question 'what must be true of *I* if its uses are to say something of the individual one is thinking about?' One way to plot the difference is to note that, plausibly, uses of *I* must refer successfully to express first-personal thinking, but they need not express such thinking to refer successfully.

Three preliminary remarks. *Independence* is not (usually) taken to hold for *all* uses of *I*. This is why Wittgenstein's *Blue Book* and other authors distinguish between the uses of *I* for which the doctrine holds (the uses 'as subject') and those for which it does not (the uses 'as object'). Nevertheless, it is usual to regard those for which the doctrine does hold as the 'central use' of first-person forms, that from which others deviate.[1]

But the inference from *Independence* to priority or centrality is not obviously cogent. For even if the doctrine holds for certain uses of *I*, it remains to be shown that we are not dealing with *special* uses; i.e. limiting cases that are variants of, or even deviate from, the truly central uses, the uses 'as object'. An argument to counter this is necessary for several reasons. The 'as subject' uses are a peculiar way for an allegedly bona fide referring expression to behave. It is notable that there is little inclination to credit uses of *other* terms (e.g. perceptual demonstratives) that appear to manifest the same features with priority-centrality status. And it would be consistent with Wittgenstein's position as expressed at various points in his career (including that immediately preceding the *Blue Book* remarks) to *demote* uses of *I* 'as subject' precisely because they counted as such.[2] For what these uses show is the redundancy (perhaps even eliminability) of the term in certain uses. Because there is no 'recognition of a person' involved in saying 'I have toothache', the subject who cries out 'toothache!' has expressed himself just as fulsomely. So the 'as subject' uses are precisely not those which we should take as our measure in elucidating first-person forms.

Second, our subject is expressive use; cases where the individual needs to know that the individual spoken about is the same as the individual thought about. For this is precisely the issue on which the doctrine stakes its claim: that in using *I*, one can know that the individual thought of is the same as the individual spoken about without having to make an identity judgement. So we will be ignoring non-central cases in which there is a merely accidental connection between what the speaker says and thinks—i.e. where someone thinks '*a* is *F*' and says '*a* is *F*', but takes himself to have thought or spoken about *b* instead. These cases are not to be described as cases of 'expressive use' precisely because they are not occasions on which the speaker *uses* a term to *express* his thoughts.

Failure to distinguish the expressive use and referring role of terms explains much current confusion about these issues: evidence relevant to one is sometimes assumed, quite falsely, to provide an answer to the other. But the differences are quite marked. An expression like *I* has a referring role when applied to things that are incapable of *any* thought (e.g. obelisks which state 'I stand at the limits of Hammurabi's realm') and used by bona fide thinkers who have no intention of expressing their own thoughts (e.g. quotation and fiction). And much less is required if one's use of a singular term is to refer than if it is to express one's thinking. This is true quite generally. So consider a term like *That*. If Abelard says, 'That bird is a hawk,' and points, it is not implausible to suppose that conventional features of the established device *That* will determine whether it refers, and

---

[1] See Evans (1982: 181; see also 221–4; 236–7); McDowell (1996: 362; 1998: 132); Brewer (1992: 30); O'Brien (1995*b*: 241).
[2] Wittgenstein (1930: 88–96).

what to, no matter whether he has his eyes or ears open, or even whether he has such a thought to express. To have such a thought to express, on the other hand, one must also (at least) have some particular object in mind when thinking *That bird is a hawk*. And one must have sufficient knowledge of the language to recognize that the sentence 'That bird is a hawk' is true if and only if this thought is what is the case.

Third, I shall delay discussion of two related matters which have greater relevance to my positive proposals: whether the use of *I* to express thoughts requires 'keeping track' of the referent, and what kind of self-awareness might ground identity-judgements in cases of self-ascription.[3]

§ 24.   *Independence* is a doctrine that has grown in the telling. There are hints in Hume that one can use *I* to express thoughts about oneself without the need to identify what is being referred to.[4] It is said that Kant thought this held for the *I Think* of transcendental apperception.[5] But the doctrine only began to achieve clear definition with Wittgenstein:

There are two different cases in the use of the word *I* (or *My*) which I might call 'the use as object' and 'the use as subject'. Examples of the first kind are these: 'My arm is broken', 'I have grown six inches'. 'I have a bump on my forehead', 'The wind blows my hair about'. Examples of the second kind are '*I* see so-and-so', '*I* hear so-and-so', '*I* try to lift my arm', '*I* think it will rain', '*I* have toothache'. One can point to the difference between these two categories by saying: The cases of the first category involve the recognition of a person, and there is in these cases the possibility of an error ... On the other hand, there is no question of recognising a person when I say I have toothache. To ask 'are you sure that it's *you* who have pains?' would be nonsensical. Now, when in this case no error is possible, it is because the move which we might be inclined to think of as an error, a 'bad move', is no move of the game at all ... To say 'I have pain' is no more a statement *about* a particular person than moaning is.[6]

We can detect at the core of this passage an argument from explanation with two simple steps. (*a*) There is a certain phenomenon: it would make no sense to ask certain questions (call this the 'nonsense-question phenomenon'; *Nonsense* for short). (*b*) To explain this phenomenon, *Nonsense*, we need to adopt *Independence*.

For Wittgenstein, *Independence* meant that there is no recognition of a person involved in certain uses of *I* ('as subject'). His two-step argument has proved remarkably durable. Peter Strawson employed it, for example, when considering subjects of experience who ascribe a current or directly remembered state of consciousness to themselves using *I*, e.g. 'I am angry':

It would make no sense to think or say: This inner experience is occurring, but is it occurring to me? (This feeling is anger; but is it I who am feeling it?) Again, it would make

[3] On the former, see Evans (1982: 175; 192–6; 236); McDowell (1996: 362 n. 4); Campbell (1994: 86). On the latter, see Shoemaker (1968; 1986; 1994; 1996); Cassam (1995).
[4] See Shoemaker (1968; 1986).   [5] See Strawson (1966: 165–9).
[6] Wittgenstein (1969: 66–7).

no sense to think or say: I distinctly remember that inner experience occurring, but did it occur to me? (I remember that terrible feeling of loss; but was it I who felt it?)[7]

These are the questions Strawson identified as nonsensical for step (*a*). For step (*b*), he argued that we should adopt *Independence*.[8] The validity of the two-step argument from explanation has been confirmed by others who have found its formulation worth improving on. The application of the basic argument has also been extended (another sign of its perceived security) to first-personal ascriptions of bodily properties and to the use of pronouns other than *I*.[9] Strawson's way of phrasing *Nonsense* has proved suggestive for this purpose. There is a judgement here, 'this experience is occurring', and it is apparently nonsensical on certain occasions to ask after its subject, 'is it *mine*?' So there are cases in which one enjoys immunity to a particular mistake: attaching a predication to its subject by a false identity-judgement. And one would not expect such a mistake to occur if there were no identity-judgement to make in the first place.

More specifically, then, there are cases in which knowing 'I am *F*' (e.g. 'I am in pain') does not depend on first knowing '*a* is *F*' (e.g. 'the man in that hospital bed is in pain') and conjoining that with the identity-judgement 'I = *a*' ('I am the man in the hospital bed').[10] And in such cases, the judgement 'I am *F*' must be regarded as independent of identification. This is said to be so for reasons Wittgenstein made familiar: that where there is no possibility of identification-*error*, there is no identification at all. As Evans expresses the point with reference to the statements in question, 'since they do not rest upon an identification, they are immune to error through misidentification'.[11]

Sydney Shoemaker has precisely defined the type of immunity to error in question. On occasion, this cannot occur: that though I know some particular thing to be F, I mistakenly assert 'I am F' because, and only because, I believe falsely that the thing known to be F is what this use of *I* refers to.[12] The improvements to Wittgenstein's basic argument can be simply rendered as distinguishing two stages to the second step:

(*a*) it would make no sense to ask certain questions;

(*b*i) to explain this phenomenon, *Nonsense*, we need to regard certain judgements as immune to error through misidentification relative to *I* (*Immunity*, for short);

(*b*ii) to explain *Immunity*, we need to adopt *Independence*.

If *Independence* is true, the central uses of *I* ('as subject') express thoughts without one's having to identify the particular individual they are about. This is common ground with *The Guarantee*, which assures us that the terms used to express such thoughts could not fail to be about that particular individual. So the doctrine would retain some measure of support after the demise of *Rule Theory*.

[7] Strawson (1966: 165).

[9] See Evans (1982: 179–92; 220–4).

[11] Evans (1982: 182).

[8] Strawson (1966: 165–9).

[10] See Evans (1982: 180).

[12] Shoemaker (1968: 82).

WHAT IS *INDEPENDENCE*?

§ 25.   In documenting *Independence*, I have emphasized the commonality of argument-form. This is partly because the consensus here is striking (though unnecessary), and partly because there is little enough consensus elsewhere—especially where it would be expected: i.e. on the question of what the doctrine *is* and what it *entails*. For *Independence* is defined in different ways, sometimes by the same author. Thus Strawson formulates the doctrine (he calls it 'criterionless self-ascription') as follows:

When a man (a subject of experience) ascribes a current or directly remembered state of consciousness to himself, no use whatever of any criteria of personal identity is required to justify his use of the pronoun *I* to refer to the subject of that experience.[13]

This evidently differs from Wittgenstein, in whose formulation the uses of *I* in question do not even count as being *about* the subject of the ascribed experience, let alone as *referring* to that subject.

Strawson's definition of *Independence* differs also from one that he himself offers elsewhere: that 'the immediate self-ascription of thoughts and experiences involves no application of empirical criteria of personal identity'.[14] This second thesis is substantially different from the first, being much weaker. It concerns only *empirical* criteria of *personal* identity whereas the first concerns *all* criteria of *subject*-identity. It makes no claim about *I* whereas the first makes a substantive claim about the use of the term. It is a claim about predication whereas the first is about reference. It concerns the 'immediate self-ascription of thoughts and experiences' whereas the first is about the ascription of 'current or directly remembered' states of consciousness. This final difference is significant since states can be current without being immediately self-ascribed. And this prompts us to note an ambiguity about both theses: what, exactly, is 'direct' or 'immediate'; the states (thoughts; experiences) *themselves* or their *ascription*? The having of them, or the knowing about them? Evans clearly interprets the doctrine as meaning the latter. In his view, the ascriptions in question 'tolerate no gap' between coming to know something is *F* and coming to know I am *F*.[15]

Advocates of *Independence* also disagree markedly about what the doctrine *entails*. As the passage quoted above suggests, Wittgenstein takes the doctrine to imply that uses of *I* 'as subject' do not refer to a person. Strawson, on the other hand, uses it to show that all uses of *I* do refer—to corporeal subjects rather than Cartesian soul-substances. Both restrict the doctrine to uses of *I* and predications of one's mental life ('inner experience'). Others extend it to the use of different terms and different kinds of predication (e.g. Evans). *Independence* for Shoemaker means that *I* is not a demonstrative, and that first-personal thought cannot fit the

[13] Strawson (1966: 165).   [14] Strawson (1966: 166).   [15] Evans (1982: 180; 220–1).

demonstrative paradigm. Evans takes the doctrine to entail the exact converse. Some claim that *all* uses of *I* are immune, so there is no such distinction between uses of *I* 'as subject' and 'as object' (e.g. Rovane). Others acknowledge the Wittgensteinian division.[16]

The debate on the final point can be fairly easily settled, unlike those stimulated by the other disagreements. It is correct to acknowledge the Wittgensteinian division. *Independence* allows that *I* can be used to express knowledge that *does* depend on making an identity-judgement, as most advocates of the doctrine admit. That this must be so emerges from thinking about present-tense uses of *I* 'as object'. The usual illustrative cases, following Wittgenstein's lead ('I could, looking into a mirror, mistake a bump on [my neighbour's] forehead for one on mine'), depend on evidence gained via looking at reflective surfaces.[17] Suppose I pick out an individual from the crowd mirrored in a shop-window. On this occasion, it would not be nonsensical to think, 'that person's shoelaces have come undone; but are they *mine*?'; and, on settling the matter in the affirmative, come to know that my shoelaces are undone precisely because I identify myself with 'that person'.

§ 26.   What explains such disagreements? Confusion about *Independence* itself, perhaps. There is certainly sufficient confirmatory evidence of that diagnosis. For example, it is often said that we need to supply Kant with a developed notion of the doctrine if we are to understand his analysis of what is wrong with Rational Psychology.[18] But this is false. Though Kant complicates the issue by offering at least three subtly different diagnoses, not one depends on *Independence* either explicitly or implicitly.[19] And the error lies precisely in a muddle about what the *Independence* doctrine is and entails. For if the doctrine applies to the use of *I* in question, the *I Think* of transcendental apperception, then that use must at least have a referring role or an ascriptive function. Yet Kant precisely denies that this use has either.[20]

Sources of further confusion are revealed by the passages quoted from Wittgenstein and Strawson. Seeing why requires a little stage-setting. The style of argument used to support *Independence* binds itself by what we might call a matching condition. The doctrine must match the specific form of the question it would be nonsensical to ask if it is to count as an explanation of *Nonsense*. Crucially, for example, *Independence* is a doctrine about identification. So the specific form of *Immunity* it explains at step (*b*ii) had better be an immunity to misidentification. And what this immunity in turn explains at step (*b*i) had better be the nonsense involved in asking identification questions. These are questions of

16   Strawson (1969: 166); Evans (1982: 179–91); Shoemaker (1968; 1986); Rovane (1993: 88; 91).
17   Wittgenstein (1969: 67). See Shoemaker (1968: 82) for the case 'my arm is moving'.
18   Strawson (1966: 165–9); John McDowell (1994: Lecture V); Andrew Brook (1994).
19   Kant (A 349–51; 402–3; B 411–12 n.; 417–20). See de Gaynesford (2003*a*).
20   Kant (A 346; 355; 381–2; B 132; 407; 420).

the form 'who, or which one, is being referred to?' They are quite different, for example, from questions of the form 'what are you saying about the one referred to?' which may be called ascription questions.[21]

It is fatal to confuse identifying the item of which something is said with saying something about that item. But it is tempting to confuse identification and ascription on the present issue because a comparable form of nonsense question arises over the latter, and it seems plausible to explain that phenomenon also by an immunity to error. If it seems nonsensical to ask 'I am in a certain state, but is it pain that I am feeling?', that may be because one cannot be wrong about whether or not one is in pain. To be clear, then: we are concerned with the claim that no identity-judgement need be made in certain uses of *I*, not the claim that no ascription-judgement need be made. So we are interested in cases where one apparently enjoys immunity to making a false identity-judgement, not where one is immune to making a false predication. Thus, ultimately, we are seeking cases where it is apparently nonsensical to ask questions of the form 'the subject of this experience is *F*; but is it *I* that am *F*?', not 'I am in some state, but is *F* the state I am in?'

The Wittgenstein and Strawson passages invite confusion here because they restrict themselves to the rare examples of sentences that seemingly enjoy immunity to both forms of error: 'I have pain'; 'I am feeling angry'; 'I remember that terrible feeling of loss.' Further confusion is evident in Wittgenstein's odd italicization of *I* on these occasions, as if what is distinctive about uses 'as subject' were audible; something we can perceive if we simply attend closely enough to what bears emphasis (or what ordinarily is emphasized; or what should be emphasized) in spoken utterance. This is not so. Sentences using *I* 'as object' bear similar emphasis. Moreover, the emphasis which is appropriate for either use has nothing to do with (mis)ascriptive features. Highlighting is provided, on occasion, as an aid to the referring-identifying task. We stress *I* when *who is being spoken of* needs emphasis, not when *what is being said* of a person needs it. Wittgenstein distracts attention from the issues of reference and identification by discussing peculiarities of the properties such sentences ascribe and how we may come to know about them. Strawson compounds the problem by calling his version of *Independence* 'Criterionless Self-*ascription*'.[22] He deliberately restricts his formulation of *Independence* and his evidence for it to the self-ascription of a very specific class of predicates; those describing 'inner experience'. This is particularly surprising since it offends against his own view that the root of 'the Cartesian illusion' lies in 'the illusion of a *purely inner* and yet subject-referring use for *I*'.[23] These are not corrigible slips but substantive views. Both authors evidently suppose that *Nonsense* is restricted to cases in which misascription is impossible.

---

[21] See Strawson (1950: 71).
[22] See also Brewer (1992: 30); Rovane (1993: 88; 91).
[23] Strawson (1966: 165–6), my emphasis.

So two issues urgently need attention. First, if the phenomenon *were* so restricted, there would be no call for *Independence* to explain it. The phenomenon would be indicative of distinctions in the nature of properties it is possible to self-ascribe and in the means at our disposal for knowing that they obtain. It would not, therefore, tell us about the nature of self-reference or our means of expressing thoughts using *I*. Hence it would not be indicative of identification-independent self-reference or identification-independent expressive use. Second, *Nonsense* is *not* so restricted. It arises in cases where misascription is possible. Thus one may be mistaken that anyone should recant, that any time is the time for repentance, that anywhere is hot, or that anything smells smoky. Nevertheless, one might say, 'I should have recanted,' 'Now is the time for repentance,' 'It is hot here,' or 'This fire smells smoky,' in circumstances where it would make no sense for one to ask, 'somebody should have recanted, but was it *me*?', 'Some time is the time for repentance, but is it *now*?', 'It is hot somewhere, but is it hot *here*?', or 'Some fire smells smoky, but is it *this* fire?'

§ 27.   Disagreements about *Independence* are explained by confusion about what that doctrine is and what it entails. If we seek a deep explanation in turn of this confusion, it is not difficult to find a plausible candidate: understandable hesitancy on the part of most theorists. For most regard the evidence in favour of the doctrine as strong, but nevertheless want to retain grasp of the default position: that *I* is a genuine singular referring term and one which is used to express thoughts about oneself. And since *Independence* puts both claims under serious threat, this is a deeply uncomfortable position.

Referring to some particular using a singular term is a kind of identification; namely, a singling out of the thing at issue from various kinds and from various instances of the kind to which it belongs.[24] *Independence* implies that certain uses of *I* are not identificatory in this sense. So it seems that anyone convinced of the doctrine should simply deny that these are uses of a term whose logical role it is to refer. As Peter Hacker writes, 'What looks like immunity from misidentification or reference-failure is in fact the absence of any reference at all.'[25] This is stronger even than Wittgenstein's position; that such uses do not refer to a person. Again, just thinking about a particular is commonly regarded as a case of identifying it, and with reason. A judgement's being directed on such an object is intelligible as the application of identity-criteria, those enabling recognition of it as the same again through changes in its properties, and individuation of it as distinct. And it is just this identity-judgement that is allegedly missing from certain uses of *I*. If one does not identify oneself in these cases, it may be assumed that one does not identify any thing. Thus *Independence* may be taken to mean that one is not then thinking about oneself, or indeed any (other) thing. Again, this is stronger even than Wittgenstein's conclusion: that, in some uses of *I*, one is not thinking *about* a person.

---

[24] Evans (1982: 218).
[25] Hacker (1993: 225). See Anscombe (1975: 154); Geach (1957: 117–20).

IS *INDEPENDENCE* TO BE PREFERRED?

§ 28.   It is some indication of the instability of a doctrine and of complications with the argument in its support that there exist such widely diverging opinions about what it is and what it entails. So we should scrutinize the two-step argument from explanation carefully. For the argument to succeed, *Independence* must be the preferred explanation of *Nonsense*. That much is clear from the summary. Showing that the doctrine is merely one explanation among many is to do little more than reveal its consistency with *Nonsense*. And it might be equally consistent to prefer an alternative and deny the doctrine. Then, far from having reason to adopt the doctrine, we would have good reason to reject it.

It is not clear that *Independence* satisfies this basic requirement. Advocates take it for granted that there is just one feature of the various example-questions raised which explains *Nonsense*. Perhaps they are right to do so. But we certainly cannot assume without argument that this one feature is the only one we are offered, i.e. *Independence*. Indeed, we have as yet no reason to suppose that this explanation is even more *likely* to be correct than the disjunction of all other possible explanations. This gap in the argument could be plugged, of course, if it could be shown that *Independence* is the only licence for the assumption it is possible to prefer. But this is not plausible. The assumption might be licensed pragmatically: by a resolution on our part, conventionally entered into, to ask whether one has got the reference right only when there is, and because there is, an evident possibility or likelihood of one's having got the reference wrong. This explanation is consistent with rejecting *Independence*, for criteria of identity retain their application here. In thinking 'I am *F*', one may be licensed to assume that one has got the reference right even though one recognizes that such criteria are applicable and may be invoked to justify one's reference. Unless this explanation and other similar alternatives are ruled out, the argument from explanation simply lapses. Independence cannot tolerate a rival, given that it is only as the explanans of *Nonsense* that belief in the doctrine is justified. Appeal to *Immunity* merely introduces an extra problem: being able to *mis*identify an item requires being able to identify it. But we are not obliged to accept the converse.

Perhaps *Independence* appeals tacitly to obvious criteria which make it the preferable explanation of *Nonsense*. But it is not wholly clear what such criteria are. Evidence of explanatory potential is one identifying feature of preferable theories. But we could not safely mount such an argument for *Independence*. If anything, evidence of this sort would be damaging and invite fresh worries. For, as we have seen, the doctrine is used to explain, support, and otherwise justify a range of different, often wholly incompatible, positions. The simplicity and economy of an explanation are also often taken to be signs in its favour. It is not always easy to decide what counts as such, of course. Is the simplest or most economical explanation the one that commits us to the clearest, the most uncomplicated, or the most intelligible theory; to the easiest, most direct, or most lucid proof; to the fewest, the most essential, or the most elementary entities (or kinds of entities)? But we need not decide the issue as it will turn out. For whichever notion of simplicity or economy we adopt, the pragmatic alternative just noted lays better claim to being the satisfying explanation.

By speaking of the pragmatics of utterance I mean to remain agnostic about what fundamental semantic properties, such as truth-conditions and reference, should be ascribed to: tokens or types. Some theorists have followed Reichenbach in formulating 'concrete expression theories' (as Garcia-Carpintero calls them), ascribing fundamental semantic properties to tokens, i.e. individual utterances (e.g. Crimmins; Perry). Others have adopted 'abstract expression theories', ascribing such properties to types-in-context, sentences, 'occurrences' (e.g. Richard; Braun). We can afford to remain agnostic about which approach is correct, for either holds at a level where we can still either assert or deny *Independence* and the other doctrines composing *Purism*.[26]

WHAT DOES *INDEPENDENCE* EXPLAIN?

§ 29.   We are asked to adopt *Independence* because we need that doctrine to explain *Nonsense*. One objection is that the doctrine is not well founded unless it can be shown that there is no other explanation that is equally good or better. Another would be that it is insufficiently clear or determinate what the doctrine is being called on to explain. For if it is unclear what it would be to explain *Nonsense*, we certainly cannot say that *Independence* succeeds in doing so.

Nonsense is the claim that, in certain cases, it would be 'nonsensical' for the subject to wonder about *which* thing his use of a referring expression picks out. If *Nonsense* fixes on any doubts, it surely also makes nonsensical the subject's wondering about *what* (kind of) thing he is. For if *I* is indeed a referring term, there is good reason prima facie to suppose that being able to pick out *which* object some particular thing is plausibly requires at least knowing *what* it is. This is to say: being a singular referring term, sortal (mis)identification bears on one's use of *I*. One fails to ascribe some property, *F*, in saying, 'this is *F*,' unless one could answer the question 'what kind of thing does your use of *This* refer to?' Similarly, one would fail to self-ascribe that property in saying, 'I am *F*,' unless one could answer the question 'what kind of thing does your use of *I* refer to?' Certainly, it would appear a minimal condition on *I*-use that the user be the kind of being to which it makes sense to ascribe thoughts and experiences. And, like Proust's narrator, one might use *I* taking oneself to be, and to be referring to, a church, a string quartet, or the rivalry between Francis I and Charles V.[27] Suppose one

---

[26] Garcia-Carpintero (1998); Crimmins (1995); Perry (1997); Richard (1993); Braun (1996).
[27] Proust (1913: 3).

thinks one is a steam-train. It might seem nonsensical to ask 'some particular thing is turning a bend, but is it me?' when the first phrase expresses knowledge.

It is worth being clear on the issue. So consider a different way of expressing the essential point, one that focuses on Strawson's version of *Independence*, i.e. 'Criterionless Self-ascription'. For that thesis is inconsistent with Strawson's own claim that self-ascription requires knowing what kind of thing one is. Strawson himself considered one such consistency problem: if *I* can be used without criteria of personal identity, how can it be regarded as referring at all?[28] The problem of the misconceiving *I*-user raises a similar issue. It is plausible to suppose that a subject might consistently misconceive what kind of thing he is, but not so uncomprehendingly that he would be judged unable to entertain thoughts of the form 'I am *F*'. Now suppose that *Independence* is correct for the reasons given by the two-step argument from explanation. Since asking 'someone is *F*, but is it me?' would be nonsensical for the subject, it must be the case that he is able to self-ascribe such thoughts without application of personal identity criteria. But claiming that he is able to self-ascribe such thoughts at all seems to run counter to the plausible position that being able to self-ascribe thoughts and experiences requires being able to pick out from all other things that to which the thought or experience is ascribed; something that in turn requires knowing what kind of thing one is. For this subject precisely does *not* know what kind of thing he is. It might be objected that the type of case I have offered all too briefly is not in fact conceivable. Misconception problems certainly require more stage-setting than I have offered here.[29] But to make much of this in the present case would be to overlook the crucial point: the *weakest* link is not conceivability but the claim that *Nonsense* is in good enough order to ground *Independence*.

It might seem nonsensical to *ask*, 'some particular thing is chuffing round the bend, but is it me?' But does that mean the question is *indeed* nonsensical? If not, why should we suppose it is nonsensical in the examples raised by advocates of *Independence*? If it is, is that because *I* is so radically unlike other referring expressions that it maintains only the most tenuous link with them—it singles out a particular thing without concern for kind? Or is it because kind is not the concern of the *I*-user? Or is it because, appearances to the contrary, 'no error is possible' here either? None of these options are particularly attractive and it is quite unclear which we should adopt. But we need not concern ourselves with that question for the main point *is* now clear. *Nonsense* is not in sufficiently good order for us to be confident that *Independence*—or any other doctrine—explains it. So we lack good reason to adopt the doctrine.

We might be tempted to treat these points as simply illustrative of the peculiarity of *I* rather than as revealing the inadequacy of the *Independence* doctrine. But this is not a sound option. As we have noted, *Nonsense* is not peculiar to certain uses of *I*. 'This is red,' for example, may be stated in circumstances where it might

---

[28] Strawson (1966: 165).   [29] See Cassam (1997: chapter 4).

seem to make no sense to say, 'something is red, but is it *this*?'[30] And the same sortal issues which make *Independence* inadequate in the case of *I* recur here. Is the question still nonsensical even if the thinker reveals himself ignorant or just wrong when asked 'this *what*?'?

IS *INDEPENDENCE* NECESSARY?

§ 30.   There are aspects of *Nonsense* which can be made more determinate, but this holds out little hope for *Independence*. For two things become clearer as the phenomenon becomes more determinate: what is required of the explanatory task and why the doctrine is unsuitable for it.

As we have seen, *Independence* is a particularly striking claim to make about a term that refers and that may be used to express thoughts about particular objects. So the evidence for it had better be at least equally striking. In the quoted passages, we are told that what make no sense are the questions *themselves*—e.g. 'This experience is occurring, but is it occurring to me?' But that is misleading. These questions are clearly meaningful. Certainly there are occasions on which it might make no sense for the subject to *ask* such questions—senseless in the way some kinds of violence are said to be (i.e. without a sound purpose), rather than in the strict way that, for example, baby-talk might be. But that gives the phenomenon a rather different complexion. For it is now clearer what follows: that there are occasions on which subjects are entitled to *assume* answers to certain questions. And *Independence* seems altogether too massive a hammer to crack *that* nut.

This suspicion has other causes. If we have to call on the weight of *Independence* to explain *Nonsense*, then it really must be *nonsensical* to ask these questions. The phrase is often loosely applied, but here it must be strictly meant. It cannot simply be that these questions are readily answered, for example. Not if (as *Independence* claims) they are asking after an unnecessary identity-judgement. But it is not obvious that it *would* be strictly nonsensical to ask these questions on any occasion. If there are situations—no matter how atypical—on which it is sensible to ask these questions and demanding to answer them, then it would *never* be strictly nonsensical to ask them. On many or even most occasions, these questions might be ignored or answered without difficulty. But that is a different matter calling for a different kind of explanation (one I shall come to).

There are occasions when sentences quoted as examples of the use of *I* 'as object' manifest features characteristic of the 'as subject' use. Wittgenstein's 'My arm is broken', for example, could be (perhaps usually would be) stated by someone who could not fail to know whose arm it was—perhaps because it expresses the same kind of knowledge about who is suffering certain bodily sensations as grounds statements like 'I am in pain'. (Recall the irrelevance of the fact that the subject

---

[30] See Shoemaker (1986: 130).

may be wrong about whether his arm is in fact broken; it is immunity to error through mis*identification*, not mis*ascription*, that is at issue.)

And there are occasions of the converse sort. More specifically, each of the sentences standardly held up as examples of *Nonsense* may be used to issue statements where asking the identity question would be quite demanding to answer and would call on knowledge that depends on making a (defeasible) identity-judgement. To see how such cases can be constructed, consider Wittgenstein's examples of 'uses of *I* as subject'. 'I try to lift my arm' might fail to manifest the general features allegedly characteristic of the use. For it could be stated by someone who knows 'someone is trying to lift my arm' but who misidentifies who that person is—if the subject's arm were numb and he observes it moving involuntarily, he might suppose (falsely) that it is nevertheless he who is trying to move it.

Wittgenstein also alludes to the sentences '*I* have toothache' and '*I* have pain.' But these sentences are peculiar in being seemingly immune to error through *misascription*. The subject cannot be wrong about whether it is in fact *toothache* or *pain* that is being felt. As a class, such sentences are restricted in another sense: to those predicating mental attributes. Hence they are not those regarded by *Independence* theorists as 'central uses' of the first-person form and may be set aside. (I am assuming that one need not have teeth to feel toothache. If one rejects this view, then 'I have toothache' will not be an example of a claim that is immune to error through misascription; it will join that other category of claims which includes 'I try to lift my arm'.)

Precisely similar circumstances explain why Shoemaker's candidate use 'as subject' ('I am waving my arm') can also express uses 'as object'.[31] The statement might be true in circumstances where the subject's knowing this depends on his making an identity-judgement. For example, my knowing the truth of '*I* try to lift my arm' when I have no feeling in that arm may be the result of my knowing the truths 'the completely bandaged man reflected in the mirror is trying to lift my arm' (I know this on the testimony of a nurse who has told me 'the completely bandaged man reflected in the mirror is trying to lift your arm') and 'I am the completely bandaged man reflected in the mirror' (again, on the testimony of the nurse). Again, my knowing the truth of '*I* think it will rain' may be the result of my knowing the truths 'that man I can see on the closed-circuit television with an umbrella thinks it will rain' and 'I am that man I can see on the closed-circuit television' (if I was not sufficiently consciously aware of picking up the umbrella). In this case, I recognize the legitimacy of the question 'some particular thing—the man I can see on the closed-circuit television—is *F*; but is it *I* that am *F*?' And I settle the issue precisely by appeal to an identity-judgement—*I* am that particular thing—making knowledge of the truth of the first-person judgement identification-*dependent*.

[31] Shoemaker (1968: 82).

This case and others that mirror it should be distinguished from counter-examples to which theorists properly object.[32] There might be a deviant causal chain linking Abelard's body with Bernard's brain, on which basis Bernard states, falsely, 'I am being tickled'—the statement is false because it is Abelard, not the referent of this use of *I* (Bernard), who is being tickled. Theorists are surely right to object that this case does not reveal the possibility of the precise kind of error picked out by the *Independence* doctrine. For it is not the case that Bernard asserts, 'I am being tickled,' knows some particular thing to be being tickled, but is wrong about what the use of *I* refers to. Given the causal deviance, it is not correct to regard his assertion as expressing *knowledge* that some particular thing is being tickled. As Evans puts it, 'it is not sufficient for knowledge that a true belief be causally dependent on the facts which render it true'.[33] In my cases, however, the subject's assertion undoubtedly *does* express such knowledge. Furthermore, unlike the deviant case, 'the question' would not even seem nonsensical to the subject.

So we may doubt that *Nonsense* is the kind of phenomenon which it takes the weight of the *Independence* doctrine to explain. The sentences in question can be used to issue statements of which, on occasion, it would be sensible to ask the identity question. So the possibility of misidentification remains a live issue for their users. It might be *otiose* to raise this question on almost every occasion. What matters is that it would not be *nonsensical*.

§ 31.   The fact that this question *is* otiose on almost every occasion leaves a phenomenon to be explained, of course—however unimposing it may be by comparison with the one advocates of *Independence* needed and advertised. The explanation can afford to be equally trivial. Indeed, it must be if it is to match the phenomenon. And the pragmatic alternative alluded to above seems perfectly suited to this task. It rests on the idea that we have good reason to avoid redundancy in reporting on our own states to ourselves and to others. In cases such as those picked out by Wittgenstein and others, avoiding redundancy means not saying who or what has been referred to when it is perfectly obvious.

This is straightforward in reporting to ourselves. Pragmatic considerations justify it in cases where such sentences are used in reporting states of affairs to others.[34] For there is a cooperative resolution on all our parts to be relevant and perspicuous in our discourse. This involves avoiding obvious redundancy. The resolution is pragmatic because wholly unnecessary repetition of information is confusing and makes communication difficult. One assumes the speaker is trying to *implicate* something by not choosing the more concise options. If we say, 'This feeling is anger,' for example, we do not usually add 'and it is I who am feeling it' any more than if we say, 'This room is hot,' we add 'and it is hot in here'. That is not because there is *never* occasion to say the longer sentences, of course. It is

---

[32] See Evans (1982: 221); Cassam (1997: 62–3); O'Brien (1995*b*: 240).
[33] Evans (1982: 245).
[34] See Grice (1961: 66–78).

because someone who says them implicates that he is *not* thinking of his own state by 'this feeling', or of 'here' by 'this room'. In the first case, he might be alluding to a state shared by two different persons: 'this feeling' which he observes in another, and 'it' which he ascribes to himself. In the second case, he might be alluding to two different rooms, 'here', where he is speaking from, and 'this room' where he is not (the latter being a room whose temperature is represented on a gauge 'here'). These are interpretations we are licensed to assume. It is the only way to preserve the hypothesis that the person speaking is a competent user of the language and observing the pragmatic principles of relevance and perspicuity governing communication.

Now this pragmatic explanation is consistent with rejecting *Independence*. For one may be licensed to *assume* that one has got the identification right when thinking '*a* is *F*' (where '*a*' is a singular term like *I* or *This*), even though it would be appropriate to call on criteria of identification to justify one's use of the term to refer. Moreover, this explanation is preferable by criteria of simplicity and economy. It explains matters in a clear and intelligible way, and commits us to fewer and cheaper materials. The question of quite *why* in these cases there is no evident possibility or likelihood that one has got the reference wrong is the subject matter of the next chapter. As we shall see, pragmatics again offers a cogent explanation of this security.

WHAT DOES *INDEPENDENCE* IMPLY?

§ 32. It is as well that *Nonsense* turns out to be a lesser phenomenon that can be explained by lesser means, for *Independence* is a taxing doctrine. We have already noted the pressure it places on the claims that *I* refers and can be used to express thoughts about particulars. Consider two more sensitive areas.

I is a device for giving information to others. Some theorists have stressed the *priority* of this role, but it is sufficient for my point that it is just one amongst others.[35] Strawson, for example, notes that

In one sense, indeed, there is no question of my having to *tell who it is* who is in pain, when I am. In another sense, however, I may have to *tell who it is*, i.e. to let others know who it is.[36]

Criteria are ways of telling. If, in using *I*, there is a sense in which I must tell who it is who is *F*, when I am, then there is a use of criteria. These criteria are of the relevant kind to be challenged by *Independence*—i.e. criteria of personal identity. For the point is that, in using *I*, I have to let others know, provide them with ways of telling, which person is thus referred to. And criteria of personal identity are precisely ways of telling whether someone—in this case, the referent of a use of *I*—is identical with some person A.

[35] See Evans (1982: 208).   [36] Strawson (1959: 100).

Thus *Independence* threatens the view that, when a subject ascribes a current or directly remembered state of consciousness to himself—e.g. 'I would like to go swimming'; 'I remember there is a good beach in that direction'—*some* use of criteria of personal identity is required, the satisfaction of which justifies use of the pronoun *I* to refer to the subject of that experience. Ordinary features of use, combined with the definition of *I*, are usually sufficient to satisfy these criteria and thus justify the use—these features provide others with ways of telling that the referent of a use of *I* is identical with some person A.

The whole point is nicely illustrated by the slightly unusual case where the mere act of saying *I* is insufficient for a person to have himself picked out by others as the subject of some state of consciousness. In a crowd of others, for example, *I*-sayers will automatically augment ordinary features of use, perhaps by sticking their hands in the air. As the *I*-sayer, the gesture is precisely one's acknowledgement that there is a sense in which I must tell who it is who is *F*, when I am. The gesture is my acknowledgement that *I* is a referring expression. As such, my use of it must forestall the question 'who is being talked about?'

§ 33.   Independence also threatens to sever the links between uses of *I* and empirical criteria of personal identity, at least in the usual way such criteria are understood to operate; i.e. that uses of *I* refer to a corporeal object among others in an objective world.[37]

These links would be cut if, so far as our understanding of *I* is concerned, the term might refer to something less than a corporeal object—for example, a subject of experience, capable of making objectively valid judgements and of conceiving what it intuits as representations of an objective world, which, though spatio-temporally located, is neither impenetrable nor force-exerting (something with the physical presence of a hologram, perhaps). If Kant is right, that both impenetrability and force-exertingness are 'thought' in the concept of corporeality, such an object would not then be corporeal.[38] If there were some requirement that personal identity criteria be applied in using *I*, and if it were held that persons are in fact corporeal objects, then that would be a safeguard. So the call for empirical criteria of personal identity turns out to be a call for criteria of the identity of corporeal objects.

But suppose there were no such requirement on certain uses of *I*, as the *Independence* doctrine asserts. What is to prevent there being bona fide referents of *I* that are something less than corporeal objects? We can ignore the problem of less than full-blooded uses of *I* here—the seemingly first-personal output of computers, answer-phones, and speak-your-weight machines may be classed alongside quotation, fiction, and other conniving uses of *I* as limiting cases of no pressing interest. The question at issue here is whether we are proof against the possibility of less than full-blooded beings—sub-personal, non-corporeal items.

Appeal might be made to Strawson's comment that '*I* can be used without

37 See Strawson (1998: 147).   38 Kant (A 8; B 12).

criteria of subject-identity and yet refer to a subject because, even in such a use, the links with those criteria are not severed'.[39] The idea is that, even though personal identity criteria need not be invoked for these uses of *I*, links between such criteria and the use remain. These are the links by which others identify the item to which my uses of *I* refer, and Strawson notes two of them.

First, the use of *I* 'issues publicly from the mouth of a man who is recognisable and identifiable as the person he is by the application of empirical criteria of personal identity'.[40] But appeal to this link does not solve the problem. For a use of *I* may issue publicly from the mouth of a man without referring to him—if, for example, the man is merely used as a mouthpiece, his vocal organs manipulated by another. And, for all Strawson shows, this other might not be a human being or corporeal object at all.

Strawson's second link is that the use of *I* 'is used by a person who would acknowledge the applicability of those criteria in settling questions as to whether he, the very man who now ascribes to himself this experience, was or was not the person who, say, performed such-and-such an action in the past'.[41] This confuses a semantic issue (whether *I* may be used to express thoughts independently of identification and still count as the referring term it is) with a pragmatic issue of communication (what an audience requires to understand the speaker's utterance). Moreover, by fixing on an *I*-user who is a person, this evidently begs the question against the spectre of a sub-personal *I*-user. If the *I*-user is a person then the use of *I* refers to a corporeal object and the links between *I* and empirical criteria of personal identity are un-severed. For any use of *I* refers to its user, and a person is a corporeal object. But perhaps the *I*-user is not a person.

So this extended discussion brings us to a simple set of conclusions. First, if we are to have good reason to adopt *Independence*, then (*a*) the doctrine must be the preferred explanation of the phenomenon (*Nonsense*) that gives rise to it; (*b*) it must be clear what explaining *Nonsense* requires; (*c*) the explanation must match the phenomenon to be explained; and (*d*) the explanation must be no more problematic than the problems it explains. But, second, none of these requirements (*a*)–(*d*) are satisfied. Third, we have an alternative explanation which is independently preferable given a wholly appropriate parsimony. Pragmatics is a better match for the phenomena in question and fully accounts for them in a less costly way. Finally, we have discovered good reasons to reject *Independence*. The doctrine threatens to undermine the referential character of *I*, its expressive use, its communicative role, and the nature of the items to which it refers.

---

[39] Strawson (1966: 165); See McDowell (1998).   [40] Strawson (1966: 165).
[41] Strawson (1966: 165).

4

Questions of Logic

§ 34. So *Independence* fails. In fact, its demise was made unavoidable by the failure of *Rule Theory*. But this is clear only now that the strands have been unravelled. For if the reference of *I*-uses is not sufficiently determined on their user, then using them to express thoughts must be more demanding than is consistent with *Independence*.

Granted, *I* is atypical. The individual *by* whom the thought is expressed is usually the individual such thoughts are *about*, and this is not usually the case with other terms. But it is worth stressing these two occurrences of 'usually'. For susceptibility to myths about *I* is fostered by a curiously well-entrenched assumption that the term is *always* exceptional in these respects. Sometimes the person expressing a thought using *I* is being employed as the 'mouthpiece' of the one whose thought it is. Sometimes what expresses the thought is not a person at all but a mechanical speaker. Conversely, one can consciously and intentionally refer to oneself using a variety of terms other than *I*. Abelard might do so in saying, '*This man* must write his autobiography,' or '*He* must write his autobiography,' or 'The lover of Heloise must', or 'Abelard must', or 'This very speaker must'. In each case, the thoughts are expressed *by* the same individual they are *about*.

Moreover, recognizing the identity of the person using *I* to express thoughts with the person thought about is not effortless, a matter of observing that this same individual is 'the user' in both cases. For it is not just *as* the one using *I* that the one using it to express thoughts is referred to. One needs to know more than that one is the user to know one is the referent. In short, there is a gap between one's awareness that one is using *I* and one's awareness that one is the referent of that use. So the expressive use of *I* depends on identification. And a stark light is thrown on this requirement by the dissolution of *Rule Theory*.

We reach down now to the oldest and most firmly wedged of the doctrines concerning the first person: *The Guarantee*. Grappling with this doctrine is impossible without first removing the others which jam it in. For how *could* any such use fail to refer, we might ask, if *Rule Theory* is true and each use of *I* has a user? Or if *Independence* is true and the expressive use of *I* need not fulfil the usual identification requirements? But we can set these doctrines aside now, and this leaves us a free hand with *The Guarantee*.

Some phrase *The Guarantee* positively. As a matter of the meaning of the term, any use of *I* is logically guaranteed to refer successfully. So Castañeda claims:

> a correct use of *I* cannot fail to refer to the entity to which it purports to refer; moreover, a correct use of *I* cannot fail to pick up the category of the entity to which it refers … a self *qua* self.[1]

Others make *The Guarantee* a negative claim. As a matter of the meaning of the term, any use of *I* is logically guaranteed against failure to refer. Strawson for example writes,

> *I* is guaranteed against two kinds of failure … it is guaranteed against lack of reference, and it is guaranteed against mistaken or incorrect reference (i.e. against lack of coincidence between the intended reference and the reference conventionally carried, in the circumstances, by the expression used).[2]

The distinction may not appear immediately significant (perhaps explaining why advocates of the doctrine make no fuss about it). But the difference it marks is crucial. Someone who denies that uses of *I* genuinely refer must reject *The Guarantee* in the first formulation but may appeal to the second for decisive evidence. If it is a fact that uses of *I* are logically secured against failure to refer, that may indicate they do not actually refer at all.[3] We shall be discussing authors who hold this view. So the second phrasing of *The Guarantee* is to be preferred.

The Guarantee sets out to explain why uses of *I* cannot fail to refer—why they are 'secure', for short. It tells us that such uses are *logically* secured against such failures. The doctrine is 'generally agreed', as Strawson says. Its deep significance is also commonly recognized. Some have regarded the doctrine as sufficient to show what the referent of *I* must be. From this doctrine, as we have noted, Descartes drew his conception of the self as a single unanalysable entity whose one essential property it is to think. And Russell and McTaggart inferred by similar means that the self is a simple whose essential nature it is to be aware of things, or to perceive things.[4] But we are principally interested in what *The Guarantee* shows about *I*. And the doctrine, if true, reveals deep features of the logical character of the term.

Some take *The Guarantee* to show that *I* is not a genuine referring expression (e.g. Anscombe; Hacker). Given *The Guarantee*, if uses of *I* refer, they must have very special objects as their referents. But such objects could not exist. So the doctrine shows that *I* is not a referring term. Others draw the less hyperbolic conclusion that *I* is not a term for which we can find a satisfactory referent (e.g. Wittgenstein).[5] Most commonly, however, *The Guarantee* is taken to show that *I* is not a *Deictic Term* (e.g. Kaplan; Campbell).[6] For *I* is invulnerable to reference-failure while terms like *You*, *He/She*, and *This/That* are not.

---

[1] Castañeda (1968: 160–1). [2] Strawson (1994: 210).
[3] See Hacker (1993: 225); Anscombe (1975).
[4] Russell (1912: 28); McTaggart (1927: 76–7). [5] Wittgenstein (1958: § 410; 1993: 226).
[6] Kaplan (1989); Campbell (1994: 121–31).

Abelard might produce an utterance purporting to be about some particular woman, Heloise; the one he takes himself to be gesturing towards when he says, 'She is beautiful.' But there may be no woman at all for him to indicate in this way; he is hallucinating the presence of Heloise. In which case, Abelard would have failed to refer through lack of reference. Or it may be that two or more women are picked out by his use of *She* and the gesture, where he wrongly believed there was only one. Then he would have failed to refer through reference-splitting. For *She* is a singular term, which is to say that it has exactly one referent or none at all. False or insufficient information about the actual states of affairs in the user's perceptual environment is usually responsible for such failures. But according to *The Guarantee*, the meaning and logical character of *I* are such that one will continue to refer successfully, no matter how deluded or ignorant one is, either about oneself or about one's environment.

It may be that so-called 'Mixed Demonstratives' (i.e. those formed in combination with a sortal, like *This F/ That F*) are vulnerable to another form of reference-failure. One may get the sortal wrong, attempting to refer to an item which is not-*F* as *That F*. To suppose reference fails in such cases is to assume the problem is referential, an instance of misidentification. This may be the wrong diagnosis. It would be if the problem were predicational instead, an instance of misascription. But we need not decide the issue here. The problem could not arise for *I* or for any of the other terms centrally at issue (*You*; *He/She*). For none could be combined with a sortal to form a mixed demonstrative.

§ 35.   When advocates of *The Guarantee* say that uses of *I* are *logically* secured against failure to refer, they do not simply mean that reference-failure *could not* occur. For that would be consistent with claiming that the security at issue is not a matter of *I*'s meaning, but of the metaphysics of the items to which it referred, or of the epistemology of identifying that reference, or of the pragmatics of issuing statements containing the term. In particular, we could not draw any conclusion about whether or not *I* is a referring term, or whether or not it is a *Deictic Term*. For it might be odd that uses of *I* never fail to refer. But that would be a strange feature of *I*'s *referents*, or of what it takes to *recognize* its referents, or of its *context*. It would not be an oddity of the term itself.

To illustrate this point. Suppose that there is a special kind of object which uses of *I* single out; one which could not but exist and could not but be successfully picked out when any attempt using any relevant term is made. Then security would tell us much about the metaphysics of the objects to which *I* refers, but nothing about the term's logical character. Or suppose there are infallible ways of singling out the right object when using *I*, kinds of self-awareness that are peculiar to oneself (e.g. proprioceptive awareness of one's body, its temperature, balance, homeostatic condition, or, for a Cartesian, some non-sensory analogue of these). Then security would be an epistemological phenomenon. Or again, suppose background circumstances peculiar to occasions of uttering *I* ensure that, simply by doing this, exactly one individual is always singled out as its referent. Then security would tell us about the pragmatics of *I*-use, but nothing about the meaning of the term so used.

The Guarantee, on the other hand, is supposed to show that *I* is certainly not a *Deictic Term*, and may not be a referring expression at all. The doctrine is capable of revealing these features of the meaning of *I*, its logical character, only because it claims that security is a matter of meaning, of logical character. As Kaplan says, 'one need only understand the meaning' of sentences using *I* to see that they could not fail to refer. Someone who denies or otherwise fails to grasp *The Guarantee* has simply failed to grasp the meaning of *I*. It is logically impossible for uses of *I* to fail to refer because *The Guarantee* is part of the meaning of the term.[7] So adopting *The Guarantee* is not to espouse security but a particular attempt to *explain* security. If the doctrine holds, alternative explanations must be excluded. Security must be a *semantic* truth, part of the 'special logic' of the term.

The point is laboured because it is crucial to determining strategy in what follows. It is not by showing that *I can* fail of reference that we expose *The Guarantee* as a myth. So we shall not be devising examples where security fails. *The Guarantee* is a myth, not because it says *I* cannot fail of reference, but because it says the *reason I* cannot fail of reference is logical, part of the meaning of the term. As we shall see, no one gives us good reason to accept this explanation, and we have excellent reasons to reject it. Indeed, when authors take themselves to be advocating *The Guarantee*, it is actually a *different* explanation of security that they have in mind, and one that should be preferred. So we are free to reject *The Guarantee* while *accepting* the security of *I* against reference-failure. And we are free to explain this phenomenon while accepting what authors have *actually* endorsed.

WHAT IS *THE GUARANTEE*?

§ 36.   *The Guarantee* sets out to explain security against reference-failure. But beyond emphasis of the point that that security is a semantic phenomenon, it is not clear what that explanation is. Charged with a key role in elucidating the logical character of *I*, the doctrine has a curiously opaque form in the literature. It is seldom if ever presented with the kind of detail and definition necessary to being the object of confident assertion or denial. Some follow Descartes and simply assume the doctrine without formulating it (e.g. Peacocke; Shoemaker; Hacker). Most regard it as just obviously true and offer no supporting argument (e.g. Anscombe; Castañeda; Kaplan).[8]

---

[7] Kaplan (1989: 509).

[8] Descartes (1984: ii. 17–18); Peacocke (1983: 175–9); Shoemaker (1986: 126–7); Hacker (1993: 223); Anscombe (1975: 149; 151–2); Castañeda (1968: 160–1); Kaplan (1989: 509).

Significant differences of opinion emerge with formulations of *The Guarantee*. As already noted, for some the doctrine states that any use of *I* is logically guaranteed to refer successfully (e.g. Castañeda). For others, it states that any use of *I* is logically guaranteed against failure to refer (e.g. Strawson).[9]

Some claim that the doctrine guarantees the existence of the object meant by any use of *I*. So Anscombe writes, 'if *I* is a referring expression at all, it has both kinds of guaranteed reference. The object an *I*-user means by it must exist so long as he is using *I*, nor can he take the wrong object to be the object he means by *I*.' Others extend the doctrine no further than the logical character of the term itself; its reference cannot fail (e.g. Strawson).[10]

Some claim that the doctrine applies to all *Pure Indexicals* (e.g. *I*, *Now*, and *Here*). Kaplan's claim that 'One need only understand the *meaning* of ["I am here now"] to know that it cannot be uttered falsely' depends on this extension.[11] Others regard *The Guarantee* as special to the peculiar self-referential logic of *I* (e.g. Anscombe).

Some regard *I* as guaranteed against reference-failure whatever intentions the speakers have. Anscombe and Strawson hold this view, as is clear from the passages quoted. There is no need to appeal to any intention the speaker may have to characterize *The Guarantee*. Others claim that speakers need to intend that the referent of their uses of *I* be the self qua self, i.e. qua him or herself. Castañeda evidently holds this view in the passage above. O'Brien presumably concurs when she writes, 'uses of *I* will always succeed in referring to something and, what is more, to refer to that thing the subject intended to refer to—viz. themselves'.[12] If these authors are correct to ascribe this property to the logical character of *I*, it is another oddity of the term. For it does not seem to hold across the board. Having decided to name whoever was the first person to send a message by e-mail 'Mercury', I may refer to him saying 'Mercury is a world-historical figure.' There is such a person, and I intend to refer to him or her, but I do not know who that person is. Thus I succeed in referring to the item I intend to refer to without knowing what (or who) that item is.

Some insist that *The Guarantee* applies to *I* when 'correctly and genuinely employed' (e.g. Bermúdez). Others, like Strawson, impose no such restriction.[13]

In short, the truth of the doctrine is evidently not so straightforward that it should obtain immediate assent, even from those already inclined to give it.

§ 37. If disagreements about *The Guarantee* manifest the qualms of its advocates, this would be understandable. For the security it provides comes at heavy cost; one that is particularly onerous, and perhaps impossible, for a theory of genuine referring expressions to bear.

---

[9] Castañeda (1968: 160–1); Strawson (1994: 210).
[10] Anscombe (1975: 151–2); Strawson (1994: 210).
[11] Kaplan (1989: 509).   [12] O'Brien (1995*a*: 236–7).
[13] Bermúdez (1998: 9); see below for discussion.

It is the role of singular terms to single out who, or which one individual, we are thinking of or speaking about. We established this when promoting the default position that *I* is a genuine singular referring expression. This singling-out role, which gives such terms their logical character, is also a semantic role. For in singling out what one thing the predicate must be true *of* if the whole utterance is to be true, such expressions help determine the meaning of sentences in which they are embedded. So if *I* is indeed a genuine referring expression, it is a semantic truth that its uses single out individuals. If *The Guarantee* is correct, it is also a semantic truth that its uses could not fail to single out individuals. And for reasons that follow, it may seem that the one cancels out the other. In brief: it is difficult to see how building security into the very meaning of *I* does not strip it of its referring role.

To be clear, the problem is not: 'If *I* is a referring term, then security must be false; it must be possible for uses of *I* to fail to refer.' Worries of this sort are often mounted. As we have seen, they have led some to deny that uses of *I* refer at all (Anscombe; Glock and Hacker), and some to deny that uses of *I* depend on identification (Hacker).[14] They stem from a remark of Wittgenstein's which, though generalizable, occurs in the midst of an extended argument concerning *I*:

when in this case no error is possible, it is because the move which we might be inclined to think of as an error, a 'bad move', is no move of the game at all.[15]

The assumption is that, if *I* is a referring term, it must at least be possible to conceive of its uses as *succeeding* in referring. And this is not possible precisely because such uses cannot *fail*. But this line of thought seems overly fastidious. Fifth-century Stylite saints like Simeon squatted for fifty years on pillars in the midst of the Antiochene desert. We might not want to deny that they succeeded in referring whenever they pointed in any direction and said *This Desert*, even though they could scarcely have failed.

The problem is rather this: 'If *I* is a referring term, then security may be true; but it cannot be a semantic truth.' Suppose the owner of a chicken-sexing firm puts his incompetent son on the payroll, insisting that whatever he pulls out and calls *Female Chick* is to count as a female chick. Sometimes one cannot fail to single things out even though one *is* singling them out. That is the case with Simeon's use of *That Desert*. Sometimes one cannot fail to single things out precisely because one is *not* singling them out. That is the case with the feckless son's use of *Female Chick*. (If application of Wittgenstein's maxim were restricted to cases of this latter sort, it would encapsulate the point.) The father builds security into the very meaning of *Female Chick*, at least in the mouth of his offspring, and hence strips it of its singling-out role. *That Desert* is made secure by the circumstances of its use rather than any such semantic truth. That is why it may still be said to single things out.

[14] Anscombe (1975: 153); Glock and Hacker (1996: 103).   [15] Wittgenstein (1969: 66–7).

Here is another way to make the distinction. A crossbow might be fixed to a frame a yard from its target so that any quarrel fired by it cannot but strike the bull's eye. Alternatively, the bow might be freed from its frame and used to shoot aimlessly; a flunkey then draws a bull's eye around each embedded quarrel. Though not particularly sporting, we would not deny that the quarrel hits ('finds') its target in the first case. In the second, this is precisely what we would deny.[16]

So, prima facie, genuine reference and security against failure exclude each other when considered as properties of the logic of *I*. If *I* is indeed a referring expression, then its uses single out individuals. It may be that its uses cannot fail in this task. But if they are to be considered as even carrying out the job, this security cannot be the semantic truth *The Guarantee* requires. We are not thereby deprived of possible explanations, however. As we shall see, like Simeon's *This Desert*, it may be that the circumstances in which *I* is used protect it from failure.

There is an additional problem with *The Guarantee* for those who hold that genuine referring expressions do not single out individuals. It is people who do so using such terms.[17] On this view, in order to refer using *I*, people have to be able to individuate the item they are referring to (i.e. themselves). But *The Guarantee* entails that the *I*-user (we might hesitate to call him a subject) will refer correctly to himself when uttering sentences of the form 'I am F' even if he does not know:

(i) *who* he is

(an amnesiac on waking perhaps; or someone in receipt of mnemonic information gathered in the course of another person's experiences—supposing, for the sake of the argument, that such cases of 'quasi-memories' are intelligible in the way described)[18]; or

(ii) *what* he is

(an insane person, for example; someone who has always considered himself a she-wolf; a wave; an immaterial soul); or

(iii) *where* he is;

someone deprived of any and all perceptual information, for example; the extreme solipsist who believes nothing else exists but himself.

The problem is that the beliefs of *I*-users in categories (i)–(iii)—beliefs about themselves and about their surroundings—seem radically discontinuous with the kinds of information necessary to individuating *any* object from among others with a referring term. And it is doubtful that a being who knows neither who, nor what, nor where he is, and is furthermore without the resources to indicate in other ways what or which one item is being spoken of, may nevertheless single

---

[16] See Hacker (1993: 223).   [17] See Strawson (1950).
[18] See Shoemaker (1970); Parfit (1984: 226).

himself out sufficiently to be able to use *any* term to self-refer successfully. And if *The Guarantee* entails a falsehood, of course, it must itself be false.

WHAT DOES *THE GUARANTEE* EXPLAIN?

§ 38. Security is a semantic truth, according to *The Guarantee*. It is to be explained by the meaning of *I*, not the metaphysics of its referents, the epistemology of its users, or the pragmatics of its use. The strongest arguments for the doctrine take the form Strawson proposes:

Anyone who is capable of formulating [a thought using *I*] will have mastered the ordinary practice of personal reference by the use of personal pronouns; and it is a rule of that practice that the first personal pronoun refers, on each occasion of its use, to whoever then uses it. So the fact that we have, in the case imagined, a user, is sufficient to guarantee the reference, and the correct reference for the use.[19]

So mastery of *Rule Theory* is a necessary condition for the use of *I*. And this in turn explains the security of any use of *I*. Others model their support for *The Guarantee* on this form of argument. For example, Bermúdez claims,

It is commonly and correctly held that the practices and rules governing the use of the first-person pronoun determine what its reference will be whenever it is employed, according to the simple rule that whenever the first-person pronoun is used correctly, it will refer to the person using it. It follows from this rule that the correct use of *I* is enough to guarantee both that it has a referent and that the referent is the user. So it is impossible for the first-person pronoun (correctly and genuinely employed) to fail to refer or for it to refer to someone other than the person using it.[20]

It is not surprising to find that the standard argument-form appeals to *Rule Theory* to support *The Guarantee*. For if *The Guarantee* is true, as we have found, security must be explained by the meaning of *I*. And the standard account of that meaning is *Rule Theory*. As Campbell writes, 'Anyone who uses the first person manages to refer using it. This is a straightforward consequence of its being governed by the [simple] rule.'[21]

There are three points to be made about this dependence on *Rule Theory*. First, circularity threatens. Campbell continues: 'But when we leave this rule behind, the datum that reference-failure is impossible is hard to understand.' So our reason for holding *Rule Theory* is its harmony in ordinary practice with *The Guarantee*, and the truth of this latter doctrine depends on the truth of *Rule Theory*. So the reason we have to believe that *I* behaves as it does (i.e. under *The Guarantee*) is because *Rule Theory* is true. And the reason we have for regarding *Rule Theory* as true is because *I* behaves as it does (i.e. under *The Guarantee*). That

---

[19] Strawson (1994: 210).   [20] Bermúdez (1998: 9).   [21] Campbell (1994: 125).

the doctrines are consistent with each other and may entail each other is not at issue. This is now a familiar feature of *Purism*. The problem is that we are not offered a reason independent of either doctrine to believe the other.

The second point relates to the frequency with which 'correct' is used in the Bermúdez passage. It obscures important differences of sense. In particular, we should distinguish carefully between what makes *Rule Theory* (in)correct about *I* and what makes an employment of *I* (in)correct. The passage might make it look as if the latter question is decided by the former, when the reverse is the case. It is what counts as 'correct employment' of *I* that determines whether *Rule Theory* is correct, whether it correctly represents the referring role of *I*. So we cannot just appeal to the 'simple rule', together with a distinction between correct and incorrect uses of *I*, to settle the matter in favour of *The Guarantee*. We have first to decide whether *Rule Theory* is correct, whether it describes what counts as 'correct and genuine employment' of the term. If it does not, *The Guarantee* lacks the support it is here attributed.

The third point follows from the second. Arguments for *The Guarantee* imply *Rule Theory*. But the latter doctrine is false, as we know. So the former must fail. Moreover, the reasons why *Rule Theory* fails impinge directly on *The Guarantee*. For the 'simple rule' is not sufficient to determine the reference of *I*-uses. So the mere fact that we have an *I*-user could not be sufficient in every (perhaps *any*) case to guarantee a successful reference for the use. Hence these passages offer no explanation of security *at all*, let alone an explanation that makes security a semantic truth.

IS *THE GUARANTEE* SUPPORTED?

§ 39.   There are independent reasons to doubt arguments in support of *The Guarantee*. If the doctrine is true, then there must be an exclusive explanation of security which makes it a semantic truth. But this conclusion does not follow from the standard arguments, even if *Rule Theory* were true. For these arguments are consistent with and even *endorse* an alternative explanation (however unwittingly). To see why, assume for the present that *Rule Theory* is true and that a 'simple rule' gives the meaning of *I*. Carol Rovane argues for *The Guarantee* as follows:

I refers to the speaker, and any speaker who has mastered the term knows this rule. Presumably, any speaker also knows that she is speaking when she uses *I*, and if she knows this she surely knows that there is a speaker. Which is just to say that, in any use of *I*, the referent (the speaker) is guaranteed to exist, and, moreover, speakers know this.[22]

---

[22] Rovane (1987: 153).

Suppose that security is indeed explained by this coincidence between what competent speakers know about the meaning of *I* and what they know about themselves in the context of use (i.e. that they are speaking). This is dubious, of course. For the attempt relies on several questionable assumptions: that anyone who speaks will know both that there is a speaker and who that speaker is; that merely speaking *I* is sufficient to give the use determinate reference; that knowing the 'simple rule' and knowing that one is speaking are sufficient for one to know of which spoken use of *I* one is the referent (an assumption on which I will put particular pressure in Part II). Still, whatever security is afforded by this applica-tion of *Rule Theory* is not explained by *The Guarantee*. For this explanation makes security an oddity of the epistemology and pragmatics of *I*-use, not of the term itself. The meaning of *I* is merely incidental to the account. Security is not a semantic truth.

The problem is one of divergence between formulation and justification. There is a mismatch between what would have to be the case if *The Guarantee* were true and what is shown to be the case if the argument is sound. The quoted passage of Strawson offers another example of divergence, as does the Bermúdez passage, and for the same reasons (unsurprisingly, since he explicitly follows Strawson). The problem is less obvious because the passage is opaque on a crucial question. Security is explained by appeal to a coincidence arising between the meaning-rule for *I* and the fact that we have 'in the case imagined' a user. But Strawson does not clarify the status of this fact.

If the user's existence is merely a contingent feature, one that fortunately obtains in this particular case, then we do not even have an explanation of security, let alone a semantic explanation. For it would permit occasions on which no such user exists. In such cases, for all the meaning of *I* (i.e. the 'simple rule') tells us, there would be uses and no user for them to refer to. So the user's existence had better be necessary. If this is because features of any occasion of utterance ensure that no use of *I* could fail to have something that counted as its user, then we would have an explanation of this odd security. (Indeed, one that we shall find offers the best explanation of security and the best interpretation of what Strawson is getting at, however unwittingly.) But at best it would be explained by a coincidence between the meaning of *I* and the pragmatics of utterance. At worst the oddity would be a matter of pragmatics alone and the logical character of *I* would be left merely incidental. For security to be the semantic truth required by *The Guarantee*, the necessary existence of the user would have to follow from the meaning of *I*, from the simple rule 'the first personal pronoun refers, on each occasion of its use, to whoever then uses it'. If this could be shown, it would offer the best argument available for *The Guarantee*. So the suggestion is worth pursuing in the detail required.

§ 40.   This 'simple rule' is interpretable in various ways, and this creates an immediate problem. It might mean no more than that, where there is a use of *I* which refers and a user, the use refers to the user. And a rule of this sort does not even guarantee that any use refers, let alone that it will have a user. Alternatively, it might mean that, where there is a use of *I* and a user, the use refers to the user. Again, however, the user's existence is merely contingent. If the rule is to make the user's existence necessary to the use, it is clear that it should be interpreted in order to imply the following: for *every* use of *I* there must be a user to whom it will successfully refer. This is another point at which the vaunted simplicity of *Rule Theory* evaporates, of course. If *this* is the rule which gives the meaning of *I*, it is certainly not straightforward. It also stretches the imagination to suppose that *this* is the rule that 'anyone who is capable' of first-personal thinking 'will have mastered', the one that describes 'ordinary practice'. But our focus is at present on *The Guarantee* and so we may ignore these difficulties with *Rule Theory.*

Having arrived at this stage, the solution may seem simple enough. Security may appear to be implied by two claims,

1. Any use of *I* refers to its user.
2. For any use, there is a user.

This pair of claims seem to tell us that every use of *I* has a referent, and the referent is the user. Moreover, this would be a semantic truth, as *The Guarantee* must be. For (1) gives the meaning of *I* and (2) gives (part of) the meaning of (1); it elucidates the component words 'use' and 'user'. So the explanation of security does not appeal beyond the meaning of *I*. It is a semantic truth, just as *The Guarantee* requires.

But this most viable interpretation of the Strawson argument fails to explain security. One problem is that even *Rule Theorists* may deny that (1) gives the meaning of *I*. Recall that, on occasion, the referent of *I* is precisely *not* its user (e.g. it is its *producer* instead). As we found, reformulating (1) and (2) in terms of 'the producer' encounters the same problems in reverse. And the inclusively disjunctive 'the producer or the user' is no option either. In cases where both exist but differ, reference would fail through splitting.

But the main problem is this: (2) is ambiguous between (2) 'For any use, there is *at least one* user' and (2*) 'For any use there is *at least and at most* (i.e. *exactly one*) user.' (2*) cannot give the meanings of 'use' and 'user'. This is evident from the fact that it would not be contradictory to deny it. So we can only appeal to (2) in elucidating (1). But it is precisely (2*) which is needed to explain the impossibility of reference-failure. For if a use of *I* refers successfully, it must have *at most* one referent. *I* is a singular term, one that cannot tolerate reference-splitting. So the pair of claims would need to ensure this in all cases if they are to explain security. But when we ask what *I* means, we are told only that uses of the term refer to their users (1) and that each such use must have at least one user (2). Being a singular term, *I*'s uses have *exactly one* referent or none at all. So the pair of claims could not tell us that every use of *I* has a referent *at all*, let alone that *the* referent is *the* user.

There is a further problem which depends on the earlier discussion of *Rule Theory.* To obtain *The Guarantee* from (1) and (2), we need to interpret 'user' in such a way as to single out an item on any occasion of *I*-use that will count thereby as the referent of that use. Otherwise, there would be the possibility that the combination of (1) and (2) gave two or more items equal right to count as the referent of a use of *I*, thus violating *The Guarantee* by splitting the reference. But the elucidation by (2) of 'use' and 'user' in (1) does not secure a single item. As we have seen, any number of things have equally valid claims to being related by use to linguistic tokens, even on occasions of successful reference (an individual body, person, or human being; a certain set of lips, tongue, or teeth; and so on). So, for all the elucidation (2) shows, (1) allows that there may be innumerable users for any one use of *I*. Hence (1) cannot show that any use of *I* *succeeds* in referring, let alone that no use could *fail* to refer.

This was our task: to make the necessary existence of exactly one user for every use follow from the meaning of *I*. Only so could security be the semantic truth required by *The Guarantee*. But suppose we continue to pretend that the 'simple rule', (1), gives that meaning. It is not sufficient to ensure that when we have *at least one* user of *I*, we have *no more* than one. Perhaps features of any occasion of utterance ensure that every use of *I* has exactly one user. We might then have an explanation of security, but not one that made it a semantic truth. The problem is exactly the same as that besetting the earlier attempt to account for the necessary existence of an *I*-user. Security would be explained at best by a coincidence between the meaning of *I* and the pragmatics of utterance, and at worst by pragmatics alone. In either case, the logical character of *I* would be incidental. We could draw no conclusions from security about whether *I* refers, what kind of term *I* is, and so on.

WHY HAS *THE GUARANTEE* SEEMED CONVINCING?

§ 41.   So we have a puzzle to grapple with. There is an apparently irresistible sense that uses of *I* are secure against reference-failure. There is an almost universally held explanation of that security which makes it a semantic truth, a deep feature of the logical character of the term. But when we enquire into the details of that explanation, we encounter significant disagreements among its advocates. And when we ask after arguments for the explanation, we discover that there are none. This gap is particularly poignant since those who take themselves to argue for *The Guarantee* actually support quite different (usually pragmatic) explanations. What explains the systematic deflection of those attempting a semantic explanation? And what *does* explain security?

Solutions emerge from a summary of the foregoing. We have no reason to suppose that security *is* a semantic truth, for the reasons offered fail, diverge, or depend on a false doctrine, i.e. *Rule Theory*. And we have no reason to suppose that security *should be* a semantic truth, for other explanations of security are not ruled out. On the other hand, we have reason to believe that security is not and could not be a semantic truth. To suppose otherwise undermines the logical status of *I* as a genuine singular referring term. This may explain why professed advocates of *The Guarantee* appeal to other explanations (in fact, if not in design). It is as if they were reluctant to adopt the doctrine but could see no clear way to an alternative. And there is good reason to be both drawn to the doctrine and repelled by it. For *I*-uses reveal a remarkable resistance to reference-failure which any explanation must match. And building security into the very meaning of the term certainly answers to this requirement. On the other hand, by making security a semantic truth, *The Guarantee* places under grave threat the default position on the logical character of *I*. In short, the doctrine is *more* than a match for the phenomenon it explains. And a sense of this dangerous superfluity, however inchoate, accounts for the systematic deflection of the doctrine's advocates.

Recognizing that *The Guarantee* is more than a match for security, we are encouraged to ask whether a pragmatic alternative—along the lines suggested by the deflected theorists, perhaps—might not be simply *equal* to it. The idea would be that features of any occasion of utterance ensure that no use of *I* could fail to refer. Now these features will not suffice if *I* is taken for a *Pure Indexical* governed by *Rule Theory*; a term whose reference is sufficiently determined by the 'simple rule'. Together with this rule, pragmatic features will certainly ensure that there is at least one thing that might count as referent for any *I*-use—i.e. the user-producer. But a use must be determined on exactly one referent if it is to refer at all. It must pick out not just *something*, but the *right* something. And, as we know, the 'simple rule' is variously indeterminate on this point. There is nothing about features of the occasion of use that would help fix matters more finely. Indeed, far from determining precisely which individual counted as *the* user-producer, focusing on such features would tend to *increase* our estimate of the proliferating candidates. So it is no wonder that theorists tempted to explore a pragmatic explanation of security find themselves blown back onto *The Guarantee*. For if *I* is a *Pure Indexical*, only a semantic explanation will do. Pragmatics and the 'simple rule' will not suffice to explain how every (or, indeed, *any*) use succeeds in referring. So security had best be built into the meaning of the term.

§ 42.   But we have the means to escape this infernal 'attract-repulse' perpetual motion machine. For the demise of the three doctrines forces us to give up taking *I* for a *Pure Indexical*. If *I* is nevertheless an indexical, it is presumably of the 'Impure' variety—i.e. a *Deictic Term*; one whose reference is partly determined by demonstration. The doctrines had prevented *I* taking its place here, among the other singular personal pronouns, *You* and *He/She*. For it was not plausible to say of *You* or *He/She* that a simple rule determines their reference, or that their use involves no identification, or that they are logically secured against reference-failure. But we have found that it is not plausible to say these things of *I* either. So we are free to contemplate the possibility that *I* is a *Deictic Term*. The details remain to be filled in, of course. But we already have the resources to appreciate the implications for security.

Briefly, then, pragmatics can be made to explain security if *I* is taken for a *Deictic Term* and not mistaken for a *Pure Indexical*. For features of the occasion of use, in the form of demonstration, determine the reference of uses of *Deictic Terms*. If *I* is such a term, then its use on some occasion refers to the deictically signified individual. It is plausible to suppose that simply doing what is necessary to utter the term is sufficient demonstration to determine one as that individual. Thus just doing what is necessary to count as using the term ensures its success. Uttering *I* determines reference on something, and the right something. So one's uses will never fail.

This security is unusual among *Deictic Terms*, of course. But it is not unique. It is not ruled out by the logical character of such terms, for example. For security is a feature that *This* and *That* would share also if the individual effecting sufficient determining demonstration by uttering were also always the referent. And there are ways to make sure this is so. Consider a *Deictic Term* like *This Very Speaker*, where 'very' makes the whole self-reflexive in the way required. In all circumstances, and simply because of what is involved in utterance, the referents of its uses cannot help being sufficiently determined as such. But it is still a *Deictic Term*; one whose reference is determined by that security-conferring demonstration of utterance. These are features which *This Very Speaker* and *I* have in common. Other features distinguish them sharply. *I* is not a mixed demonstrative, and it does not refer exclusively to speakers (even when the use of *I* is spoken; the speaker need not be the reference-maker).

If this picture is roughly correct, it is no accident that theorists who try to support *The Guarantee* find themselves drawn to the pragmatics of utterance. For a pragmatic explanation gives us all the security we need and no more than we should wish for. Rejecting *The Guarantee* means replacing the standard conception of *I*'s logical character. We *can* explain the security of *I* pragmatically. And we can *only* do so if we give up taking it for a *Pure Indexical*. Dim outlines of a replacement conception are becoming apparent. The security of *I* is explained by features of its use. Security is not built into the meaning of the term, so the default position is safe. *I* is a referring term. The features which explain the security of *I* also determine the reference of its uses. They are deictic features. So *I* is a *Deictic Term*, like *You* and *He/She*.

In Part II of this book, we shall see how to make good on this proposal.

5

Interim Conclusion

SUMMARY

§ 43.   We now know:

1. *I* is a genuine singular referring expression. It is a linguistic counter whose meaning indicates which one particular thing is relevant to the truth-value of the sentence containing it.

This is the default position at present. It will receive independent support in an argument from inference in Part II.

2. *I* is a device with varying referents (a 'variant device'). *I* may be used by anyone to refer to themselves; everyone who uses *I* can only refer to himself; context disambiguates which object is referred to by any use, not which term is in use.
3. *I* is not a proper name or descriptive term.
4. *I* is not a *Pure Indexical*; no rule entirely gives its meaning and sufficiently determines its reference in context.

Phrases like 'any use of *I* refers to whoever uses-produces it' usually offer an accurate statement of the reference of *I*-uses. But they help identify the user-producer, not determine the referent.

5. When used to express thoughts, uses of *I* are not independent of identification of the individual thought about. As with other terms, it would be unconventional for the user to ask which individual is identified when there is no likelihood of misidentification.
6. Uses of *I* are secure against reference-failure; but this is not part of the meaning or logical character of the term.

PURISM

§ 44.   The meaning of *I* is like Plutarch's Mediterranean: 'a well-mixed bowl of myths'.[1] At the depths of this bowl lies the hopeful thought that the

---

[1] *De defectu oraculorim*, 421 A. Quoted in Brown (1978: 7).

meaning of *I* is simple and its explanation uncomplicated, undemanding. Bertrand Russell gave expression to this cheery optimism when he asserted that *I* is a term 'which we all know how to use, and which must therefore have some easily accessible meaning'.[2] *Purism* benefits directly from this expectation of easefulness because it satisfies the desires thus generated. Separately and together, its three component doctrines offer a straightforward answer to the basic question, 'How does *I* refer?': to the user, directly, and always successfully. *Purism* seems uncomplicated, in stark and flattering contrast with accounts that ascribe *I* the features and requirements common to other variant terms. If we add reciprocal endorsement by the component doctrines, it is not surprising that the position has been deeply attractive.

We have seen what is wrong with *Purism*. It is a contradictory position founded on doctrines that turn out, when defined, to be false. More poignantly, it is a fragile position. The history of debate about *I* led directly to its current dominance over our conception of *I*. But beneath the surface unanimity, self-professed advocates support divergent and incompatible interpretations of the three component doctrines.

There is also much amiss with the assumption of straightforwardness from which *Purism* benefits. For it is merely a conjecture, held by some like Russell, and denied by others. Wittgenstein, for example, rejected such optimism as ungrounded, observing that use of *I* is 'one of the most misleading representational techniques in our language.'[3] Russell tries to make his position appear the conclusion of an argument. In the sentence quoted above, he claims that access to the meaning of a term must be trouble-free if its use is effortless. But his strident tone reveals the bluff. For it is evidently not true that, if we enjoy a common familiarity with the use of an expression, we will be able to provide a ready and fluent account of its meaning. St Augustine famously remarked on this, taking *Time* as his example. Translated in such a way as to bring out the consonance with the Russell passage, he notes: 'We are always talking about time and times ... They are the most accessible and commonly used words, and yet they are also profoundly obscure; their meaning remains to be discovered.'[4] But the evidence is ubiquitous: young children deal faultlessly with words whose meaning anyone would experience the greatest difficulties in accounting for (*True, Believe, Mind, Good, Beautiful*).

Given what we now know about *I*, expectations of ease should be relinquished. If after investigation the meaning of *I* turns out to be uncomplicated, all well and good. But we should not prejudice the enquiry by stating in advance that this must be what we will find.

---

[2] Russell (1914: 164).   [3] Wittgenstein (1930: 88).   [4] *Confessions*, XI. xxii.

AN ALTERNATIVE CONCEPTION

§ 45.   If myths are widely mistaken for true doctrines, it is usually because they contain distorted truths. And this is certainly so in the present case.

Rule Theory, as we have found, turns a platitude into a falsehood by elevating the 'simple rule' to the position of sufficient determinant. But rules of this sort are true enough and occasionally helpful in their original role: providing another means of identifying the referent of *I*-uses. *Independence* distorts a feature of interest for the pragmatics of utterance (i.e. *Nonsense*), turning it into a phenomenon that only a weighty claim like *Immunity* could explain. Similarly, *The Guarantee* distorts another pragmatic feature (i.e. security), reading out of it a substantial semantic truth.

So we know that *I* is unusual in various ways. It is secure against reference-failure. It expresses thoughts where there is no likelihood of misidentifying what one has thought about. These phenomena are not unique to *I*-uses. So we should seek an explanation that embraces other terms also. These phenomena do not occur with every use of the terms in which they are found. So the explanation should not appeal to features that do. This rules out appeals to the meaning or logical character of the terms concerned and instead draws attention to the circumstances in which they are used.

The demise of *Purism* can be made to reveal more than this. For it creates a strong presumption in favour of regarding *I* as a *Deictic Term*. This is to put the matter conservatively. For on the standard view, the demise of *Purism* would *entail* that claim. If variant terms are either *Pure* or *Impure Indexicals*, and *I* is not a *Pure Indexical*, it must be *Impure*; i.e. a *Deictic Term*. But the standard view may be incorrect. We may not be justified in drawing this conclusion. So two major questions have now arisen which will dominate the rest of our enquiry:

(A) What is it to say that any expression is a *Deictic Term*?
(B) Is *I* a *Deictic Term*?

If *I* were a *Deictic Term*, it would belong to the same group as the other singular personal pronouns, *You* and *He/She*, together with *This (F)* and *That (F)*. Certainly, we have as yet no reason to deny the claim. For if *I*'s reference is not sufficiently determined by definition-in-context, it may require other means (like demonstration), just as *You* and *He/She* do. It is no less anti-conventional in certain circumstances to ask after their referents. And it is no more possible in certain circumstances for their reference to fail.

To say that *I* is a *Deictic Term* is not to say that it is synonymous with any other such term, just that it falls into the same class. This should be obvious. But it is often just assumed that, if *I* were a *Deictic Term*, like *This F*, it would have to *mean* something like *This F—This Body*, perhaps; or *This Mind*; or *This Subject of*

Experiences. So Campbell argues that if *I* were a *Deictic Term*, it would have to have 'something of the force of *This Body*'. And Heal thinks the claim would imply that *I* is semantically equated with *This Mind* or *This Subject of Experiences.*[5] The inference is not licensed in the case of other members of the class. Agreeing that *You* or *He/She* are *Deictic Terms*, for example, does not commit us to thinking that *they* must mean, or have the force of, *This F.* So the conclusion does not follow for *I* either.

The point rests on a deep fact that we will investigate in Part II: semantic and syntactic features distinguish *Deictic Terms* from each other as well as from other, non-*Deictic Terms*. For example, some can be combined with a sortal to create a 'mixed' expression (e.g. *This (F)*; *That (F)*). Some cannot (e.g. *I*; *You*; *He/She*). *This* often implies proximity whereas *That* implies distance. *He/She*, unlike *This* and *That*, are inherently gendered. These terms are all deictic though they possess distinctive features and contribute different information to the content of sentences in which they are included. *I* is no exception, something that we will later turn to our benefit. For our task is to elucidate the term in all its specificity. And this is not something we could achieve by concentrating solely on what *Deictic Terms* have in common, what sets them apart from non-deictic expressions. We also need to discover what sets *I* apart from other *Deictic Terms*, from expressions *within* the group to which it belongs.

Some have tried to use the fact that *I* is unlike some other *Deictic Terms* in some respects to argue that it is not a *Deictic Term* at all. They point to the fact that we can respond to the use of *This/That* in a sentence like 'This is full of water' with the question 'This *what* (or *which*)?', but it is not possible to pose a well-formed question of the same kind when *I* is used.[6] Again, the inference is not licensed because other bona fide *Deictic Terms* are the same in this respect. When *You* or *He/She* are used, for example, we need not be prepared to answer 'You/He/She *which*?' or 'You/He/She *what*?' For the questions are not well formed and make no sense. And in all such cases, the same explanation presents itself. Questions of this sort are not well formed because of the fact that, unlike *This/That*, the *Deictic Terms* in question cannot be combined with sortals to form a 'mixed' expression (e.g. *This (F)*; *That (F)*).

When *Deictic Terms* are used, we might occasionally ask '*which* He/She?', just as we ask '*which* this?' or 'this *what*?' And this same question is perfectly appropriate for uses of *I*. In all these cases, we are asking 'of what kind is the item to which you are referring' or 'which person/thing is being spoken of?' And it is possible to ask this question in relation to uses of *I*. Moreover, the question can be shortened and made specific in the usual manner: '*which* I?' This is particularly obvious in cases where one asks among a group of people for the attitudes of some. Those that will respond will tend naturally to accompany their uses of *I* with some obvious identifying gesture.

---

[5] Campbell (1994: 145); Heal (1996: 19).   [6] See Anscombe (1975: 148).

That they do so to forestall a '*which?*'-question is made obvious by situations in which the gestures are not produced and that question has to be asked. For example, in response to their teacher's question, several children wishing to own up to some offence might distinguish themselves in the bustling innocent crowd by raising their hands when saying, 'I did it.' Suppose they wish to be difficult and *merely* utter these words without raising their hands. Then sufficient deixis would not have been provided, *ex hypothesi*, and the teacher might ask, 'which of you said that?' ('which of you are being spoken of?'). What makes the question 'which?' appropriate here is the fact that the speaker has not provided sufficient demonstration for the audience to identify the referent. Granted, we rarely need to ask this question of uses of *I*. But that cannot be because such uses do not depend on demonstration for the communication of their reference. For then the question *could* not be asked. It must be because it is unusual for uses of *I* to lack sufficient demonstration to achieve this purpose. And *that* is readily explained by the fact that mere enunciation is usually sufficient. (These matters will be discussed in the necessary detail in Part II, where the fundamental features governing communicative reference for the whole group of *Deictic Terms* are established.)

So this is our task in pursuing the investigation: to discover whether the presumption in favour of regarding *I* as a *Deictic Term* can be converted into full affirmation. And with (A) and (B) we have isolated the main issues to be resolved. What is it to say that *any* referring expression is a *Deictic Term*—what is distinctive about the logical character, inferential role, referential function, expressive use, and communicative role of such expressions? And why might we regard *I* as such a term?

In answering these questions, we can expect to resolve other questions also, and shed further light on what we now know about *I*. Two issues in particular have become prominent as a result of earlier discussions:

(C) Uses of *I* express thoughts where there is no likelihood of misidentifying what one has thought about. This may be explained pragmatically rather than by appeal to the meaning of the term. But we do not yet know what accounts for the phenomenon.

(D) Uses of *I* are secure against reference-failure. This also may be explained pragmatically. But we are similarly ignorant, as yet, of what accounts for the phenomenon.

Our point of departure should be the last stage reached: the logical character of *I*. We may then work back, exposing the meaning of *I* fold by fold, from the heart of the matter to its outer reaches.

Part II

THE MEANING OF *I*

6

Logical Character

§ 46.   *I* has obligatory deictic reference. This is a fact about logical character whose existence and significance are of the first importance to the meaning of the term, though it has gone unrecognized in the literature.

To appreciate this fact takes some stage-setting. So consider the class of so-called 'variant devices': singular referring expressions with varying referents like *I*, *You*, *He/She*, *This*, *That*, *Now*, and *Here*. The same individual may be picked out regularly enough by uses of *She*, for example. But there is no single woman, A, such that A is the referent whenever *She* is used. The chief contrast is with proper names: invariant terms whose referents do not change with different uses. Whenever the proper name *Abelard* is used, one and the same individual is such that he is its referent (preserving the simplifying fiction that where proper names like *Abelard* are concerned, there is a single such name and a single individual so baptized.)

Now consider the following uses of variant terms; *Herself* in

(1) Heloise loves herself [i.e. 'x loves x']

and *The Former/ The Latter* in

(2) If Heloise and Abelard elope, the former risks imprisonment and the latter death [i.e. 'If x and y elope, x risks imprisonment and y risks death'].

These uses are obliged to refer anaphorically: their reference is systematically determined in relation to a 'source'-term; they refer to whatever that term refers to. In (2), for example, *The Former* refers to whoever *Heloise* refers to in this way.

We should exercise care in characterizing anaphoric terms. They are sometimes described as expressions intended to be understood as being co-referential with a referring expression occurring elsewhere in the sentence.[1] This is too broad, since two terms can be intentionally co-referential without being anaphorically related. It is also too narrow, since two terms can be anaphorically related without occurring in the same sentence. (It would also be too narrow if anaphora were a relation that extended to *non*-referential terms, e.g. pronouns and variables with quantifier antecedents, though nothing in my arguments turns on this; they

[1]   e.g. Evans (1985: 214).

would be unaffected if the modifier *referential* were added to uses of *anaphora* throughout.)

These features are important for what follows. For we need to know what the first feature tells us: that anaphora is not *identical* with co-reference, but one way (amongst others) of *achieving* co-reference. In the sentence 'Peter Abelard was accused of heresy in 1140, but the renowned author of the *Logic* appealed to Rome,' for example, the use of the definite description *The Renowned Author of the Logic* is intended to be understood as co-referential with the earlier occurring use of the proper name *Peter Abelard* without being anaphorically related to that term—its reference is determined quite independently. We also need to be aware of what the second feature reveals: that anaphora is not limited to the inside of one sentence. For cross-sentential anaphora is often used to ensure the validity of arguments composed of several sentences. So this feature enables anaphoric uses of singular terms to play their inferential role. And the implications of the present discussion for the inferential roles of singular terms in general and *I* in particular form the main focus of this part of the chapter.

Another characterization of anaphoric terms is closer to the mark: they refer to whatever their antecedent refers to.[2] But 'source' is preferable to antecedent, since it does not imply that the dependent term be positionally consequent. In the sentence 'He is very witty, that Parisian philosopher we hear so much about,' the anaphoric pronoun (*He*) is positioned before its logical antecedent, the source-term *That Parisian Philosopher*. For the purposes of this discussion, then, anaphora embraces cataphora. Nothing hangs on sentential positioning of this sort.

More precisely then,

Anaphora: One singular term *a* is anaphorically dependent on another such term *b* (its source) if and only if *a* refers to whatever *b* refers to in a systematic way and with this implication: *a*'s contribution to the truth-conditions of the whole sentence in which *a* occurs is not evaluable from *a*'s immediate sentential context alone, but depends on evaluation of the context in which *b* occurs.

Some uses of variant singular terms may be described as 'free' with respect to the manner in which they refer. The use of *He/She* in sentences like (3) offer examples:

(3) If Heloise elopes, she must leave Paris.

The sentence is ambiguous, depending on whether the use of *She* refers anaphorically to Heloise—so that (3) has the form

(3) [If x elopes, x must leave Paris]

or whether it refers to another female (perhaps her accompanying friend)—so that (3) has the form

(3*) [If x elopes, y must leave Paris].

---

[2] See Evans (1985: 225).

In (3), the reference of *She* would have been gained intra-sententially, by pointing to another piece of language-use—the source-term as it occurs in the (sentential) context, i.e. *Heloise*. In (3*), on the other hand, *She* gains its reference extra-sententially, by appeal to something salient about the (non-sentential) context in which the utterance occurs—e.g. the presence of the individual referred to. Uses of this sort are commonly called 'deictic' from the Greek δεικνυμι (to show, point out) and its adjective δεικτικος, a term used by ancient grammarians and translated by them with the Latin *demonstrativus*.

In order to focus on the formal aspects of deictic uses, we shall postpone examination of major related questions to the chapters following—such as what makes an individual salient, and how salience is made discriminable. One secondary consideration may be dealt with immediately however. Some claim that *She/He* are disguised complex demonstratives of the form *That Female/Male*. If this were true, it would greatly complicate the application to them of the anaphoric-deictic distinction. The idea that *She/He* are to be understood in this fashion, and that sentences like 'That woman is studious' are consequently to be treated as synonymous with 'She is studious,' is said to follow from the claim that *She/He* have a hidden indexical component.[3] But the arguments are quite unconvincing. For suppose we acknowledge hidden indexicality. First, this evidence does not settle the question of primacy. It gives us no more reason to regard *She/He* as proxy for *That Female/Male* than vice versa. Hence we have as much reason to regard *That Female/Male* as disguised *simple* demonstratives of the form *She/He* as the converse. Second, this evidence gives us no reason to regard the *meaning* of the terms in question (their logical character, inferential role, referring function, expressive use, and communicative role) as given by the *meaning* of *That Female/Male* or *That Woman/Man*. Doubtless the sortal question (which gender?) is *answered* by *She/He*; but that is a different matter. Third, the claim of synonymy is incorrect: sentences of the form 'She is that woman' have fully informative uses that 'She is she' do not.

The difference between anaphoric and deictic uses shows up clearly when we try to evaluate the contribution they make to the truth-conditions of the sentences containing them. In the anaphoric use of *She*, that contribution is evaluated by appeal to the sentential context in which the source-term occurs. In the deictic use, the contribution is evaluated independently, by appeal to its extra-sentential context.

This/That are 'free' in the sense specified, though they are usually used deictically. Dashiell Hammett offers a complex example of an anaphoric use in this conversational fragment:

[Sid Wise] 'Why don't you get an honest lawyer?'
[Sam Spade] 'That fellow's dead.'[4]

---

[3] See Corazza (2002: 174).   [4] Hammett (2002: 112).

Finally, some uses of variant referring expressions are obliged to gain their reference deictically. An example of the use of a term with such obligatory deictic reference is *Her* in

(4) Heloise loves her ['x loves y'].

We should be careful to note that it is this particular use of *Her* that has obligatory deictic reference, and separate it from the free use of the same term in

(5) Heloise loves her mother ['x loves x's mother' or 'x loves y's mother'].

I is another term whose uses have obligatory deictic reference. (Thus *I* is crucially unlike the so-called 'first person plural' if, as some argue, *We* 'leaves room for anaphora and binding'.[5]) But there is no need to separate deictic and free uses, as with *He/She* and *Him/Her*. For, as with *The Former/The Latter*, no uses are free. Unlike those terms, however, all uses are deictic. If *He/She* are *Deictic Terms* because they have deictic uses, then *I* is a kind of super *Deictic Term*; it has no non-deictic uses. This is the key fact about the character of the term. Drawing out the deep implications of this fact and finding it confirmed in the referential role and expressive use of *I* will occupy us for the rest of this chapter. So it will be as well to substantiate and illustrate it first.

HOW *I* BEHAVES IN SUBSTITUTION INSTANCES

§ 47.   The standard case of non-deictic reference for variant terms is a sentence with a quantified antecedent, like

(6) Every woman loves her mother.

It has been said that whenever we substitute a singular term for the quantifier in sentences of this kind, we arrive at a sentence in which the pronoun can be interpreted as anaphoric.[6] There are two striking features about this widely accepted substitution claim. The first is that *I* presents a clear counter-instance: substituting this singular term for the quantifier in (6)

(7) I loved *her* mother

results in a sentence in which the pronoun (i.e. *Her*) only has a deictic reading. The second striking feature is that *I* is almost alone in this regard—singular *You* is another case. The existence of counter-instances to the substitution claim is obscured by the prevalence of confirmation from all types and uses of singular terms. As is readily appreciable, proper names (*Heloise*), demonstrative terms (*That F*), singular personal pronouns (*She*), and definite descriptions (*The Woman in Front*) all produce sentences that manifest the phenomenon when

---

⁵ Vallée (1996: 230).   ⁶ Evans (1985: 215–16; 219; 229).

they substitute for *Every* in (6). In each case, the pronoun *Her* is used ambiguously; each may refer deictically or anaphorically. If the use is anaphoric, its form will be [x loved x's mother]; if it is deictic, it will have the form [x loved y's mother].

Since anaphora is not to be identified with co-reference but merely with one way of achieving it, it is no surprise to find that co-reference is possible in the deictic interpretation also. We obtain (8) by substituting *Heloise* for *Every* in (6)

(8) Heloise loved *her* mother.

And suppose that *Her* is being used deictically by the speaker, who points out a particular woman; a woman who, it so turns out (and unbeknownst to the speaker), *is* Heloise. Then the terms *Heloise* and *Her* would co-refer; their value or referent would be the same. The same might be the case with the use of *I* in (7), though it would be as unusual as any case in which one refers deictically to oneself without knowing that it is oneself one is referring to. (Heloise might say (7) using *Her* deictically, pointing out a female form that she takes for her sister's, but which is in fact a reflection of herself.) The point can be extended by application to *I*. Suppose we change the profile of the quantifier sentence so that the substituted term and the pronoun come out undoubtedly co-referential. We would arrive at

(9) I (You) loved *my* (*your*) mother

by substituting *I* (You) for the quantifier in the sentence 'Every woman loved my (your) mother.' The point is that, however co-referential with the substituted term, the pronoun *My* (*Your*) still has only a deictic reading. Its contribution to the truth-conditions of the whole sentence does not depend on evaluation of the context in which the substitute occurs, but (like that substitute itself) is evaluated independently, by appeal to its extra-sentential context. Even in (9), then, *I* (*You*) is a counter-instance to the substitution claim.

Castañeda-type examples of alleged anaphoric uses of *I* fail for these reasons. 'I think that I am in danger' is supposed to mirror 'He thinks that he (himself) is in danger' in such a way as to make the second occurrence of *I* anaphorically dependent on the first. But the reference of either use of *I* is determined independently of the other; i.e. this is a case like 'I loved my mother' where uses of the same type-term are synonymous without being anaphorically related. The same holds in the complex case of extended fictional narratives where *I* or *You* are introduced to substitute for a definite description or quantified phrase. Suppose Abelard engages in re-enactment to work out what Heloise is thinking. In the first part of the project, he states whatever relevant information he has about her doings using a name (*Heloise*), or a definite description (*The niece of the canon*), or a quantified phrase (*Some student*). In the second part, he promotes the imaginative task by replacing each such term with *I*. Finally, he tries to see how things look from that perspective. It is perhaps not implausible to regard the uses of *I* introduced in the second part of the project as *co-referential* with those introduced in the first. But if so, they are certainly not *anaphorically* dependent on them. For it is not on different parts of the *sentential* context that their contribution to truth-conditions depends, but on features of the *extra*-sentential context, and particularly *who* is engaging in the imaginative project, *what rules* govern it, and so on.

These points also hold for truth-functional sentences; a feature that will accumulate significance as we proceed. So suppose we take the quantifier sentence

(10) If any woman elopes, *she* must leave Paris.

As we have seen (i.e. with (3)), this sentence is ambiguous if the quantifier is replaced by *Heloise*. *She* may be used anaphorically or deictically. But it is not ambiguous if the quantifier is replaced by *I*; it must have the form [if x elopes, y must leave Paris]. *I* may appear suspiciously alone in this regard, but that is not so. As already noted, the same applies to singular *You*. The same obligatorily deictic reference for both first- and second-person forms occurs when substituted either for the antecedent expression in (10):

(11) If I (You) elope, she must leave Paris

or for the consequent expression:

(12) If any woman (Heloise) elopes, I (You) must leave Paris

or for both antecedent and consequent:

(13) If I (You) elope, I (You) must leave Paris.

In each case, even if the values of the variables turn out to be the same (as they must in (13)), the sentences have the form [If x elopes, y must leave Paris].

In brief: *I* is a counter-instance to the substitution claim; and that is because it has an obligatory deictic reference.

Many linguists now hold that deictic and anaphoric pronouns should be interpreted by the same general strategy. This may suggest, together with our conclusion, that anaphoric pronouns are to be thought of as a limiting case of deictic pronouns.[7] It is certainly plausible enough to regard anaphora as reference to a contextually salient individual. For example, we might say that the pronoun in 'Heloise loved her mother' is not ambiguous between readings on which it refers to a salient or a non-salient individual. It is ambiguous between readings on which what *makes* an individual salient differ. Is it extra-sentential context (e.g. the one pointed at) or sentential context (i.e. the one referred to by the source-term)? In both cases, we may say that the term is deictic; it makes 'a reference to an object rendered salient in some way'. After all, isn't that precisely the role of the source in anaphoric reference: to render the object contextually salient by referring to it elsewhere in the sentence? For example, in the sentence 'If Heloise and Abelard worked hard, the former will benefit,' *The Former* might be analysed as referring precisely to the object made salient by the earlier occurrence of *Heloise*. And if it is

---

[7] Heim and Kratzer (1998: 239–41); Lasnik (1976: 1–22).

true that anaphora can be given a deictic analysis but not conversely, then demonstration is the more fundamental phenomenon. (In Chapter 7, I shall continue considering various kinds of reducibility claim as they impinge on *Deictic Terms*).

WHAT MATCHING CONSTRAINTS REVEAL

§ 48.   There are various ways in which it might be thought possible to challenge this argument.

First, it might be said that the pronouns in (7), (9), and (11)–(13) *can* be read as anaphorically dependent on the terms substituted for the quantifier. But I doubt anyone's intuitions could be sufficiently flexible to make this option tenable.

Second, it might be argued that *I* and *You cannot* be counter-instances to the substitution claim: the claim applies to the substituting in of singular terms, and they are not singular terms. But though a few regard *I* suspiciously (without good reason), as often noted, no one denies that singular *You* is such a term.

Third, it might be urged that *I* and *You should not* be allowed to form counter-instances: the claim should be altered so that it only covers certain singular terms. Apart from being ad hoc (to exclude counter-examples is not to disarm them), this move would do nothing to disturb the main point. Indeed, it would highlight it. It is precisely *because I* and *You* have an obligatory deictic reference that a viable substitution claim would have to be phrased in such a way as explicitly to exclude them.

Finally, it might be argued that the counter-instances are illegitimate. We have trouble accommodating them because they violate certain matching constraints, not because of anything obligatorily deictic about their reference. This is obviously the strongest challenge and is worth investigating.

If the substitutions are to be legitimate, so it could be argued, they must match in gender, number, and person. And there are three relations relative to which such matching constraints might exist: quantifier phrase and pronoun; quantifier phrase and substitute singular term; substitute singular term and pronoun. The first of these relations presents no mismatch: (6) and (10) make perfect sense. And we may ignore the relation anyway. We are looking for matching as a constraint on the substitution of terms like *I* and *You*. This relation obtains prior to substitution. As for the other two relations, Number is not the cause of the trouble. For confirmatory instances of the singular claim show mismatch between quantifier phrase and substitute singular term (e.g. (8)), and we obtain the same counter-instances if we make quantifier, substitute singular term, and pronoun agree—e.g. obtaining the problematic (7) from

(14) Exactly one woman loved *her* mother.

The problem is not caused by gender either. *I* and *You* are genderless terms—which is just to say that there can never be a gender-mismatch with gendered quantifier phrases like *Every (Any) Woman* or gendered pronouns like *Her*. There are languages in which all personal pronouns are gendered and where predicates reflect the gender of the terms with which they are concatenated. But this does not show that *I* or *You* are gendered terms, only that there is no precise equivalent for them in these languages. And this is a feature of surface grammar which can be ignored here. For when gendering is held steady in such languages, e.g. Hebrew, substitution instances still fail in the cases discussed. So the problem extends across the board at the depth it arises.

There may be mismatches of person. But, again, resolving them does nothing to solve the problem. We have already seen that (9) is a counter-instance. Yet there is person-agreement between the substituted singular term and the pronoun, and we may obtain (9) from a sentence in which the quantifier also agrees:

(15) Some of you loved your mother.

This last sentence illustrates what would be wrong with one last challenge: that *I* and *You* are problematic because they are matched with different kinds of singular term in the counter-instances. In the move from (15) to (9), there is no such mismatch. Indeed, the uses at issue are not only uses of the same *kind* of term (indexical). They are uses of the same *term*.

Thus we obtain a table of relations in which the only mismatches may be discounted (Table 1). And so we may conclude that mismatching is irrelevant to the point at issue: the substitution claim is false. And that is because *I* and *You* have obligatorily deictic reference. This means not just that *I* is a *Deictic Term* after all, like the other personal pronouns, but that it is a *pure* Deictic Term. *He/She* have deictic uses but are otherwise free with respect to their referential roles. *I* and *You* have nothing but deictic uses.

Table 1.

Mismatching?	Relation 1: quantifier phrase and pronoun	Relation 2: quantifier phrase and substituted term	Relation 3: substituted term and pronoun
Gender	Ignore	None	None
Number	Ignore	Discounted	None
Person	Ignore	Discounted	Discounted
Kind of term (Indexical)	Ignore	Discounted	Discounted

7

Inferential Role

§ 49. Discovering that *I* is an obligatorily *Deictic Term* unlocks the logical character of the expression. As for any term, the logic of *I* is fundamentally a matter of the contribution its uses make to the inferential relations of the sentences containing them; to what would entail those sentences and what would be entailed by them. Being a sub-sentential expression, *I*'s role here is indirect. For direct contributions to what entails what are made by the use of whole sentences in statements; items which can count as the premisses and conclusions of arguments. But the ability of statements to make such systematic contributions to inferential relations is conferred on them by the sub-sentential expressions they contain. And to characterize the inferential role of a term like *I* is to specify the ways in which its uses thus contribute to entailment relations.

HOW THE INFERENTIAL ROLES OF VARIANT TERMS ARE DISTINGUISHED

Singular referring terms are one sort of sub-sentential expression whose occurrence has (indirect) inferential significance. It is not simply that they help determine the meaning of the sentences that embed them. For predicates and plural terms are sub-sentential expressions that contribute in this way to entailment relations. Singular terms are distinctive in the manner by which they determine meaning: singling out that one thing from all others of which the predication must be true if the whole statement is to be true on any occasion of use. *I* has precisely this form of indirect inferential significance, as we have found. There are important differences in the way in which singular referring expressions single out individuals, as I shall argue. But what makes them all count as such is plain enough.

Different singular terms have different ways of carrying out their essential function of singling out individuals. And determining the way in which any such expression fulfils this function, its inferential role, is to establish its logical character. *I* refers deictically, as we have found, in each of its uses. To discover the inferential role of *I*, then, requires investigating the ways in which *Deictic Terms* quite generally contribute to entailment relations.

§ 50.   In order to distinguish the inferential role of a *Deictic Term* from the use of other expressions, it is necessary first to establish the relevant notion of inference. The validity of an argument of the form:

(1) *a* is *F.* Therefore *b* is *F*

depends on ensuring co-reference between the singular terms in the premiss–conclusion set. Thus '*b* is *F*' follows from '*a* is *F*' only if *a* and *b* co-refer. Evidently, the inference in (2) is not, on the face of it, good:

(2) 'I am *F. NN* is *G*. Therefore I am *F* and *G*'

(where *NN* stands for the user's proper name; in my case '*M de G*'). There are two questions that could be asked here: What is required to make the argument formally valid? And what is required for knowledge of the conclusion to count as the result of knowing the premisses? The answers differ. It would be sufficient to make the argument valid to add a premiss that rendered the set inconsistent (e.g. '*M de G* is not *G*'). For the conclusion would then be true in any interpretation (assignment of semantic values) in which the premisses were true. But since knowledge is factive and the premisses are contradictory, there would then be no 'knowing the premisses' for knowledge of the conclusion to rest on. We are interested in the second question, in the way that we may move from knowledge to new knowledge by means of argument.[1] So the advancement of knowledge is essential to the notion of inference we are interested in here. A good inference is one that would take one from knowledge of the premisses to knowledge of its conclusion.

§ 51.   The mere fact that *a* and *b* are co-referential is not sufficient to make (1) a good inference (however sufficient it may be for formal notions of validity). For one may know '*a* is *F*' without knowing '*b* is *F*', precisely because one does not know that '*a* = *b*'. Different kinds of singular term require different measures to ensure knowledge of their co-reference. So we may distinguish the inferential role of *Deictic Terms* like *I* from other expressions by distinguishing the different ways required by each such term to ensure knowledge of co-reference.

The co-reference of some singular terms is guaranteed by the mere fact that they are uses of the same type-term. This holds for most proper names. Thus 'Abelard is mad, bad, and dangerous to know' follows from 'Abelard is mad,' 'Abelard is bad,' and 'Abelard is dangerous to know.' But this is precisely not the case for the category of terms with which we contrasted proper names in Chapters 1 and 6: devices with varying referents like *I, You, He/She, This, That, Now,* and *Here.* This has immediate consequences for inference. Consider *She.* Since each use of the term might single out a different individual and thus refer to different females, if 'She is mad and bad' follows from 'She is mad' and 'She is bad,' that cannot simply be because the same type-term is involved. Uses of the same type-term are sufficient for valid inference

---

[1] See Campbell (1994: 73–826).

in the case of invariant devices like proper names. But for variant devices, something more is required.

Anaphora is one means of augmentation. For the inference 'She is mad; she is bad; hence she is mad and bad' *would* be good if it were specified that the various uses of *She* were anaphorically related to each other. Given this sentential means of gaining their reference, anaphoric uses of terms would be guaranteed to co-refer with their sources. For example, if *She* is used anaphorically, as in (3),

(3) She is mad. ↔She is bad. Hence ↔She is mad and bad

(where the horizontal arrow represents the intra-sentential nature of this form of referential dependence), each dependent use must refer to whatever its source-term refers to. So the inference is good. Anaphora is the guarantee ensuring not only that each use of ↔*She* co-refers, but that knowledge of the premiss takes one to knowledge of the conclusion. And since it is anaphoric relations which make the inference good, the inferential role of these uses of *She* may be characterized as anaphoric.

§ 52. If *Deictic Terms* like *I* do not gain their reference anaphorically, they cannot appeal to such a structure. Such terms have inferential roles, nevertheless. This is obvious if we focus simply on the operation of anaphoric chains like (3). The first *She* is a deictic use whose inferential role it is to provide the source for the subsequent anaphoric uses. Consider the cases discussed above, distinguishing *I*'s obligatory deictic reference from free uses of variant terms. From a sentence of the form 'If x elopes, x must leave Paris', we need only 'x elopes' to infer directly that 'x must leave Paris'. But the form of these sentences

(4) If I (You) elope, she must leave Paris
(5) If any woman (Heloise) elopes, I (You) must leave Paris
(6) If I (You) elope, I (You) must leave Paris

is such that an extra premiss is required to make that conclusion formally valid. The premisses 'If x elopes, y must leave Paris' and 'x elopes' will not get us to 'y must leave Paris' without an identity-judgement of the form 'x = y'. Far from taking one from knowledge of the premiss to knowledge of the conclusion, it is not even guaranteed that the singular terms co-refer. Consider (3) again. The sentence (without markings) is clearly structurally ambiguous. Suppose the subsequent uses of *She* refer deictically like the first (i.e. '↑She is mad. ↑She is bad. Hence ↑She is mad and bad'; where the vertical arrow represents the extra-sentential nature of this form of referential dependence). Since they gain their reference independently and are independently truth-evaluable, each use might refer to a different person. Hence the inference would not be good. The problem arises even in sentences that contain more than one use of the same *Deictic Term*, like that involving *I* or *You* (i.e. (6)). Being deictic uses, they gain their reference independently of each other and are independently truth-evaluable. So each use might refer to a different person.

So we have need of a mechanism that would serve to overcome this threat of fallacy; one that would take us from knowledge of the premiss to knowledge of the conclusion when variant terms like *I* are used in this deictic way. The guarantee of co-reference might be supplied in an extra premiss: specifically, an identity-judgement. Where (3) is interpreted deictically, for example, the addition that would make it a good inference might be:

(3*) She$_1$ is mad. She$_2$ is bad. She$_1$ is She$_2$. Hence She$_1$ is mad and bad.

(where She$_1$ and She$_2$ denote that the same type-term has been used non-anaphorically and the accompanying demonstration differs). Without an identity-judgement or some other similar means of knowing that the uses do co-refer, an inference based on more than one deictic use of a term would not be good. Another mechanism for achieving the same end may be the subject's ability to keep track of an item over the course of an inference. We shall explore these options with specific reference to *I* below.

WHAT IS REQUIRED FOR THE VALIDITY OF *I*-INFERENCES

§ 53.   Beyond the fact that the uses of terms in the premisses to an argument co-refer, there is a further question to be asked when deciding on the validity of inferences employing *Deictic Terms*: do those employing the argument *know* that the uses of the term in the premisses co-refer? This is obvious when we consider inferences like (3), when *She* is used deictically throughout. (The definition of validity at issue here, recall, is one that will secure knowledge-advancement—knowledge of a conclusion from knowing the truth of its premisses.) It is less clear that this further question arises when one uses *I* in inference. Consider the argument 'I am mad. I am bad. Hence, I am both mad and bad.' Is the inference valid given only that the terms co-refer; that the same person was in fact responsible for each use of *I*? We now have sufficient resources to address this question.

Note first that there are obvious similarities between the issue at present under discussion and the issue raised in Chapter 3. The former is about identifying oneself as the individual referred to by several different uses of *I*. The latter is about identifying oneself as the individual thought about and the individual referred to by an *I*-use. Given the similarities, it is tempting to confuse the two. But given the differences, this would be disastrous. For what is fundamental to the first issue is what relates utterances to each other, while what is fundamental to the second is what relates utterances to thoughts. And these are two very different kinds of relation.

Compare three different inference-forms: the one just mentioned, i.e.

(7)   I am *F.* I am *G.* Therefore I am *F* and *G.*

and two others that we have already looked at: the combination of *I* with a proper name in

(8) I am *F. M de G* is *G*. Therefore I am *F* and *G*.

and the combination of deictic and anaphoric uses of *She* in

(9) ↑She is *F.* ↔She is *G*. Therefore ↔she is *F* and *G*.

Compare (7) with (8). The inference in (8) is not good (so long as we define a good inference in terms of knowledge-advancement) even if the uses of *I* and *M de G* co-refer. It is enthymematic, resting on a suppressed identity-judgement: 'I am *M de G*.' The judgement is required because knowing the conclusion depends on knowing that the two terms *I* and *M de G* co-refer. And, without knowing 'I am *M de G*', it is not known that this is the case. (7) is not like (8) however. The only possible identity-judgement is merely a tautology: 'I am I.' So knowledge of the premises cannot fail to secure knowledge of the conclusion for lack of an identity-judgement.

Suppose it were assumed that there must be some explicitly co-referential relation in (7) to be exploited, one that allows its thinker to trade directly on co-reference. That would explain the unwillingness to regard the behaviour of *I* in inference as conforming to that of other *Deictic Terms*. But the assumption is false; it ignores the contrast between (9) and (7)–(8). (9) differs from (7) because the subject-terms in the former are anaphorically related while those in the latter are self-standing. Evaluating the truth of the phrase '↔She is G', as it occurs in this argument, requires interpretation of the phrase containing its source-term, i.e. '↑She is F.' By contrast, the phrase 'I am G' is independently truth-evaluable. It does not require interpretation of any other such phrase. This is because the reference of each subject-term in (7) is determined independently of any of the others. In (9), however, reference is determined inter-dependently. And this is crucial to explaining the virtue of the inference in (9), as the following contrast between (9) and (8) brings out.

(9) clearly differs from (8): it requires no identity-judgement to make it a good inference. Anyone who knows the truth of the premises will know the subject-terms are co-referential. What enables the thinker to trade directly on co-reference is anaphora. The inter-relation between the subject-terms presents an explicitly co-referential resource that the thinker exploits. For the uses of the subsequent anaphoric ↔*She* only obtain a reference dependently on the use of the initial deictic ↑*She*.

I is a *Deictic Term*. Each of its uses refers to the individual salient in the extra-sentential context. So having the right to conclude that each use of the term *I* refers to the same individual requires knowing who is salient for each use. If knowledge of the conclusion in (7) is not dependent on knowing an identity-proposition (unlike (8)), nor made possible by a direct trading on co-reference (unlike (9)), how is it achieved? Usually, one is right to take the different uses of *I* in (7) as co-referential, to judge that each use of the term refers to the same thing. How so? The most plausible route to an answer notes this fact: one is aware of and sensitive to one's own salience in ways that one is not sensitive to that of others. (How to characterize this awareness and what makes it possible is a different matter, and one that we shall investigate below, in Chapter 11.) It is because of this asymmetric awareness that an identity-judgement is not required in (7) but required in (8). And it is because there is nevertheless a *need* for sensitivity to one's own salience that (7) is unlike (9): there are no anaphoric relations to rely on. Thus the behaviour of *I* in knowledge-advancing inference confirms what we have found when investigating the formal aspects of its reference: that *I* is a *Deictic Term*. For someone who uses such a term in inference needs to know that their uses succeed in referring to the same item.

We have arrived at details which will occupy us more fully later on. For the moment, it is sufficient to review the following principles. The logical character of *I* is fundamentally a matter of its inferential role. The inferential role of any singular term is to be characterized by appeal to the different mechanisms each requires to guarantee co-reference in a knowledge-advancing way. *I* is a term whose every use refers deictically. Therefore it lacks the sentential reference structure which guarantees the co-reference of variant devices used anaphorically. It depends instead on identity-judgements and other means of guaranteeing co-reference in a knowledge-advancing way. The knowledge-advancing validity of inferences using *I* is like that of any *Deictic Term*: one must know that the uses co-refer.

HOW THE REFERENTIAL CHARACTER AND INFERENTIAL ROLE OF *I* ARE RELATED

§ 54.   *I* is a term with obligatory deictic reference and the inferential properties of a *Deictic Term*. How are these two features of *I* related, its referential character and inferential role?

Very closely, it seems, since either seems perfectly appropriate as an answer to the fundamental question 'on what does the significance of the term depend?' We might, at least on the face of it, say with equal justice: 'on the contribution that *I*-uses make, by referring, to the truth-conditions of the sentences containing them' or 'on the inferential inter-relations that the inclusion of *I*-uses enables sentences to maintain'. The former puts stress on the referential character of *I*; its ability to single out (represent; be directed on) particular individuals existing *outside* the sentential context in which the term itself occurs. The latter emphasizes the inferential role of *I*; the opportunities it confers on items *within* that sentential context (i.e. on those sentences which include it), to realize logical forms, particularly the conditional, and to support material-inferential properties. To represent the logical character of *I* accurately, we need to know whether these two aspects of the term are indeed equally fundamental or whether one explains the other. And we are now in a position to address the question.

In general terms, to suppose that one aspect is 'basic' with respect to some other is to suppose that the first is prior in the order of explanation or elucidation; that the first can be explained without appeal to the other; but that the other cannot be explained without appeal to the first. What would this mean more specifically for the aspects in question? If the referential character of *I* is basic, then understanding the significance it confers on sentences containing it must be independent of understanding any inferential use those sentences might have. Now much of the significance of such sentences lies in the fact that they can be used to make assertions of the form 'I am *F*.' So one implication would be this: by making referential character basic, we would have to make intelligible to ourselves the concept and practice of assertion using *I* without appeal to the concept and practice of inference. And it is difficult to see how this could be possible for reasons that have been sufficiently expressed in the literature and need no addition here.[2]

Briefly, then, two kinds of problem arise. The first is that assertion is a property of sentences, not sentence-parts. This line of criticism is particularly associated with the opening sections of Wittgenstein's *Philosophical Investigations*, and his attack on the notion that we could work up to an account of the meaning and function of whole sentences from treating word-meaning as basic and as the object for which the individual word stands. As we have seen, understanding the ability of *I* to combine with other words to form sentences depends on understanding its inferential role. But suppose we can make sense of genuinely meaningful sentences containing uses of *I* ('*I*-sentences') independently of inference. The second problem is that assertion is not characteristic of all sentences, only those participating in specific forms of linguistic behaviour with their own function and role. Assertions are sentences that enter into certain kinds of relation with other sentences. The fact that assertions negate other sentences, for example, distinguishes them from questions and commands. And these relations are inferential. Recognizing that some *I*-sentence counts as an assertion is to think of it as offering rational support to other sentences and as calling for such support (if only tacitly) from other sentences.

§ 55.   Confronted with these difficulties, we are prompted to see whether the explanatory order should be reversed. If the inferential role of *I* is treated as basic, it might be possible to comprehend the significance of sentences containing it without appeal to their referential character, and then understand referential relations in terms of inferential relations. This is a strong variant of inferentialism. For it takes the inferentialist insight: that assertions have content partly by virtue of their inferential context; and adds: we can conceive of inferential relations

---

[2] See Sellars (1953: 318; 327–34; 1954: 332–3); Brandom (1994: ch. 7).

without appeal to referential character at all.[3] Robert Brandom, who has offered the most finely developed and precise formulation of the strong variant, makes explanatory order its defining feature:

> The major explanatory challenge for [strong] inferentialists is to explain the representational dimension of semantic content—to construe *referential* relations in terms of *inferential* ones.[4]

There are various ways to challenge this strong variant. The weakest is simply to remain inferentialist and decline the addition: since seeing what is wrong with making referential character basic does not require reversing the explanatory order, we should treat inferential and referential relations as *equally* basic.[5] The conclusion is true, as I shall show in a moment. But this argument for it seems too weak, quietist even. Given a plausible parsimony, if we *can* make inferential relations intelligible to ourselves without appeal to referential relations (i.e. by appeal to anaphora alone), *shouldn't* we? At any rate, avoiding the charge of intellectual Luddism requires that we stay to see whether the trick can be pulled off. That it cannot be pulled off follows from what we now know about *Deictic Terms*. This is a different, and sufficiently robust way of responding to the strong variant.

Sentences are so articulated that they are capable of entering into entailment relations with other sentences. And uses of *I* make systematic contributions to this inferential articulation, as we have seen. So this is one implication of making inference prior: the indirectly inferential role of *I*-uses has to be made intelligible without appeal to the ways in which singular terms represent and single out individuals existing in an extra-sentential context. And that leaves only one kind of relation which holds between singular terms to which we could appeal: anaphora. Anaphoric relations support inferences, as we have seen. And they hold between sentential items only. So it is in terms of anaphora alone that we would have to make the referential character and inferential role of singular terms intelligible. Brandom acknowledges this constraint and tries to make a virtue of the necessity.[6] But it is impossible to carry out this task for reasons that we can now fully appreciate.

Consider referential character first. The substitution claim that we examined above failed precisely because an anaphoric explanation was not sufficient to explain all variant terms, let alone all singular terms. *I* itself is the standing counter-example here, together with any term whose deictic reference is obligatory (like singular *You*). It cannot be said of these expressions—as it might of those with 'free' reference (*He/She*, for example)—that their deictic use is explanatorily subordinate to their anaphoric; for they *have* no anaphoric use. It is true that

---

[3] See Frege (1879: 3); Carnap (1937: 4; 168); Sellars (1953: 318; 327–34; 1954: 332–3); Brandom (1994: 466; 1997: 154–5).

[4] Brandom (1997: 156).   [5] See McDowell (1997: 160).

[6] Brandom (1994: 462–3; 1997: 155; 181).

Deictic Terms are used on occasion as the source-terms for anaphoric chains. But this is not their only use (consider 'If I (You) elope, she must leave Paris'; 'If any woman (Heloise) elopes, I (You) must leave Paris'; 'If I (You) elope, I (You) must leave Paris'; i.e. (4)–(7) above). So this is false: 'to use an expression as a [*Deictic Term*] is to use it as a special kind of anaphoric initiator.'[7] Acting as source-term cannot be their only use since, as we have found, there are no anaphoric inter-relations between repeated uses of obligatory *Deictic Terms* like *I*.

Moreover, even if there were some enforced restriction so that *Deictic Terms* were only ever used to source anaphoric uses, it would not follow that the referential character of the former presupposed or was intelligible only in terms of that of the latter. This is partly because *Deictic Terms* like *I* refer independently of that on which the reference of anaphoric uses depend: the sentential context within which a particular expression is salient as the 'source'-term. And partly because there is no common referential character in terms of which anaphoric uses might elucidate a *Deictic Term* like *I*. For if anaphoric uses of terms possess a referential character at all, it is only in an etiolated and dependent sense. It is not they but their deictic source which fulfils the essential referential function of singling out items (in any context, sentential or non-sentential). Anaphoric uses inherit references once made and pass them on. In no sense do they refer to their source-term, and it is only in this weak sense that they may be said to refer to whatever that source refers to.

The inferential role of obligatory *Deictic Terms* like *I* is also inexplicable by appeal to anaphora. The *nature* of that role is non-anaphoric: the (indirect) inferential significance of deictic uses depends on their singling out individuals in the extra-sentential context. The *possibility* of that role is non-anaphoric: the validity of arguments involving deictic uses depends on alternative mechanisms to ensure co-reference, measures that we investigated above. It is true that, as their source, *Deictic Terms* are involved in the inferential role of anaphoric uses. But this is not the only occasion on which they have an inferential role (again, consider (4)–(7) and (3*) above). And even on those occasions where they are so involved (e.g. (3)), the underpinning given to anaphoric uses does not exhaust their inferential role. The initial, deictic, use of *She* makes an independent contribution to entailment relations in (3), for example. If the subsequent anaphoric relations failed for any reason, the sentence containing it might still be used to ground a different inference.

§ 56.   So anaphora is not basic to the referential character or inferential role of *Deictic Terms* like *I*. Indeed, if we should be parsimonious, there is good reason to reverse the explanatory order.

Consider referential character first. Deictic uses of variant terms might subsume anaphoric uses since all are cases in which reference is made to contextually salient individuals. In deictic uses, an individual is singled out as salient in the

---

[7]   Brandom (1994: 462–3).

extra-sentential context (e.g. being the one pointed at). Anaphoric uses form the limiting case where *sentential* salience is also involved. In such uses, reference depends on singling out an individual made salient in the extra-sentential context (e.g. being the one pointed at) by singling out that same individual as salient in the sentential context (i.e. being the one to whom the source-term refers).

The same explanatory subordination might operate with regard to inferential role, for the inferential significance of anaphora depends on the contribution made by deictic uses, but not vice versa. It is true that some term, a, might not be directly dependent on a source-term but on a term, b, which is itself anaphorically dependent on c, and so on. Indeed, it is conceivable that there be long inheritance chains of anaphorical dependence. But anaphoric relations are asymmetrical. If some term, a, is anaphorically dependent on another, b, then b cannot be anaphorically dependent on a. To inherit a reference, there must be a reference to inherit. If there *is* a reference for an anaphoric chain a–y to inherit, it must correspond to the use of a source-term at the end of the chain, z. Consider the deictic source and subsequent anaphoric uses of *She* in (3). Without the initial use underpinning the chain, the others would lack reference, would be evacuated in the delivery, could not contribute to the truth-conditions of the sentence in which they occur, and hence could play no inferential role. So for any anaphoric chain (of no matter what length), either there is a source-term which is not itself anaphorically dependent, or none of its terms refer. And if there is such a source-term for a chain, simply by virtue of being that source, it must play the dominant inferential role.

Another argument points in the same direction. Consider the inference 'If Heloise worked hard, she will benefit. Heloise worked hard. Hence, she will benefit.' The first premiss and the conclusion are clearly structurally ambiguous, depending on whether *She* refers anaphorically or deictically. This ambiguity directly affects the inferential roles of the first premiss and conclusion—i.e. the contribution they make to entailment relations. If *She* refers anaphorically, then co-reference between premisses and conclusion is guaranteed and the inference is (formally) valid. But if *She* refers deictically, then the inference is enthymematic— the guarantee of co-reference would have to be supplied in an extra premiss: specifically, an identity-judgement of the form 'She is Heloise.' Now suppose it were false to say that some non-anaphorically dependent uses of singular terms play an irreducible inferential role. And suppose it were true that deictic inferential roles are reducible to anaphoric ones. Then we could recognize no such distinction between anaphoric and deictic uses of terms and the separate contributions each kind of use makes to the inferential roles of the sentences containing them. But recognizing the ambiguity in the inference as presented calls for such a distinction. And it is an ambiguity we recognize. So it must be true that some non-anaphorically dependent uses of singular terms play an irreducible inferential role and false that deictic inferential roles are reducible to anaphoric ones. In short: if this were not so, we could not explain how the inference as presented is ambiguous. But we can; and hence it must be so.

To sum up: the inferential role of *Deictic Terms* like *I* is not explanatorily prior to their referential character. If it were, then the character and role of such terms would have to be explicable in terms of anaphora. And this is false for reasons that have to do with the issues investigated in this chapter: the obligatory deictic reference of *I*; the failure of the substitution claim; the mechanisms required to guarantee co-reference of *I* across different uses; and so on. Indeed, if there is any ordering here, the reverse has a chance of holding. This is because we depend on deictic uses not only to explain what anaphoric uses are, but to account for what they can do. This reversal would be strictly local, a matter between demonstration and anaphora alone. It would not imply, for example, that the referential character of *I* is prior to its inferential role. We have already seen what is wrong with that claim. Local reversal would simply mean that there are particularly strong reasons to reject any explanatory ordering in the other direction.

To help clarify matters, compare the position we have arrived at with the strong variant of inferentialism which prompted our discussion. As Robert Brandom summarizes that variant:

The substitutional structure of the inferences sentences are involved in is what the contentfulness of their subsentential components consists in. At the lowest level, unrepeatable tokenings (paradigmatically deictic uses of singular terms) can be understood as involved in substitution inferences, and so as indirectly inferentially contentful, in virtue of their links to other tokenings in a recurrence structure. The key concept at this level is anaphora. For taking an unrepeatable tokening to be contentful requires associating it with a repeatable structure of the sort that can be the subject of substitutional commitments. Anaphoric inheritance by one tokening of the substitution-inferential potential of another does just that. The articulation characteristic of specifically discursive commitments is to be understood most broadly in terms of inference, the details of which require attention to substitution, the details of which in turn require attention to anaphora.[8]

We can distinguish three claims here:

(a) A content is conceptual just in case it plays an inferential role—e.g. a sentence expressing a premiss or conclusion;

(b) A sentence plays an inferential role just in case its sub-sentential expressions do—e.g. the singular term(s) it contains.

(c) A singular term plays an inferential role just in case it plays an anaphoric role.

(a) and (b) state the kind of modest inferentialism I have espoused here. (b) has been particularly important, providing sufficient grounds to regard *I* as a genuine singular term. It is (c) which makes the whole position a strong variant of inferentialism. But (c) is false, and the failure of the substitution claim shows why. It may be true that unrepeatable tokenings have an inferential role partly in virtue of their links to other tokenings in a recurrence structure. It may be true that

---

[8] Brandom (1994: 472–3).

co-reference must be guaranteed if unrepeatable tokenings are to have an inferential role. But anaphoric relations provide only *one* such guarantee. Identity-judgements certainly provide another, and the subject's ability to keep track of an item over the course of an inference possibly provides a third. This is just as well since the recurrence structure for some terms *cannot* be anaphoric. These are terms like *I* and *You* whose reference is obligatorily deictic.

§ 57.   These investigations reveal much about the logical character of *I*. Its significance (i.e. the contribution its uses make to the truth-conditions of the sentences containing them) depends on the existence of referential relations between its uses and individuals existing in extra-sentential reality and salient in that context. Moreover, we can acknowledge this consistently with regarding the significance of any referring expression as (also) a matter of the inferential inter-relations which its uses confer on the sentences containing them.

For this is the deep message of the failure of anaphoric explanation: the systematic contribution made by *I* to inferential articulation is simply unintelligible without appeal to the ways in which its uses represent and single out individuals existing in an extra-sentential context. The manner in which sentences including *I* are so composed that they are capable of entering into entailment relations with other sentences has, by virtue of that inclusion, an essentially and irreducibly deictic aspect. It may be that the significance of *I*-sentences is in the first instance a matter of their inferential articulation. But we depend on referential relations to explain what such inferential articulation is and to account for what it does. It is only by being about or directed on the extra-sentential world that sentences including obligatory *Deictic Terms* like *I* fulfil their inferential function. In the same way, it is only by being related to *Deictic Terms* that sentences including expressions which appeal directly to their intra-sentential context (i.e. anaphors) fulfil *their* inferential function.

We can express the inter-dependence by saying that *I* has an irreducibly deictic inferential role. It is by virtue of singling out objects made salient in the extra-sentential world that its uses contribute systematically to what entails what.

To summarize what we now know to be the case about *Deictic Terms*, given logical form and the structures of inference. (Here, as usual, I am including in the group of *Deictic Terms* expressions with non-deictic uses. If this is a terminological slide, recall that it has no potentially confusing or otherwise deleterious effects on the main thesis. For *I*, like *You*, has no *non*-deictic uses.) The class comprises expressions like *I* and singular *You* whose every use is deictic, and expressions whose uses are only sometimes deictic, like *He/She*. Deictic uses of such terms refer to individuals salient in the extra-sentential context. The inferential role of such uses is irreducible. It is by virtue of singling out objects made salient in the extra-sentential context that they contribute systematically to what entails what.

8

Referential Function (I)

§ 58.   Investigations into logical form and the structures of inference lead to the most intricate issue of the enquiry: how *I* refers. For we have rejected the standard answer to this question: that the 'simple rule' in context is sufficient to determine the reference of any *I*-use (i.e. *Rule Theory*). So we need to find the correct alternative determinant for *I*.

Coming to grips with this problem requires an enriched conception of what it is to be a *Deictic Term*. For although a formal and abstract notion of such terms has been sufficient up to this point, it is not sufficient to elucidate all aspects of the meaning of *I*. It is one thing to say what is deictic about the term's logical character and inferential role; quite another to specify the deictic aspects of its referential function. And once we have an answer to that question, we will still be some way from explaining how the reference of an *I*-use is determined. For we will only have established what *I* has in common with other *Deictic Terms*. And we need to know what is distinctive about *I* if we are to explain its referential function completely. But as we shall find, this is a relatively straightforward matter once we recognize *I* as having the referential function of a *Deictic Term*. So let us concentrate for the moment on what it is for *any* expression to have such a function, and whether *I* satisfies the requirements.

One might think the answers to these questions are obvious, given what we now know. Logical character and inferential role have shown that uses of *I* refer to the individual salient in the extra-sentential context. Does this not entail that salience is the fundamental factor here; that it is *by being salient* that an individual is determinately singled out as the referent of any *Deictic Term*? This does not follow. For there may be a shortfall between logical character and the way a term fulfils its referential function. An analogy pinpoints the problem. Masters of the Paris Schools might wear some distinctive gown. If a particular man, Abelard, is wearing one, that is a reliable indication that he is a Parisian master. Even so, it is not *by wearing such a gown* that Abelard is a Parisian master. Possibly the same should be said of *I*. Its uses refer to individuals with whole sets of properties. One of those properties is salience, and that is relevant to the logical character and inferential role of the term. But it may nevertheless be by possessing some other property that a particular individual is singled out as the referent of some particular *I*-use.

§ 59.   Indeed, there is a presumption *against* taking salience as fundamental to the determinant of *I*, given our investigations so far. For we rejected the claim that *I*-uses have a 'simple rule' as their determinant. But the classificatory position to which the claim partly appeals has been left unchallenged. This position implies that indexicals whose reference is not determined by a rule-in-context alone depend instead on a demonstration. So perhaps it is by being associated with an ostensive gesture of this sort, rather than by being salient, that an individual is determinately singled out as the referent of an *I*-use. Or perhaps the individual is singled out by being demonstrated *and* by being salient—the former is a means of achieving the latter. Or perhaps the demonstration merely makes manifest the real determinant of the term, which is something else altogether; something connected with the speaker's intentions, for example. These positions are not straw men. In the earlier part of his career, Kaplan claimed that all deictic uses are determined by demonstration. Later, he claimed that demonstrations have a communicative role but no referential function. But he has always regarded demonstration as criterial of *Deictic Terms*. His founding principle, which he claims to find throughout the literature on this subject, is that 'The referent of a demonstrative depends on the associated demonstration'. His views have simply changed on the question of *why* demonstration should be regarded as the mark of the deictic: from 'because they determine reference' to 'because they make manifest what determines reference'.[1]

If we are to narrow these options down to the correct view, we must investigate the general question to which the classificatory position gave an answer: what is it for an expression to have a deictic referential function? Only then can we say whether what logical character and inferential role indicate is in fact true; namely, that the referential function of *I* is deictic. And in order to avoid circularity or prejudice, we should answer the general question without appeal to cases involving *I*. Equipped with an answer as to what is distinctive of deictic reference in general, we will be able to see whether *I* belongs to the class of *Deictic Terms* in this respect also. And equipped with an answer as to what is distinctive of *I*'s deictic reference in particular, we will be able to see what sufficiently determines the reference of the term's uses.

There are beneficial side-effects to this enforced order of investigation: finding out about the referential function of *Deictic Terms* and then examining *I*. For the class of *Deictic Terms* includes expressions which differ from each other in deep ways, as we have already seen. And unless we constantly compare uses of *I* with other terms, it will not be possible to say which discovered features are unique and which are characteristic of the whole class. It is not just that, unless we adopt these procedures, there is great risk of creating a specious uniformity where there is evidence only of comparability. Without adopting them, there will simply be no telling whether or not what we have achieved is a fiction of this sort. For example, we might concentrate on one *Deictic Term*, like *I*, and extract from it a unified

---

[1] Kaplan (1989: 492). For the later view, see (1989: 582–4).

theory of the whole class. Or we might treat spoken uses as basic and then extrapolate from that evidence alone to conclusions about other kinds of use. Then it would be easy to mishandle peculiar features of the parts.

Spoken uses of *I* fail to come into focus unless seen as one among many possible ways of referring to the same kinds of individual and even on occasion to the same individual. If we are to give due weight to the fact that there *are* many such ways, and that these ways *differ*, then we need to compare uses of *I* with uses of other referring expressions, and specifically other *Deictic Terms*.

WHAT REFERENTIAL FUNCTION REQUIRES

§ 60.   Like other *Deictic Terms*, *I* is a singular referring expression. Its meaning indicates which one particular thing is relevant to the truth-value of the sentence containing it. So we can elucidate that meaning by asking about how it indicates that thing. This is to ask after the referential function of the term, a subject that requires a little scene-setting.

The use of a singular term refers only if it singles out exactly one individual, no less and no more. So to say that a use of any such term refers is to imply determinacy. Nothing would count as 'reference' that was either indeterminate or non-determinate. We can capture something of this by saying that a (spoken) use of such terms refers if there is a positive answer to the question '*which* individual (or *who*) is being spoken of?' Indeed, it is precisely the referential function of a singular term to provide a positive answer to this 'which?' question.

The answer must be positive. For suppose Abelard says, 'She is betrothed to me,' and (for whatever reason) either no woman corresponds to the use of *She* or many do. Then his use does not single out exactly one individual, it fails to refer and does not discharge its referential function. We might nevertheless say that there is *an* answer to the 'which?' question in this case—'No one'. But if a singular term fulfils its referential function, there must be an answer of the sort 'Heloise'; or 'Her'; or a gesture that points out some individual. Answers of this sort are positive because they implicitly respond to a background question in the affirmative—*is* anything referred to?—while other answers to the 'which?' question respond in the negative.

§ 61.   As I shall use the phrase, there is no *more* to referential function than providing a positive answer to the 'which?' question. This is to help distinguish the subject at issue so that we can focus on it and exclude for the moment closely related matters.

It would be false, quite generally, to say that if a question has an answer, someone must know what it is. The question 'How many lectures did Abelard give?' has an answer, for example. To say this does not imply that anyone has ever known it or ever will know it. Indeed, some questions may have an answer even though it is not even *possible* to know what it is. This general point holds for the present case also. If Heloise says, 'He is betrothed to me,' pointing at Abelard when her audience are blind, for example, there is a positive answer to the 'which?' question but none of her hearers know what it is. The use of a singular term may provide a positive answer to the 'which?' question without anyone actually knowing what it is, or being in a position to know, or even ever being able to find out.

So we should distinguish between determinacy (what is required for reference) and what is required for *understanding* reference; what we can call 'discriminability'. 'Discriminate' and 'discriminable' are sometimes used ambiguously. Some talk of speakers discriminating an item by demonstrating it, for example. Others talk of demonstrations as discriminating items. Some, confusingly, talk in terms of both.[2] As I shall use the term, a reference is discriminable if it is possible for someone to single out an individual as its referent. So discriminability of reference is about conditions on the possibility of understanding reference. Determinacy of reference, on the other hand, is about conditions on the success of making reference. Both are achievement-terms; we use them when the relevant criteria for success have been met. So Abelard's utterance failed to meet the former set of conditions and Heloise's utterance failed to meet the latter, at least for her audience. Hence Abelard's attempt to refer failed while Heloise's attempt succeeded. It was her attempt to have the reference understood which failed. It is tempting to identify discriminability with the conditions on communicating reference successfully. But this is a mistake. Heloise's reference is discriminable and would have been even if it was quite incommunicable. It is enough that *someone*—even if only the reference-maker—could single out an individual as the referent.

Close connections exist between determinacy and discriminability. For something to be understood, there must be something to understand. An attempt at reference is not discriminable unless it is successful. But cases like Heloise's utterance suggest the converse is not true: it is possible to fail in the attempt to produce discriminable reference even though one has succeeded in referring. Some regard determinacy of reference as dependent at a deeper level on discriminability. Others think this makes semantic issues unacceptably dependent on epistemology.[3] Those who hold any of the positions (a)–(e) will tend to the former view:

(*a*) The key to elucidating the semantics of a referring term is to ask for the conditions for an *audience's understanding* its uses on occasions of use.

(*b*) Referring terms are ultimately characterized by their *communicative function* between speaker and audience.

---

[2] Reimer (1991: 179).   [3] See Kaplan (1989: *passim*).

(c) The meaning of words is dependent on their *social function*, and from a social perspective the survival value of singular terms is as devices which enable an audience to pick out items uniquely.

(d) It is only in the context of our *interpretative practices* that any semantic notion acquires a sense; it is from those practices that the meaning of words derives.

(e) It is people/agents who refer; referring terms are just used by them to do so.[4]

These are deeply controversial questions; but they need not detain us here. For we can treat the relevant issues while remaining neutral about the relationship of semantics and epistemology. Discriminability will be investigated in its turn. But our business now is with determinacy; that is why the phrase 'referential function' is restricted. Here understood, this function is discharged if there is a positive answer to the 'which?' question.

WHAT DEMONSTRATION IS

§ 62.   Singular terms discharge their referential function in different ways. Indeed, this is one way to distinguish *Deictic Terms* from proper names, definite descriptions, and other kinds of indexical. Ensuring that there is only one individual who could possibly be the referent for any use of a term is one route to determinacy. This is how proper names (*Abelard*) and definite descriptions (*The author of the* Sic et Non) can fulfil their referential function. Such terms provide a positive answer to the 'which?' question prior to any use.

Deictic Terms have no such assistance. Prior to their use, anyone is a potential referent for *I* or *You*; any male/female for *He/She*. And it is possible that every use of such terms has a different referent. We can imagine a world in which *She* is only uttered five thousand times, but on each occasion singles out a different female. *Deictic Terms* provide no answer to the 'which?' question prior to any use. There may *be* such an answer, of course—imagine a world containing only one female where *She* will always refer to her, if at all. But the prior answer will have been provided contingently, not by *She. Deictic Terms* are quite unlike other singular terms in this respect. *Abelard* will go on referring to the same man no matter how the world teems with men. We might explain this by saying that the determinant of *Abelard* exists prior to any use as a property of the term itself.

§ 63.   So it must be in their use that *Deictic Terms* discharge their referential function. And this is one reason why demonstration has standardly seemed a good candidate for what determines their reference.

---

[4] For (a), see Wittgenstein (1958: §§ 1–89; pp. 143–243); Searle (1969: 79); Evans (1982: 143–5). For (b), see Strawson (1950: 11–18). For (c), see Quine (1960: 5–8; 56). For (d), see Davidson (1984: *passim*). For (e), see Strawson (1950: 11–18).

On the one hand, it explains how the use of a *Deictic Term* might positively answer the 'which?' question—by singling out exactly one individual as the one demonstrated. And on the other, it explains why *Deictic Terms* are distinguished from proper names and definite descriptions—by fulfilling this referential function in a different way. For if what determines reference is a particular ostensive gesture associated with a particular use, it does not exist prior to that use, as a property of the term itself. Moreover, the use requires the demonstration to answer the 'which?' question positively. Other kinds of term depend on gestures (if at all) for other kinds of reason. So one might gesture at an individual when saying *Abelard*, for example. But this would be for emphasis or as an aid to communication. This will usually be because the audience do not know who Abelard is. Very exceptionally, it might be because there are several people called Abelard present and the audience do not know which one is being referred to. Even here, however, the demonstration should not be regarded as the determinant. It provides an answer to the question 'which proper name is being used', not 'which individual does this use refer to'. Of course, the audience only know the answer to the second question if they know the answer to the first. But that is a different matter; one that concerns discriminability and, as a further sub-set, communicability. No demonstration is necessary to achieve determinacy of reference for *Abelard*.

The notion that demonstration might determine the reference of *Deictic Terms* is therefore worth considering carefully. It will be helpful to have an example. So suppose that, calmly and deliberately, with a movement of his arm and index finger, before an audience, Bernard points at Abelard while uttering the words 'He is a heretic.' He performs a paradigm demonstration: an ostensive gesture.[5]

Gestures of this sort are perceptible bodily actions that are regarded as (more or less) part of a person's willing expression. They involve movement of the hands, fingers, head, face. Other cases need not involve gestural action by the person referring. While lecturing, Abelard might say, 'This is Rome,' while an assistant points to the spot on a map.[6] Some count stress as another form of demonstration. In speech, for example, exaggerating levels of pitch, accent, timbre, tone, loudness, and rhythmic variation. But the usual examples taken to show this are not persuasive, so I shall ignore this possibility. It is true that deictic uses of the sentence 'He shot an arrow and then he died' are distinguished from anaphoric uses by whether or not the second *He* is stressed.[7] But here stress is not a demonstration, for it in no way fulfils (or even helps fulfil) the referential function. It is there to tell us *what kind of use* is at issue, not *which thing* the use refers to.

Demonstrations obey a system of form constraints. There are differences between ways of pointing that are well formed and ways that are not well formed, for example. They reveal a flexibility that is only partly linguistic in character. On

---

[5] See McNeill (2000: 1–10).   [6] See Kaplan (1989: n. 9).   [7] See Lyons (1977: 658).

the one hand, it is easy to reverse a pointing gesture. On the other, there is no way reliably to negate one, and demonstrations are not syntactically combinable with other gestures. Moreover, demonstrations are (only) partly conventionalized. There are socially constituted group standards telling the speaker something about the form an act of pointing must take in various contexts to count as such. It is because our interpretative practices are partly governed by convention, for example, that we can recognize the 'index finger straight, other fingers bent' hand-shape as a (the?) paradigmatic pointing-act. But, unlike the iconic thumbs-up sign, convention does not regulate which hand-part we use or exactly how. Indeed, we need not use our hands to point at all, since we can point with our feet and with non-bodily objects like sticks.

Not all ostensive gestures are demonstrations. There is support here for the notion that demonstration determines the reference of *Deictic Terms*. For we naturally distinguish gestures like Bernard's pointing from other ostensive signs, and we do so precisely by appeal to their referential function. To see this, consider three other types of ostensive gesture.

Gesticulation: Abelard might hold his hand above his head saying, 'The man who attacked me was *this* tall.'

Dumb show: if asked, 'how are you feeling?', Heloise might simply draw down her mouth to 'say' she is sad.

Iconic form: a more buoyant Heloise might respond to 'how are you feeling?' by giving the thumbs-up sign.

These gestures answer the question 'what are you saying about the thing referred to?' So they fulfil an ascriptive function where the role of demonstration is referential. If Abelard says, 'The man who attacked me was *this* tall,' and does not gesticulate, for example, it is not that his words will have failed to pick out an item. They will have failed to describe the item in the way they specified they would. If Heloise offers no dumb show or iconic form when asked how she is, she will not have failed to single herself out. She will have failed to describe herself. Contrast these cases with Bernard's pointing while saying, 'He is a heretic.' The situation may have been such that the pointing was necessary: many candidate males may have been present, none of whom were made conspicuous by the utterance alone. So if Bernard had not pointed, his words would not have provided a positive answer to the 'which?' question. They would have failed to refer. Hence what distinguishes demonstrations from other types of ostensive gesture is not simply that they form part of the use of *Deictic Terms* (even if that use is unspoken). Demonstrations help secure determinacy of reference where other kinds of gesture describe the individual referred to.

There are occasions in which someone asks 'Who is Abelard?' and he 'answers' by putting his hand up. It is an open question whether the questioner's mode in asking the question provides sufficient speech-context to regard speech as nevertheless present in the required sense when the *I*-user is silent. What is of interest, however that issue is decided, is that the gesture operates as a way of making an unspoken use of *I*. For there is evidence here of a claim that will become central below: that what is essential to the use of *I* in the spoken utterance '*I*' is what provides its referent with sufficient salience. In this case, it is a gesture, a demonstration, that counts. Perhaps this is always the case in spoken contexts where the *I*-user is silent. It is difficult to see how a determinate use of *I* could be effected in such a context without speech or gesture.

Demonstration does not figure in the standard ways linguists and psychologists distinguish ostensive gestures. Part of the purpose of this present discussion has been to plot the place of demonstration by reference to categories that *are* usually recognized. Presenting the results in schematic form may help summarize the points made. So consider a modified version of the model defined by Adam Kendon and presented by others under the label 'Kendon's continuum'.[8] The model plots ostensive gestures on the continuum by their answers to three basic questions: must speech be present? are the properties of the gesture linguistic? and is the gesture conventionalized? In the case of gestures studied by linguists— gesticulations, dumb shows, iconic forms, autonomous gesture-based languages—the answers are as in Table 2.

As we have found, demonstration answers these questions as in Table 3.

So demonstration is quite distinct from other forms of ostensive gesture. A separate place needs to be found for it in linguistic studies.

WHY DEMONSTRATION IS NOT THE DETERMINANT

§ 64.   To say that demonstrations have the role of determining the reference of *Deictic Terms* is to make a claim about all demonstrations, not about all *Deictic*

Table 2

Gesture type	Speech present?	Linguistic properties?	Conventionalized?
Gesticulations	Yes (obligatory)	None	No
Dumb shows	No (obligatory)	None	No
Iconic forms	Optional	Some	Fully
Autonomous gesture-based languages	No (obligatory)	Fully linguistic	Fully

Table 3

Gesture type	Speech present?	Linguistic properties?	Conventionalized?
Demonstrations	Usually—often obligatory	Some	Partly

[8] See McNeill (2000: 2–6).

Terms. It tells us that if some gesture does not have such a role, it is not a demonstration. It does not tell us that if some use of a *Deictic Term* is not accompanied by a demonstration, its reference is not determined. This is just as well since many uses of *Deictic Terms* provide positive answer to the 'which?' question when no individual is demonstrated.

This fact is most obvious in non-spoken modes of use; in soliloquy and writing for example. Such modes occasionally have a place for ostensive gestures and their parallels. Abelard might write, 'My lecture will be in this room,' on a note with an arrow attached to it. But most deictic uses in the written mode require no such 'gesture'. In the case of soliloquy and silent thought, it is important not to mistake perceptual uptake (that in virtue of which one can single out the item in question from all others) for demonstration. It is often necessary that there be some kind of perceptual uptake if a particular object is to be salient to a thinker. When I *think*, 'That tree has borne no fruit this year,' on an occasion where *saying* this would require demonstrating a particular tree in the environment, for example, it is perhaps essential that I be in receipt of perceptual information about a particular object sufficient for me to identify it and single it out from others as precisely *That Tree*. But there is obviously nothing that counts as *demonstration* here.

Demonstration has its home in speech. Yet it is clear that here also uses of *Deictic Terms* provide positive answer to the 'which?' question when no individual is demonstrated. Suppose we lived in a one-tree world. Then no demonstration would be necessary when saying, 'That tree is dying, but those branches look healthy enough.' Yet *That Tree* is a *Deictic Term*. The question 'which?' has a positive answer given only the uniqueness of the individual referred to. This uniqueness is relative to the utterance: it is some particular tree being spoken of and there is but one tree in existence.

The case is unusual, of course; but utterance-relative uniqueness is not. In the exceptional case, it is the world which limits the number of possible candidates. In the usual case, that task is undertaken by the deictic utterance itself. Suppose Abelard says, 'She is beautiful,' and no gestures accompany the utterance. In most cases, an utterance of this sort implicitly specifies the domain of individuals potentially spoken about. That domain is not the whole world of existing things but some restricted set. In this instance, for example, the set might consist of human beings within common perceptual range of speaker and hearer. If Heloise were the only female member of this set, then the 'which?' question is provided with a positive answer. It is some particular female being spoken of and there is but one such in the domain specified. Abelard did not gesture because he did not need to. Implicit set-specifications for deictic utterances are usually perception-based, being variations on 'individuals within the current field of vision (hearing; touching; tasting; smelling) of the reference-maker, or reference-maker and audience'.

Utterance-relative uniqueness can be achieved in various ways. Sometimes it is not the implicit domain-restriction which clinches the matter. Suppose there are two birds on the scene, Sparrow and Robin. Abelard points at Sparrow saying, 'This bird is hungry,' going on immediately to say, 'That bird is colourful,' but without pointing at anything. Given the domain, there are two candidates for referent. But when the same speaker utters *That F* immediately after uttering *This F*, the individuals referred to must differ. This is a rule which competent speakers know. Hence Robin is determined referent by being the unique candidate.

§ 65.   Utterance-relative uniqueness is not the only means by which *Deictic Terms* discharge their referential function without demonstration. Two others are worth noting. Both come into operation in circumstances where implicit specification of the domain leaves more than one candidate as referent for a *Deictic Term*. So suppose Heloise says, 'You should be wary of my relatives,' before a number of people and without gesturing. It is some particular addressee being spoken of since this is a singular use of *You*. But there is more than one addressee in the domain of individuals spoken about. In this instance, nevertheless, there is an answer to the 'which?' question. For suppose Heloise's utterance is an answer to Abelard's query 'How do your relatives feel about me?' Given the utterance alone, he is one among several candidate referents for Heloise's *You*. Given this surrounding discourse, however, he is the *leading* candidate and hence reference is determined on him. Discourse has various ways of making individuals count as the leading candidate. Suppose there are a large number of birds on the scene. Abelard points at Sparrow saying, 'This bird is hungry,' going on immediately to say, 'This bird is colourful,' but without pointing at anything. Given the utterance and domain-specification alone, there are several candidates for the use of *This Bird*. But when the same speaker utters *This F without* gesturing immediately after uttering *This F with* a gesture, the individuals referred to must be the same. Again, this is a rule which competent speakers know. Hence Sparrow is determined referent by being the leading candidate.

These points refer back to Chapters 6 and 7, where we noted that there is some reason to think of anaphoric reference as a particular form of deictic reference. The phenomenon of leading candidacy given surrounding discourse enables us to round out that suggestion. Consider how we may now explain what makes some object, *O*, the one denoted by the anaphoric use of *It* in the sentence 'This is dying; it needs watering.' It is the object referred to by the antecedent use of *This*. So it is the leading candidate given surrounding discourse; and hence it is the object denoted by the anaphoric use of *It*.

Surrounding discourse is one means of making a leading candidate out of several individuals. The surrounding perceptual environment is another. About to lecture in a room crowded with students, Abelard might say, 'You; please shut the door,' without gesturing. Implicit specification of the domain leaves any number of candidates for the reference. But there is a leading candidate: Clovis, who is the most prominent addressee. In this instance, he is the most prominent because he is the only one on his feet. But being the most prominent individual is thoroughly context-sensitive. He might have been the only one sitting; or the only one speaking; or the furthest away from the speaker; or the closest to him. In other contexts, the most prominent individual may be the largest or the smallest of the set; the best or worst illuminated; the most still or the most frantic. The permutations are endless but the point is clear. Given features of the perceptual field in which a deictic utterance is produced, there may be a positive answer to the 'which?' question without need of demonstration.

§ 66.   So we have found nothing that is common about the referential function of *Deictic Terms*. We have discovered a variety of ways in which uses provide a positive answer to the 'which?' question: by (*a*) *Demonstration*; (*b*) *Utterance-relative uniqueness*, in relation either to the world, or to the utterance (implicitly or explicitly); (*c*) *Leading candidacy*, in relation either to the surrounding discourse, or to the perceptual environment.

Nothing yet about referential function distinguishes *Deictic Terms* as a group. Some forms of leading candidacy might be effected by quasi-gestural means—Abelard might vocally mimic the individual referred to when saying 'He is a poor student', for example. But there need be nothing gestural about utterance-relative uniqueness. If we stretched *Demonstration* so that something counting as such could be associated with every spoken, communicative, soliloquizing, written use of a *Deictic Term*, we would merely have a contradictory concept with inconsistent application and a grotesque distortion of what is ordinarily meant: ostensive gesture.

And this is exactly what we find in current literature, which is devoted to making demonstration the mark of *Deictic Terms*. Kaplan even enshrines this claim in the first of his two founding principles.[9] There are three major points of contradiction and distortion produced by the attempt to make demonstration criterial in this way.

Sometimes we would need the demonstration to be simply the gesture itself (e.g. Bernard saying as he points, 'He is a heretic'). Sometimes we would need it to be a contextual feature indicated by a gesture (e.g. Abelard saying, 'This is Rome,' while looking at his assistant who is pointing to the spot on a map). Most of the time, however, the demonstration could be no gesture at all.

Second, instances of demonstration would have to form both part of the context and part of the syntax of the verbal expression they accompany. Kaplan usually restricts demonstration to context, but slides towards incorporating it into syntax when he says that demonstration is 'a (visual) presentation of a local object discriminated by a pointing' and when he accepts that 'demonstrations may . . . require no special action on the speaker's part'. Frege tentatively put forward the incorporative view: 'mere wording, which can be grasped by writing or the gramophone, does not suffice for the expression of a thought . . . The pointing of fingers, head movements, glances may belong here too.' Kaplan follows him in this, describing uses of demonstratives without their demonstrations as 'incomplete'.[10]

---

[9] Kaplan (1989: 492).   [10] Kaplan (1989: 490; n. 9); Frege (1918: 24).

Third, on occasions where there are no other means of making a particular item salient, the demonstration would need to be regarded as part of the expression of the *Deictic Term*. On other occasions, where demonstration is offered merely as emphasis, for example, it would need to be regarded as part of the context instead. On the first kind of occasion, we would need to think of determining the reference of terms as the defining role of demonstration. On the second, we would need to think of demonstration as having a merely pragmatic significance, something that helped communication along. So demonstration would have to denote both the ostensive gesture and a contextual feature indicated by that gesture. Its role would be to both determine the reference of terms and merely make their reference manifest. So what counted as a sufficient demonstration would shift. That a gesture simply *does* accompany the use of a *Deictic Term* would be sufficient demonstration to determine reference. But to make the reference manifest, the gesture would have to make the referent discriminable as such, both to the person referring and to any audience.

These instances of deep contradiction force us to reject the idea that demonstration is the mark of the deictic. The benefits of renouncing any such criterial ambition for *Demonstration* are immediate. We are free to appreciate demonstrations for what they are: ostensive gestures. We need not skew our account of *Deictic Terms* by making all modes of use conform to those which suit ostensive gestures best: speech with the task of communicating reference. We will not expect all deictic uses of terms to be accompanied by such gestures. So we are in a good position to settle the matter of what makes demonstrations significant.

9

Referential Function (II)

§ 67.   Our task is to discover what distinguishes the referential function of *Deictic Terms* from other kinds of expression. And our investigations in the previous chapter have given us a clue. What we seek is the genus of which demonstrating an individual, or making it unique, or making it the leading candidate are species. What is common to seeing, hearing, tasting, smelling, and touching, for example, is what relates them as species: the genus Perceiving. One can perceive by hearing or seeing. And if one sees or hears, one must perceive. So we need to know of what φ the following is true: that one can φ by demonstrating an individual or making it unique or the leading candidate, and that if one demonstrates an individual or makes it unique, or the leading candidate, one must φ. This will tell us what is common to these modes of reference, and hence what is distinguishing about how *Deictic Terms* fulfil their referential function.

Demonstrating an individual or making it unique or the leading candidate are things one does. So is referring with uses of a *Deictic Term*. So we should explore the possibility of commonality here: that a *Deictic Term* is one whose uses refer by doing something in particular—*by φing*—in the extra-sentential context. If this were the case, of course, explaining what one means by uses of a *Deictic Term* would be linked inextricably to explaining what one does. But given the close relationship between meaning and doing, this general description holds for words that are not even singular terms. And since our task is to elucidate what is characteristic of *Deictic Terms*, we should ask what is distinctive about the role of action here.

WHAT IS DISTINCTIVE ABOUT *DEICTIC TERMS*

§ 68.   Suppose Bernard threatens Abelard in saying, 'He is a heretic.' In this illocutionary act, Bernard *does* something in *saying* something. Hence accounting for what he did, what he achieved, will involve accounting for what his words meant, what they were taken to mean. There is nothing distinctive here. Cases of the converse sort are called rhetic acts; those in which individuals *say* things in *doing* things. So Abelard might respond—saying, for example, that he has been falsely charged—in uttering noises of certain types in a certain language, corresponding to some particular vocabulary and grammar. This is a specific kind of rhetic act: it is concerned with the fact that uttering certain noises can be meaningful. So call it a meaning act, for short. Again, there is nothing distinctive here.

But consider another sort of rhetic act, one that occurs in Bernard's gestural utterance 'He is a heretic,' for example. It is not simply that he says something of an individual, Abelard (that he is a heretic), in doing something (uttering these words; gesturing), where what he says is truth-evaluable depending on how it is with the individual referred to. For that is true of any sentence using a singular term. It would have been true had Bernard used a proper name, for example, saying, 'Abelard is a heretic.' But action plays no referential role for the name *Abelard*. And this is the crucial point. It is not in virtue of actions like uttering the term or demonstrating any individual that the name refers to Abelard. For *Deictic Terms*, however, these actions have precisely this function: as we have seen, they provide a positive answer to the 'which?' question. On occasion, the only action necessary to discharge the referential function is the uttering of the term; namely, when the domain is specified and there is a unique or leading candidate. On other occasions, it is in virtue of utterance plus demonstration that a *Deictic Term* refers to an individual.

§ 69.   So what is distinctive about *Deictic Terms* is that they fulfil their referential function by action. And we can distinguish more finely still by asking what is common to the actions involved; something that connects cases in which uttering is sufficient and cases in which demonstrations of different sorts are called for. Here we may be prompted by the logical character of *Deictic Terms* to consider salience. Not salience *simpliciter*, but salience relative to the use of referring terms: referential salience. (Since it is usually referential salience that I mean in what follows, I shall simply speak of salience where it is clear that salience *simpliciter* is not meant.) For if one is demonstrating an individual or making it unique or the leading candidate, one must be making it salient. And one makes it salient precisely by demonstrating it, or making it unique, or the leading candidate.

Hence salience solves the puzzle of the genus, φ, to which demonstrations etc. belong as species. If this were not so, salience would be a polymorphous concept rather than generic. A generic concept implies its species while a polymorphous concept does not. Perception, for example, is a generic concept. One can perceive by seeing or hearing, and if one does either one must perceive. Having fun, on the other hand, is a polymorphous concept: one can have fun by running or jumping, but one can do either without having fun. Other examples of polymorphous concepts include working and thinking.[1] If salience were polymorphous, then there would be various different features the possession of one or other of which by an individual could in certain circumstances count as salient and yet none of

[1]   See Ryle (1951: 67–9); White (1964: 5–10).

which in other circumstances would necessarily count as salient. Now this certainly seems to hold true of salience *simpliciter*. Abelard may count as salient in this sense in certain circumstances by being unique (the only man in the room) or prominent (the tallest). In other circumstances, these same properties do not make him count as such. Perhaps Heloise is present and equally unique (she is the only woman in the room) and prominent (the shortest). So it is clear that, as with other polymorphous concepts, what makes salience *simpliciter* a true or false description of an individual is not anything in that item itself but in the circumstances. It is polymorphous rather than generic because it is free with respect to the circumstances of its application.

And this is the clue as to why the concept of salience we are appealing to is the genus to which demonstrations etc. belong as species. For we are not appealing to salience *simpliciter* but to *referential* salience. And referential salience is precisely not free with respect to the circumstances of its application. It is salience relative to certain highly specific circumstances in which a particular action is performed: the uttering of a referring term. Since its application to specific circumstances is bound by its meaning, the concept of referential salience is generic. For one can be made referentially salient (i.e. the salient individual relative to the use of a referring term) by being unique, or the leading candidate, or the demonstrated item. And if any of these properties truly describe one, then one must be made referentially salient.

So each use of a *Deictic Term* counts as rhetic twice over: as a meaning act and as a deictic act. For, like any such piece of speech, the use is rhetic in the sense that something meaningful is said (e.g. 'He is a heretic') in something that is done (uttering noises in a certain language). But unlike most pieces of speech, each use of a *Deictic Term* in speech is also a deictic act; it is a making-salient of an individual. What makes the act deictic is not something that *accompanies* the use of the term, as Bernard's pointing accompanied his use of *He*, for example. Rather, it *is* the use of the term. Sometimes this making-salient is simply a matter of uttering the term; namely, when this deictic act gains determinacy of reference for the use given domain-specification and the existence of a unique or leading candidate. On other occasions, this making-salient is a matter of uttering the term and demonstrating an individual. But on both kinds of occasion, the deictic act involved in the use of a *Deictic Term* is the same: the act which discharges the referential function; namely, the making-salient of an individual in relation to the use.

WHAT REFERENTIAL SALIENCE IS

§ 70.   What is distinctive about *Deictic Terms* is that they fulfil their referential function by action of a particular sort: making an individual salient. In short: salience is the determinant of *Deictic Terms*.

It may seem surprising that salience could be offered so central a role when we have not yet explicitly elucidated the concept. But this is a mistake. Sufficient elucidation has already taken place in the investigation of demonstration, utterance-relative uniqueness, and leading candidature. For referential salience is the genus of these species; they are the disjuncts of which it is composed. So to have elucidated demonstration etc. is to have elucidated referential salience. And we can gather together what we have learnt, drawing some conclusions about the overarching concept.

Salience is at home in describing items which stand (originally, jump or leap) out in some way. So it is a broad-spectrum feature, enabling it to play genus for multiform species. There is something which counts as 'making an individual stand out, etc.' in spoken and unspoken uses; in soliloquizing and communicative uses; in thought; on occasions when no demonstration is necessary for the use to single out its object; and so on.

Naturally the opportunity conditions differ with medium and context, and this will affect the means by which salience is achieved. If deictic sentences of the form 'δ is F' are to be effected in speech, for example, the circumstances making an item salient relative to that use may differ from those that would have made it salient in other circumstances (had the sentence been played back from a recording, for example, or uttered in soliloquy, or thought, or written). But these are differences of means. Salience itself is a concept equally (and well) suited to characterizing the different uses of *Deictic Terms*.

To say that salience is a broad-spectrum feature is not to extract its teeth. There are various ways in which an item can be salient. That is not to say that many items could count as salient relative to the use of a referring term. If an item is salient, it must be not merely noticeable, but conspicuous. And even this does not quite capture what is required. For being conspicuous is often a matter of degree where salience is not, at least in the referential sense to which we are appealing. If salience were a matter of degree, it would have to be possible for some item, A, to be less salient than another item, B, relative to some deictic thought or utterance, and yet both A and B remain salient. But such instances are ruled out by the concept, even in the loaded case of mixed *Deictic Terms* like *This F* where we can emphasize continuity between A and B by ensuring that they are of the same kind. Suppose the objects in question are books. A is a very large book on the table between Abelard and Heloise and is the only book either can see without moving. B, on the other hand, is a tiny book, hidden away amongst others on the bookshelf behind them. Heloise says, 'That book is particularly worth reading,' turning round and pointing to B. No matter how salient A was before Heloise spoke and pointed, B is the only book that is salient now, relative to her utterance. This is not to deny that A remains salient in other ways; with respect to size or position, for example. The point is that A does not even enter into comparison with B with respect to the deictic utterance.

§ 71. Salience bites deeper still. It is not a matter of degree, and nor is it relative to observation. This is surprising on the face of it. For there are familiar uses of salience *simpliciter* which make its application relative in precisely this way. Some item, *A*, might be salient to some observer, Abelard, because, and only because, it is this object which Abelard is looking at. If the same holds of another item, *B*, and another observer, Heloise, then neither *A* nor *B* is more salient than the other except in relation to these two individuals. For example, there might be a multitude of identical-looking and -behaving pigeons eating grain in a square, and Abelard is watching one while Heloise is tracking another. With respect to any particular deictic utterance, however, salience is not relative to observation, and for the strongest reason; namely, that an individual would remain the salient item relative to that utterance even if it were not observed at all. This is a direct implication of the distinction between the determinacy of reference and its discriminability which was discussed above. The former is not concerned with the conditions on understanding reference. So when Abelard means to speak of one pigeon (Lucky) but, momentarily put off, actually points to another (Plucky) when saying, 'He has grown fat,' it is still the unobserved Plucky that is the referentially salient item, and hence the individual on which reference is determined. This is because demonstrations can determine reference *in spite of* the speaker's intentions. We could correct for the divergence between intentions and demonstrated item by altering the former so that they necessarily converge with the latter; for example, by using a formulation like 'the speaker intends to refer to whatever he actually demonstrates'. But then, far from depriving demonstrations of semantic significance, we have explicitly endowed them with it.[2]

It is this determinacy of referential salience which enables it to discharge the referential function of *Deictic Terms*, to provide a positive answer to the 'which?' question by making a particular individual salient. On many occasions, a *Deictic Term* makes particular sorts of individual salient—males/females with uses of *He/She*; speakers with spoken uses of *I*; addressees with uses of *You*; *F*s with the use of so-called mixed terms like *This F* (e.g. *This Tree*); and so on. And since there is often just one item of that sort in the context, or one leading candidate, there is no second item that might be (however grossly or slightly) less salient relative to the utterance. Where this is not the case, as we have seen, an action to supplement the uttering of the *Deictic Term* is called for; a demonstration. Uniqueness, leading candidature, and demonstration may be absolute or relative in the referential context. If we lived in a one-tree world, for example, no individual would be more or less the salient item when one said, 'That tree is dying, but those branches look healthy enough.' If there were only one woman in the immediate utterance-environment or given conditions of observation, no individual would be more or less the salient item when one said, 'She is beautiful.' If there were only one man pointed at, no individual would be more or less the salient item when one said, 'He is a heretic.'

[2] *Pace* Kaplan (1989: 582–4). See Bach (1992), Reimer (1991).

So we can now add to what logical character and inferential role have told us about *Deictic Terms*. A *Deictic Term* is one whose uses refer by action of a particular sort; namely *by making an individual salient* in the extra-sentential context. When this claim was originally mentioned at the beginning of this chapter, it was compared to the claim that Abelard is a master of the Paris Schools *by wearing a particular gown*. That claim is false, of course. So it is worth seeing why the moral does not apply in the present instance. The gown case fails for two reasons. Although it is a sign that Abelard is a master and in most respects a reliable indication, first it is not true that if he is wearing this gown he is a master (he might be a student-impostor); and second, it is not true that if he had not been wearing this gown he would not have been a master (he might have removed it for whatever reason). Given logical character and inferential role, the fact that a term makes an individual salient is a reliable indicator of the use of a *Deictic Term*; but no more. We now know that salience passes both conditions for the 'by'-construction: that it is by making an individual salient that *Deictic Terms* fulfil their referential function. For (*a*) if an individual is made salient in relation to the use of a *Deictic Term*, there is an answer to the 'which?' question; and (*b*) if an individual is not made salient in relation to the use of a *Deictic Term*, there is no such answer.

HOW THE REFERENCE OF *I* IS DETERMINED

§ 72.   *I* is a singular term. So it has a referential function to discharge: that of providing determinate reference; a positive answer to the question 'which individual is being spoken of?' And the question has arisen, how that function is discharged. Logical character and inferential role reveal that *I* is a *Deictic Term*. But that is not enough to show that *I* fulfils its referential function in the deictic way. Does it nevertheless?

That is a way of putting the grounding problem of these chapters on referential function. In order to solve it, we have had to answer the subsidiary question: what it is for any term to fulfil its referential function in the deictic way? And in order not to prejudge the grounding problem or render any proposed solution circular, cases involving *I* have been deliberately excluded while formulating an answer. Without appeal to *I*, we have found that a *Deictic Term* is one whose uses refer by action of a particular sort; namely, the making-salient of an individual in the extra-sentential context. So we can now freely address the grounding problem; whether the same holds for *I*.

Suppose that, when accused of heresy by Bernard, Abelard says, 'I claim the right to answer the charge.' He says something of an individual, Abelard (that he claims the right to answer the charge), in doing something (uttering these words). And what he says is truth-evaluable depending on how it is with the individual referred to. This much is true of any sentence using a singular term. Particularity emerges, as it did with *He*, when we compare the sentence with one using a proper name. Suppose Abelard had said, 'Abelard claims the right to answer the charge,' instead. Of course, if no one had acted to use this sentence, no one would have been referred to by it. But that is not because, unless there is an act to use it, the name *Abelard* has no reference. There is a positive answer to the 'which?' question quite independently of the action by which this term is used on any occasion. So here is the contrast with *I*. For again, if no one had acted to use this sentence, no one would have been referred to by it. But this is so precisely because the term has no reference unless there is an act to use it. Independently of the action by which *I* is used, there is no positive answer to the 'which?' question. So action plays a referential role with *I*, as it does with other *Deictic Terms*.

§ 73.   Now this is only part of the story, of course. For as with any term, there are various ways in which one may act to use *I*. One may utter the term, write it, play back a recording; one may gesture at an individual; etc. The question is, whether it is specifically in the deictic way that the actions involved in using *I* enable it to discharge its referential function.

Here is a way to focus the issue. On many occasions, as with other *Deictic Terms*, an *I*-use need only be uttered, written, played back, etc. for the 'which?' question to be provided a positive answer. But in the case of other *Deictic Terms*, it can never be *by being uttered* etc. that their use has determinate reference. For uttering etc. fails at least one condition for this 'by'-construction. It is not true that, if such terms are uttered, there is a positive answer to the 'which?' question. When Bernard said, 'He is a heretic,' for example, uttering the term was not sufficient. That is why he demonstrated the referent. So it is only in so far as actions like uttering sub-serve another action—making an individual salient, as we have found—that they play a referential role with regard to other *Deictic Terms*. Is the same true of *I*?

We are being asked to consider what specific sort of action *I*-use depends on if it is to refer. It is a fact that the referent of *I* is not always an utterer (because speech is not the mode of use), a writer (because speech *is* the mode of use), someone playing back a recording (because the use is not mediated in this way), etc. Indeed, even if we continue to concentrate on spoken uses, the referent of *I* is not always the one uttering it. The utterer can be another person (a 'mouthpiece') or a mechanical device used by the referent. So being the utterer fails one necessary condition for the 'by'-construction: it is not true that if *x* is the utterer of an *I*-use, *x* must be its referent. Hence we cannot say that it is *by being the utterer* of an *I*-use that anyone is ever determined as its referent.

This issue, *who* is determined as the referent of an *I*-use, is dependent on another: *how* is that reference determined? So what we have learnt about the first tells us about the second; specifically, about the kind of actions which determine the reference of *I*-uses. For if being the utterer fails one condition of the 'by'-construction, that is because uttering itself fails. It is not true that, if *I* is uttered, there is a positive answer to the 'which?' question. On occasions where the utterer is not the referent, for example, the uttering alone is not sufficient to answer that question. Of course, the act of uttering is a sign that there is a positive answer to the 'which?' question for an *I*-use, and in most respects a reliable indication. But it can never be *by being uttered* that a use of *I* has determinate reference. And the same goes for writing, playing back a recording, etc. None of these actions are the determinant of *I*.

So *I* fulfils its referential function in ways with which we are now familiar from investigation of other *Deictic Terms*, like *He/She* and *You*. Often, merely uttering *I* is sufficient to provide positive answer to the 'which?' question. But sometimes this referential function is fulfilled without uttering the term. And sometimes more than uttering is required if positive answer is to be provided; for example, when the referent of a spoken *I*-use is not its utterer. Hence the actions necessary to utter *I* (or write it; play it back; etc.) are not those which determine reference. When such actions are involved, they merely sub-serve the action which does.

§ 74.   And this prompts us to ask what action that might be, the genus of these species. Now the logical character of *I* focuses on salience. So this prompts us to consider referential salience; salience relative to the use of referring terms. More specifically, we should ask whether the generic action is the making salient of an individual. And, as was the case with other terms, this prompt turns out to be confirmed by what we have already observed about *I*. For when merely uttering *I* is sufficient to fulfil its referential function, an individual is made salient relative to that use. And when uttering is not sufficient, an individual is not made salient in this way. Even on occasions where the utterer *is* the referent, the uttering alone may not be sufficient to provide positive answer to the 'which?' question. For if the utterer were a perfect ventriloquist, the *salient* item in relation to the *I*-use would not be the utterer. (This does not entail that there is no salient individual in relation to the use; only that uttering is not sufficient to make that individual salient even when the utterer is the referent.) Perfection of this sort would be exceptional. But the point it helps illustrate is simple and general. (*a*) If an individual is made salient in relation to the use of *I*, there is a positive answer to the 'which?' question; and (*b*) if an individual is not made salient in relation to the use of *I*, there is no such answer.

Hence *I* fulfils its referential function in the way we have found to be definitive of the deictic use of terms. For the same specific sort of action meets the conditions of the 'by'-construction for *I* and for other *Deictic Terms*. And it is action of this sort which determines the reference of all such terms on any occasion of their use. Each such use provides a positive answer to the 'which?' question by making an individual salient in the extra-sentential context.

So referential salience is the fundamental factor in determining the reference of *I*-uses, just as it is fundamental to the use of other *Deictic Terms*. To say this is not to claim that we have given a *sufficient* account of how reference is determined in any of these cases. For then we could not account for the fact that different *Deictic*

Terms are capable of referring to different individuals on the same occasions of use. Suppose Bernard points to Abelard and says, 'I think he is a heretic.' One individual is singled out by the *I*-use, and another by the use of *He*. Yet both individuals are salient relative to the utterance. (They must be if each is referred to, for *I* and *You* are *Deictic Terms*; and hence expressions which would fail to refer if the respective individuals were *not* salient.) So if we are to explain why Abelard was singled out by one *Deictic Term* and Bernard by the other, we must discover what *more* is required to determine reference.

§ 75.   This may seem a tough undertaking. But only if we assume it is necessary to look *beyond* referential salience for the 'more' that is required to determine reference. Actually, it is to be found by looking more closely at the materials we already have; and specifically at the different *character* referential salience assumes in relation to different *Deictic Terms*.

Abelard and Bernard have it in common that they are salient individuals. But they are distinguishable if we ask 'salient *as what* in relation to the utterance?' And here, standard dictionary definitions and linguistic rules point the way. It is by being salient as the male to whom Bernard is pointing that the reference of his *He*-use is determined on Abelard. It is by being salient as the individual uttering the sentence that the reference of Bernard's *I*-use is determined on Bernard himself. If Bernard had said to Abelard, 'You are a heretic,' his use of singular *You* would have been determined on the individual salient as the addressee of the sentence. And so on. In short, referential salience is not simply the 'fundamental factor' in determining the reference of any *Deictic Term*, it is *sufficient* to determine that reference. Employing the now-familiar term of art, referential salience is the determinant of *Deictic Terms*.

This is so despite the fact that *Deictic Terms* differ from each other. For their differences are precisely differences in the character *of* referential salience; and specifically, the character such salience has to take on if a use of any particular term is to have its reference determined on some particular individual. We have not given a full account of deictic reference until we have noted these particularities of character. But we have not gone beyond referential salience in doing so. Indeed, since these are precisely differences in the *character* of referential salience, in detailing them we have been forced to remain focused on referential salience. Consider another medieval garment analogy. Wearing a certain habit was sufficient to make one recognizable as a monk. This was so despite the fact that monks differed from each other in the orders they belonged to. For differences in order were recognizable by differences in the character of the habit worn; specifically, the particular cut, colouring, markings, etc. such a habit had to take on if any particular wearer was to be made recognizable as a monk. So a full account of what made monks recognizable as such would be forced to take such particularities of habit into account. But in detailing those particularities, it would be precisely on the habit that such investigations would focus.

It is worth noting how these findings bear out the tentative suggestion made in Chapter 2: that the most plausible explanation for the hold of *Rule Theory* over current philosophical imagination is that it exaggerates and distorts what is the case. Linguistic rules for *I* have their place, as we now appreciate. They are not sufficient to give the meaning of the term or to determine its reference. But they do help distinguish *I* from other *Deictic Terms*. For they indicate the particular character of the salience required of an individual if that individual is to have the reference of an *I*-use determined on him.

At this point, we should draw together the various threads of this discussion and restate the main conclusions. *Deictic Terms* are those whose uses refer to an individual salient in the extra-sentential context. This is what logical character and inferential role showed. Greater specificity has been achieved by noting the way uses of such terms fulfil their referential function, achieving determinacy of reference. A *Deictic Term* is one whose uses refer by making an individual salient in the extra-sentential context. (I have sometimes anticipated this claim by saying 'the deictic use of a term refers to the item which is (made) salient in the extra-sentential context'; what is outside the brackets gives the logical character of such terms; the whole sentence combines that character with their referential use, i.e. with what is necessary if they are to fulfil their referential function.) *Deictic Terms* are distinguished from each other by the character of the referential salience required of an individual if reference using some particular term is to be determined on that individual. For example, Abelard must be salient as the addressee of some utterance 'You are F' if the reference of *You* is to be determined on him.

Action has a specific referential role in deictic use, and it helps us categorize further. For some deictic uses, uttering the term is sufficient to make an individual salient. This is due to domain-specification and the existence of a unique or leading candidate. For other deictic uses, an ostensive gesture or demonstration is necessary. This distinction can be put in terms of different sorts of rhetic act. Sometimes there is no more to the deictic act of making an individual salient than the meaning act of uttering noises which mean the *Deictic Term* in question. And sometimes that deictic act also includes a demonstration.

This distinction categorizes *uses* of *Deictic Terms*. It does not categorize at the level of the terms used. For some uses of the same *Deictic Term* fall into the first group and some into the second. But it grounds that explanation of *I*'s security against reference-failure proposed at the end of Chapter 4 as an alternative to *The Guarantee*. For it is a remarkable feature of *I* that its central spoken uses—where the utterer is the referent and salient as such—fall squarely into the first category. So it is sufficient in these circumstances simply to engage in the act of using the term for its referential function to be achieved. That is, uttering the noises that count as meaningful uses of *I* will make the individual salient and hence provide positive answer to the 'which?' question. This discharges a debt incurred in Part I: to substantiate the pragmatic explanation of why uses of *I* are secure against reference-failure.

WHAT HAS IMPEDED APPRECIATION OF *I*'S DEICTIC CHARACTER

§ 76.   If *I* fulfils its referential function in the deictic way, why has that fact been under-appreciated or frankly dismissed? There are two kinds of reason for resisting the claim that *I* is a *Deictic Term*, just as there are for resisting any claim that some *a* is an *F*. Because one thinks of *a* as possessing properties that *F* could not have, and because one thinks of *F* as possessing properties that *a* could not have. Bernard says, 'Abelard is a heretic.' To rebut the charge, Abelard can either say he teaches what the church declares true, something no heretic could do. Or he can assert that a heretic teaches what the church declares false, something he could not do.

It is from the three myths examined above that resistance of the first sort springs. For if we think of *I* as characterized by *Rule Theory, Independence*, and *The Guarantee*, we will attribute properties to it which could not be possessed by a *Deictic Term*. These myths exercise a powerful grip on philosophical imagination. So it is not surprising to find equally powerful resistance to the claim that *I* is a *Deictic Term*. But they are, after all, myths. *I* is exactly like *You, He/She*, and other *Deictic Terms* in the relevant respects. No use of any of these terms is sufficiently determined in context by a simple rule. No such use is guaranteed reference by virtue of meaning or logical character. No such use is independent of identification when expressing thoughts about individuals. No such use fulfils its referential function without making an individual salient in the extra-sentential context. Like *He/She* and *You*, *I* has uses in which the only action necessary to effect referential salience is uttering the term. Or consider a particular *Deictic Term* whose similarity with *I* in this one feature we have noted before: *This Very Speaker*. Uttering this phrase will rarely fail to provide positive answer to the 'which?' question. But the reference is nevertheless dependent on making an individual salient. 'Rarely' because, in cases of perfect ventriloquism, the referent of either term is the utterer but not salient as such. *I* is unlike *This Very Speaker* in several other respects, of course. It is not a mixed term and it does not always refer to the speaker. This is obvious when the mode of use is not speech. It is also obvious when the mode is speech but the individual making the reference is not the individual uttering the words. And, as we have seen, far from counting against the claim that uses of *I* depend on making an individual salient, all these various comparisons and contrasts help prove it.

This great ease of reference shared by *I, He/She, You*, and *This Very Speaker* has been the source of greater confusion. For it is tempting to think that if uses of such terms do not *lack* the means to make an individual salient, they do not *need* them either. But this is a mistake. Little Lord Fauntleroy has it easy also. But although he does not *lack* the means to live, he *needs* them. *I* depends on means it usually does not lack; true. But that is also true of *He/She* and *You* and *This Very Speaker* when the domain is specified and there is a unique or leading candidate. In short, *I* possesses no properties that a *Deictic Term* could not possess. This explains and neutralizes one source of opposition: falsely thinking of *I* as possessing properties that no genuine *Deictic Term* could possess.

§ 77.   But it leaves the alternative in place: thinking of *Deictic Terms* as possessing properties which *I* could not. So suppose we adopt the standard definition: that *Deictic Terms* are those whose uses refer by demonstrating an individual.[3] Then we will think *I* could not possess the features of a *Deictic Term*. For it is not by demonstrating an individual that uses of *I* achieve determinacy of reference. Now this definition of *Deictic Terms* has been deeply influential in recent theorizing. So, again, it is not surprising to find deep resistance to the claim that *I* is a *Deictic Term*; resistance that survives exposure of the myths as myths. But this definition fails, as we have found. *Deictic Terms* are those whose uses refer by making an individual salient, not by demonstrating an individual. Hence *Deictic Terms* do not possess properties that *I* could not possess.

This neutralizes the second source of resistance to the claim that *I* is a *Deictic Term*. It does not quite explain it, however. For the definition we have discarded has exercised its own powerful grip on recent philosophy. And if it is false, we need to know why it has been so widely adhered to. Only so can we explain why opposition to our conclusions about *I* has found such influential support.

Adherence to the false definition is explicable once we realize that saying 'the referent of a demonstrative depends on the associated demonstration' is rather like saying 'the pen is mightier than the sword'. Both are true enough so long as we recognize that they are synecdochal. They substitute for an outcome (i.e. referential salience; military victory) the means sometimes used to achieve it (i.e. demonstration; the sword). The fact that the sentence is true gives us the best possible explanation of why it is plausible. The fact that it is far easier to forget that this useful short-cut of a substitution has taken place explains why the first sentence is only 'rather like' the second. And this ease also explains widespread adoption of the false view about *Deictic Terms*. For if it is easy to forget that the sentence substitutes in this way, it is also fatal. The sentence will be read as a plain definition and generate the confusion over *I* with which we are now familiar.

No one would ever dream of saying 'How can *that* be a conquest? No swords were used!' For, obviously enough, whether or not a conquest counts as such depends on whether it is dependent on military victory, not on the use of swords. And the use of swords is merely one way of achieving military victory. There are others (the use of guns, for example). But it is quite easy to make this same mistake when dealing with the sentence about *Deictic Terms*. Forgetting the substitution, we will read it as a plain definition; that a *Deictic Term* is one whose uses refer by demonstrating an individual. And then, faced with uses of *I*, *You*, and *He/She*

---

[3] e.g. Kaplan (1989: 492).

which fulfil their referential function by utterance alone, we will say, 'How can *that* be a use of a *Deictic Term*? No ostensive gestures were used!' If the mistake is easier to make with this sentence, the moral is still the same. For whether or not a *Deictic Term* counts as such depends on whether it is dependent on referential salience, not on the use of demonstration. And the use of such ostensive gestures is merely one way of achieving referential salience; there are others (utterance-relative uniqueness, for example, or leading candidature).

This is not to deny that relations with ostensive gesture help distinguish *I* from certain *Deictic Terms*: specifically, *This F* and *That F*. But we should be clear about what sort of gesture individuates. It is gesticulation rather than demonstration. And we should be clear about what this relation to gesture shows: that some uses of *This/That* lack a referring function, not that *I* is something other than a *Deictic Term*. To see this, consider an extreme case: *Yea* is a word whose use *always* requires completing by gesticulation. One does not mean anything by saying 'He was *yea* tall' without some gesture. Some uses of *This F/That F* are of this sort; 'He was *this* tall,' for example. Other *Deictic Terms* like *I*, *You*, and *He/She* never need to be so completed. But these gesticulation-dependent uses carry out an ascriptive rather than referential function. They provide us with a positive answer not to the 'which?' question but to the supplementary query 'what are you saying about the individual referred to?' This is obvious even if we reconfigure sentences to make it look as if the gesticulation-dependent use answers the 'which?' question—e.g. '*This* narrow was the gate.' And this fact leaves us with at least two ways to phrase the conclusion. Nothing of relevance here hangs on which we choose. Either some uses of *Deictic Terms* (*This F/That F*) are not referential, or there are homonyms of some *Deictic Terms* (*This F/That F*) which are ascriptive. Ostensive gesture helps individuate expressions, but in such a way as to promote the claim that *I* is a *Deictic Term*.

To sum up. It is definitive of *Deictic Terms* that they fulfil their referential function by making an individual salient in the extra-sentential context. *I* fulfils its referential function in precisely this way. What distinguishes *I* from other *Deictic Terms* is what distinguishes any such term from its fellows; namely, the character of the referential salience associated with it. Appreciating that *I* refers deictically means taking leave of certain well-rooted but false conjectures. For this conclusion has faced stiff resistance. Various more or less plausible assumptions have stirred controversy, implying that *I* has features which a *Deictic Term* could not have and vice versa. But these assumptions seriously misjudge the issues in various ways. By its referential function we recognize this, as by its logical character and inferential role: *I* is a *Deictic Term*.

10

Expressive Use

§ 78.   Heloise catches sight of her teacher and says what she is thinking: 'I am in love with Abelard.' *I* fulfils its referential function for a purpose: to be used in utterances that express thoughts. How the term achieves that purpose is a significant part of its meaning. So this enquiry into *I* will continue with investigation of its expressive use. Since there is a shortfall between referential function and expressive use—uses of terms must refer successfully to express thinking, but they need not express thinking to refer successfully—this requires a further broadening of focus. Earlier findings shed light on the subject. To appreciate this, it will be helpful to distinguish the expressive use of *I* from others of its uses.

On some occasions, uses of *I* do not express thoughts at all. So a probe might give information about otherwise inaccessible regions by reporting on its own states and how they are affected by its environment using *I*: 'I have a temperature of such-and-such'; 'I am positioned at such-and-such a location.' In such cases, *I* is used by individuals capable of non-intentional acts but incapable of thought. On other occasions, an individual may use *I* without thereby expressing any thought they are capable of having. So an actor playing Hamlet might say, 'I have that within which passeth show,' and think its negation without lying. Or a parrot might be trained to give apparent structure to its feature-placing reports (Hot! Hungry!) by prefacing each with a use of 'I am'.

On other occasions, individuals entertain thoughts expressible using *I* without uttering them. Heloise might have kept her thoughts about Abelard to herself out of shyness. Or she might have been struck dumb by the sight of Abelard, and hence unable to speak her love.

On yet further occasions, thoughts are expressed by *I*, but this is a matter of coincidence. The utterance is not used to express the thought. The phenomenon occurs with all referring expressions. So Abelard might have thought something Brigitte Bardot later said: 'I am in love,' or 'Paris is beautiful.' What Bardot said expressed what Abelard happened to think, but it was not used to do so. As it turns out, what is said is true if and only if what is thought is true. But this match depends on coincidence. On other occasions, an expressive match may depend on something involuntary. Thus Abelard might say, 'I am tired,' under his breath, or 'You frustrate me!', something he thinks but does not intend to say and is perhaps not even aware of having said. Again, the utterance was not used to express the thought.

In their different ways, these occasions can all be called uses of *I*. But they are not cases of its expressive use; occasions like that involving Heloise, in which her utterance 'I am in love with Abelard' attempts to, and on this occasion does, express her thought. She would not have *succeeded* in this aim unless the individual referred to by *I* is the same as the individual thought about. And she would not have counted as *having* this aim in saying what she did unless she were satisfied that the one were indeed identical with the other.

§ 79.   So this is one crucial distinguishing feature of expressive use that holds for any singular term. In expressing a thought with an utterance using such a term, one tries to make sure that the individual referred to is the individual thought about. We can separate the task into two: identifying the referent, and ascertaining its identity with the individual thought about.

This enables us to put the issue more precisely. Suppose someone, Heloise, is thinking about a particular object or individual; call it O_1. Heloise thinks of O_1 that it has some property; that it is F, for example. She tries to express this thought in an utterance using a singular term, a; so she says, 'a is F.' Call the object to which a refers O_2. Now Heloise will not have succeeded in expressing her thought unless the object a refers to (i.e. O_2) is identical with the object thought about (i.e. O_1). And she will not have tried to express her thought unless she has tried to make sure this is so. So Heloise needs to know, first, which object her use of a refers to; i.e. 'this use of a refers to O_2'. And then, equipped with that knowledge, she needs to ascertain that this object is identical to the one she is thinking about; i.e. '$O_1 = O_2$'.

And this is where our earlier investigations help. For we know three significant facts about what would be required in the case of *I*. We learnt these respectively from the failure of *Independence*, of *Rule Theory*, and of non-deictic accounts of *I*'s referential function. First, one who uses *I* to express thoughts about themselves is not absolved from the need to identify what is being referred to. This is so no matter how easily that identification is made. Second, the reference of *I*-uses is not determined on their user-producer. So it cannot be as their user-producer that the referent of an *I*-use is to be identified. Third, it is as the individual made salient in relation to the use that the referent is to be identified. For it is on that individual that the reference of an *I*-use is determined.

This tells us much in general terms about the expressive use of *I*. It is the individual made referentially salient that one has to identify in order to know what an *I*-use refers to. And it is this individual whose identity with what is thought about one has to ascertain. 'In general terms' because this applies to every expressive use of *I*. On any specific occasion, the one expressing the thought will need to know more. For suppose one knows only that the referent of this particular *I*-use is the referentially salient individual. Not knowing *which* individual is the individual made referentially salient, one could not ascertain its identity with the individual thought about. Consider Heloise's utterance, 'I am in love with Abelard', in relation to the stages noted formally above. She needs to know 'this use of *I* refers to O_2', for some *particular* individual, O_2, before she can assess whether '$O_1 = O_2$'. In short: if the reference using *I* provides positive answer to the 'which?' question, Heloise needs to know that answer.

And at this point, our earlier findings give out, offering no help. For in examining what is necessary to determine the reference of an *I*-use, we have ignored what is necessary to discriminate it. This was intentional. For we rigidly distinguished these two issues—what is required to *provide* a positive answer to the 'which?' question, and what is required to *know* the answer—so as to settle the first. So we must now investigate what is required to discriminate reference, adopting the usual method: discovering the general pattern for *Deictic Terms* before asking whether, and if so how, *I* conforms. This will tell us what we need to know in specific terms about the expressive use of *I*.

Two preliminary remarks. First, it might be thought that our examination of the logical character of *I* provides a useful clue in our present investigation. For the behaviour of the term in knowledge-advancing inference revealed that knowing one is the referent of several different *I*-uses need not require an identity-judgement. It was suggested at the time that a particular awareness of and sensitivity to one's own salience might serve here instead of an identity-judgement. It might also serve in the different case now at issue: identifying oneself as the individual thought about and the individual referred to by an *I*-use. But the appeal to special awareness was a promissory note which has yet to be redeemed, let alone extended in this way. Redemption is part of this chapter's task, but we shall see how it strengthens the distinction between the kinds of identification required for inference and for expressive use.

A second remark. What is necessary if the reference of a *Deictic Term* is to have expressive use is distinct from what is required if that reference is to be communicable to an audience. In both cases, of course, the answer to the 'which?' question needs to be known. But the expressive use of a singular term depends on the discriminability of its reference to the *reference-maker*. Whereas its communicative role depends on the discriminability of that reference to its *audience*. The distinction is significant since reference-makers may know the answer to the 'which?' question in circumstances where the audience does not. They might make an individual salient relative to an utterance by using a demonstration that the audience cannot see, for example. And the converse is also possible. The reference-maker may be unaware of which individual they have demonstrated; their audience may be in a position to correct them about what they referred to. But since our enquiry into discriminability sub-serves our interest in expressive use, we will continue for the moment to focus on the reference-maker. The communicative role of *I* and other *Deictic Terms* will be addressed separately below.

HOW DEICTIC REFERENCE IS DISCRIMINATED

§ 80. Discriminating reference tracks determinacy. For determinacy provides the answer which it is the task of discrimination to discover. Singular terms differ in the ways their reference is determined. So they also differ in the ways their reference is made discriminable.

Proper names and definite descriptions, for example, provide positive answer to the 'which?' question prior to their use. So reference-makers are in a position to know what that answer is in advance. And they can know which individual has been referred to without attending to any feature of the circumstances of use. Suppose Abelard thinks, 'Heloise is beautiful,' or 'The guardian of Heloise is over-protective.' In advance of the use, he knows which individual has been given the proper name in question, which individual uniquely satisfies the description. And so long as it is these terms he uses, he need not attend to their use to know who has been referred to.

Deictic Terms contrast deeply in these respects. Such expressions refer, if at all, to the individual made referentially salient. Prior to use, there is no term in relation to which any individual might be salient. So no one, not even the person making the reference, is in any position to discriminate deictic reference in advance of use. There is quite simply no reference to discriminate. And no one is in such a position during or after that use if they do not attend to features of the circumstances in which the *Deictic Term* is uttered. For no one will know what has been referred to unless they know which individual has been made salient by the utterance. And no one will know this unless they attend sufficiently to circumstances to know which item has been demonstrated, or made unique, or the leading candidate. This holds for all. To appreciate why it holds even for the reference-maker, and to note the implications for expressive use, compare two cases.

§ 81. Abelard might take Heloise up a prominence on the outskirts of Paris and ask her to point out the city's landmarks. Prompted by some particular church she is looking at, she might think, 'This is Notre-Dame.' She points at the building she is thinking about and says, 'This is Notre-Dame.' *Deictic Terms* are used here expressively and successfully: the reference-maker knows that the individual she is speaking about is the same as the individual she is thinking about. Now suppose the case were different in one detail only: the salient item relative to the utterance is not Notre-Dame but some other building. This can be explained variously. Perhaps Heloise is inattentive and points carelessly while uttering her sentence so that, unawares, it is quite evidently the nearby royal palace rather than Notre-Dame that she demonstrates and thus refers to. Her thought remains the same in this second case, however. If she is thinking about the particular church she is looking at in the first instance, then that is the building she is thinking about in the second. So there is evidently a mismatch in the second case between individual thought about and individual referred to.

These cases reveal two related reasons why even the reference-maker must attend to features of the circumstances of utterance: to know which individual has been referred to, and to meet the conditions necessary for the expressive use of *Deictic Terms*. As to the first, Heloise uses a *Deictic Term*. But, being inattentive, she does not know which item has been demonstrated, or made unique, or the leading candidate in relation to her utterance. So she does not know which individual has been made salient. Hence, no matter what she may have believed at the time, she does not know the answer to the 'which?' question. She does not know what she has referred to. Not knowing this, of course, she does not know whether the individual she has referred to is the same as the individual she is thinking about. Yet ensuring this is part of the expressive task. So the issue relates to the second reason why the reference-maker must attend to the circumstances of utterance. Being inattentive, Heloise fails to meet the conditions necessary for the expressive use of *Deictic Terms*. For she uses a *Deictic Term* to express her thought. And this places special requirements on the expressive task. Such terms refer to the individual made salient, irrespective of which individual the reference-maker is thinking about. So ensuring that what she says expresses what she thinks requires that Heloise carefully align her salience-making acts with a particular individual. And that requires attention to circumstance. It is precisely because Heloise is inattentive in this respect that she fails in the expressive task. The individual she refers to is not the one she is thinking about because her demonstration singles out the wrong individual.

Both these points go deeper. To know which individual is referred to by a *Deictic Term* is at least to know whether it refers. And to meet the conditions for its expressive use is at least to succeed in referring. But without attention to the circumstances of utterance, the reference-maker may fail in both respects. Heloise pointed, however casually, because she recognized that, without a demonstration, her utterance would make no individual salient. Even given implicit domain-restriction, there are a number of possible candidates for referent. Antecedent discourse may have made it plain that buildings were at issue. Perhaps Heloise was replying to Abelard's question 'which buildings can you name?' But Notre-Dame is not the unique building. Nor is it the leading candidate, given that the surrounding perceptual environment is replete with prominent buildings. Without attending to these circumstances, Heloise would not have appreciated that a demonstration was necessary to effect determinate reference. If she had been inattentive to this extent and uttered the sentence without demonstration, no individual would have been made salient. And this is a more desperate case than one in which the reference-maker is simply ignorant of the answer to the 'which?' question. For there is no knowing which individual was spoken of when none has been. So the attention of reference-makers is decisive in deictic use.

§ 82.   There is another sense in which discriminating reference tracks determinacy. On many occasions, the way in which an answer to the 'which?' question is provided is the way in which that answer is discovered. Some uses of *Deictic Terms* provide positive answer by demonstration, for example, just as it is sometimes by attending to demonstration that the reference-maker knows what that answer is. Other uses fulfil their referential function in a non-demonstrational way. This is because the utterance alone is sufficient to make an individual unique or the leading candidate, given features of the circumstances of use. And in such cases, it may also be sufficient for the reference-maker to attend to these features to know which individual has been referred to. So the same species–genus shape occurs with discriminability as with determinacy. Demonstrating an individual or making it unique or the leading candidate are all ways of making it salient. Hence it is by making an individual salient that *Deictic Terms* fulfil their referential function. In the same way, knowing which item is demonstrated or made unique or the leading candidate are all ways of knowing which individual is made salient. Hence it is by knowing which individual is made salient that the reference-maker is able to discriminate the reference and so give expressive use to *Deictic Terms*.

On some occasions, however, the way in which an individual is made referentially salient by the use of a *Deictic Term* is not the way in which that referent is discriminated. So there are points at which discriminating reference diverges from determining it. This may be so for all singular terms. Baptism or some similar fact answers the 'which?' question for a proper name like *Abelard*. However we need know nothing of these details to know who the name refers to. But it holds for *Deictic Terms* in a more particular sense. They refer by making an individual salient. And we can ask, nevertheless, both (*a*) is it by knowing which individual has been made salient that we know which individual has been referred to? And (*b*) is it by knowing the way in which the individual has been made salient that we know which individual has been referred to? I shall ignore (*a*) to concentrate on (*b*) because the implications for *I* are more significant.

Suppose Abelard has before him a crowd of pupils, among them Heloise. He does not know what is in fact the case: that she is the only woman present. Taking care to make his reference determinate, he points to her when saying, 'She is my best student.' The 'which?' question is provided with a positive answer: a unique individual is made salient in relation to the utterance (i.e. referentially salient). And the reference-maker knows what that answer is: the referent is made salient to him as such. But the way in which Heloise was made referentially salient is by being unique, given domain-specification. While it is by being the demonstrated individual that she is made discriminable.

This divergence illustrates a significant difference between referential salience and discriminability. The reference of a *Deictic Term* is determinate only if it is referentially salient, i.e. salient relative to its use in an utterance. And as we found, referential salience is not relative to anything or anyone else. In particular, it is not relative to any observer. This is because an object would remain salient relative to the uttering of a referring term even if it were not observed at all. The reference of a *Deictic Term* is discriminable, on the other hand, only if it is discriminable to someone; the reference-maker, for example, or the audience. So discriminable reference *is* relative, and standardly to the observer.

Drawing these threads together, we can augment our characterization of *Deictic Terms*: their discriminability and expressive use are dependent on attention to the circumstances of utterance. For knowing which individual such terms succeed in referring to means knowing whether an object has been made salient in relation to an utterance, and which object that is. So knowing the answer to the 'which?' question depends on such attention. And this holds for the reference-maker as well as for their audience. Using *Deictic Terms* to express thoughts means making an individual salient, and ensuring its identity with the individual one is thinking about. So the expressive use of such terms also depends on attending to the circumstances of utterance. And this holds for the reference-maker.

HOW THE REFERENCE OF *I* IS DISCRIMINATED

§ 83.   *I* conforms to this pattern for *Deictic Terms*. Discriminating its reference tracks determinacy at the same points and diverges at the same points.

When Heloise says what she thinks, 'I am in love with Abelard,' her words say something of an individual, herself, by making that individual salient. Unlike proper names and definite descriptions, then, *I* provides positive answer to the 'which?' question only in its use. There must be an act of making-salient if one's use of *I* is to refer; the using of the term. So there is no knowing the answer to that question independently of the use. And this is so in two senses. First, without that act, there is no positive answer to know; nothing has been made salient. Second, without attention to that act, there is no knowing whatever positive answer is provided. For if reference occurs, it is determined on the salient individual. And knowing which individual has been made salient depends on attending to the circumstances of use. Answering the question depends on knowing what has been demonstrated, or made unique, or the leading candidate in relation to that use.

This demand for attention to the circumstances of use falls on the one making reference with *I* as well as on the audience. And this is so for the same two reasons that hold for other *Deictic Terms*. First, it is necessary if the reference-maker is to know which individual has been referred to. For an *I*-use refers to the individual made salient in relation to the utterance. And without attending to circumstance, the reference-maker will fail to know which individual has been made salient. Second, it is necessary if the reference-maker is to meet the conditions for expressive use of *I*. For an *I*-use will only express thought if the individual made salient by that use is the same as the individual thought about. And, without attending to circumstance, the reference-maker will be unable to align their salience-making act of using *I* with the particular individual thought about.

§ 84.   The attention required for these tasks usually takes no particular effort. When Heloise says, 'I am in love with Abelard,' for example, her use of *I* refers to the individual made salient by her uttering, and that individual is the utterer. On such occasions, the reference-maker need only attend to the uttering in order to know which individual an *I*-use refers to, and in order to align their salience-making acts with the individual thought about. But these are purely contingent features of *I*-use. And we are after the meaning of *I*, what is true of the term on any occasion of use, not a description of what often happens to be the case. On other occasions, the one uttering is not the referent; Heloise uses a mechanical device to utter her words, or employs another person as her 'mouthpiece'. Moreover, on occasion, the referent is not made salient by the uttering; Heloise indulges in perfect ventriloquism, so that her words appear to come from the mouth of her companion. In circumstances such as these, greater demands are made on attentiveness. To appreciate why even the reference-maker can be affected, consider the following case.

Five bishops try simultaneously to use a single mechanical speaker to utter the sentence: 'I condemn Abelard of heresy.' This speaker is connected to a sophisticated device which edits out background noise. So although these several persons try to activate it at roughly the same moment, what the speaker itself utters is the sentence produced by whoever was fractionally first.

What we are interested in here is what is uttered by this device, not whatever causes it to produce utterances. It may, but need not, be voice-activated (perhaps the bishops type sentences onto five different keyboards simultaneously). It may be (perhaps it usually will be) that whatever causes the device to utter a sentence is itself an utterance. So suppose in the present case we think of there being six utterances, five by the persons trying to operate the device, and the sixth by the device itself. The first five utterances are irrelevant to the issue under discussion. Whether or not (and how) their referents are discriminable is not at issue. It is the discriminability of the sixth which is at stake.

The 'which?' question is provided with a positive answer. For an individual is made salient in relation to the utterance by being the one who caused the speaker to utter the sentence. But no one knows who was fractionally the first to try, not even the reference-maker. So even the reference-maker must have other means of knowing who is referred to by this use of *I*. Perhaps a light flashes beside the person responsible for the speaker's utterance. Perhaps the person responsible is recognizable to himself by the character of the voice uttering the sentence. But some such means are necessary, and the reference-maker needs to attend to them, for the familiar two reasons: to know which thing is referred to by this use of *I*, and to ensure that it singles out the same individual as the one thought about.

Variations between cases in which the speaker and reference-maker are non-identical serve to confirm these points. So we may cause various kinds of mechanical apparatus to emit statements; e.g. by talking into a microphone linked to a speaker. But we may do so without talking at all; e.g. by typing the statement into a computer that emits it via a speaker. We may even do so without bodily gestures or movements of any kind; e.g. by merely thinking the statement, if we are suitably linked up to an apparatus that can speak what we think. That apparatus might be another person, of course. It might be that two or more people are wired up in such a way that, although uses of *I* proceed from Abelard's mouth, it might be Abelard or Heloise or Bernard who is thus using the term.

We rarely lack air, so it is possible to forget we need it. It takes exceptional circumstances, like being held under water, to remind us of what is always the case. We rarely lack the free use of all five fingers on each hand, so it is possible to forget that many daily activities require unrestricted use of all five. But the smallest injury to one finger reminds us immediately that this is the case. In the same way, an exceptional instance like that of the five bishops is required to reveal what is always the case: that even the reference-maker needs to attend to circumstances to discriminate *I* and ensure its expressive use. Though exceptional, cases which draw attention to this need have a ready specification: they are cases in which the reference-maker is not the utterer (writer, etc.), or not salient as such.

The five bishops case illustrates two further points. First, as with other *Deictic Terms*, the discriminability of reference using *I* diverges at certain points from its determinacy. For the way an individual is made referentially salient by an *I*-use need not be the way that referent is discriminated. It is by being the one to activate the speaker that a particular bishop is made salient in relation to the utterance 'I condemn Abelard of heresy.' This is something he achieves by being fractionally the first to try. But the way in which that bishop is made discriminable (if the flashing light is operational), to himself and to others, is by being demonstrated. In this respect, the case is precisely akin to the example of Abelard saying, 'She is my best student.'

Second, and again as with other *Deictic Terms*, attention is necessary but not sufficient for the discriminability and expressive use of *I*. For there may be no discriminating details to attend to. Suppose no additional means of recognizing the referent are provided in the five bishops case. There are no signs (flashing lights etc.) to indicate which person is talking; the mechanical speaker makes one utterance at a time but distorts the original voices or overlays them with its own vocal character; and so on. Being fractionally the first to try activating the speaker might be the only discriminating feature. And no one knows who counts as such. In such circumstances, reference would be discriminable to no one, no matter how attentive. And it would be impossible to align reference with whichever individual is thought about.

The case is similar in the relevant respects to that in which Heloise carelessly points while saying, 'This is Notre-Dame.' Suppose Abelard had not seen where she pointed. Then there would have been a positive answer to the 'which?' question: the royal palace. But no one, not even the reference-maker, would have known what that answer was. Heloise continues to believe falsely that she referred to Notre-Dame (and Abelard, if he believes anything, probably believes

Heloise). The difference is that, in this case, attention would have corrected the problem. In the five bishops case, where no means of discriminating the referent are available, it would not.

To emphasize: saying that uses of *I* might be *discriminable* to no one is not saying that, in these cases, reference has *failed*. For we are maintaining the distinction between determinacy of reference and its discriminability; the latter is not necessary for the former. Perhaps a more complex case could be devised on similar lines which *did* put pressure on the determinacy of some uses of *I*. The idea would be that, in causing various kinds of mechanical apparatus to emit statements so that the reference-maker is not made salient by the utterance itself, it is possible for there to be a genuine *I*-use and yet no determinate answer to the question 'who has been singled out?', no such 'fact of the matter'. In such a case, there would have to be more than one candidate for the referent of that use and yet none would be sufficiently salient in relation to it to count as its referent.

Suppose we deepen the original case, for example, by stipulating that the people at the news conference all use a single speaker to utter their thoughts (i.e. without even speaking into it), and that nothing that might achieve salience for the referent is supplied—no enunciation, no signs of any kind to indicate which person's thoughts are being spoken; the machine emits one utterance at a time in its own voice; etc. Again, all of the participants might try at the same moment to activate the same apparatus and have some *I*-statement said. The point can be made in truth-conditional form: a use of *I* may fail to single out which one particular item is relevant to the truth-value of the sentence containing it for this precise reason; that the putative referent lacks salience.

It is not easy to know what to say about arguments of this sort and the cases on which they depend. One might respond that, even in the worst such cases, there *is* a 'fact of the matter' about who is made salient and thus referred to; namely, whoever caused the utterance actually produced. On the other hand, this response depends on treating the (self)-referential relation in a problematic (if not untenable) way; i.e. as if it were merely a causal relation. The simplest and most decisive reason for considering this questionable is that something can be self-referring without being self-causing—the sentence 'This sentence contains five words' is an example. More generally, treating reference in this way problematically gives explanatory priority to reference over truth.

Whatever we should say about cases of this sort, however, we should remain clear on one matter: as we have seen, what is criterial of *Deictic Terms* is that they depend on the salience of their referents, not that they depend on any one means of providing for that salience, such as demonstration. So, whatever interest such eccentric cases might have, we certainly do not need to devise them to show off the deictic component in spoken uses of *I*.

WHAT FORMS OF ATTENTION ARE REQUIRED

§ 85.   Whether some object is referentially salient depends on a complex of features of which even the reference-maker may be only partially aware—including the layout of objects in that environment, the content of antecedent discourse, the actual demonstrata of the utterer's bodily movements, and communication-constraints like principles of economy and relevance. So no one will know which individual has been made salient, let alone whether that individual is the same as the one thought about, unless they attend to the circumstances of use. It is distinctive of *Deictic Terms* that their discriminability and expressive use depend on attention in this way. This requirement is worth examining since it plays so crucial a role and throws light in turn on the meaning of *Deictic Terms* in general and of *I* in particular.

Reference-makers who wish to refer to the objects they intend to refer to must learn to suit their actions to their words. In using a *Deictic Term* to express a thought, they must be attentive, and in both senses of that phrase: attending to the circumstances of use, and being attentive about that use. In the first sense, being attentive is akin to observation or scrutiny. So call it scrutiny-attention. In the second, it is a matter of exercising caution or care, of taking trouble over doing something. So call it care-attention.[1]

One can make almost anything the object of one's scrutiny-attention: events, individuals, states of affairs, actions, feelings, physical objects, etc. This is just as well if one is to know which individual has been made salient in relation to the use of a *Deictic Term*. For that will require attending to an individual on every occasion (i.e. the one made salient). But on some occasions, it will also require attending to an event or action (e.g. those which demonstrate the individual). On some occasions, it will also require attending to a state of affairs (e.g. the uniqueness of an individual which makes a demonstration unnecessary). On other occasions, it will require attending to some presupposition (e.g. the do-main-specification on an utterance which reduces the number of possible candidates). And on yet other occasions, it will require attending to pragmatic assumptions (e.g. those governing implicature in discourse which can make an individual the leading candidate). These are the ways that discriminating reference depends on scrutiny-attention.

There are a limited number of things to which one can be care-attentive. I cannot be care-attentive except towards activities, and my own activities at that. I cannot be care-attentive to my body, for example, since my body is not something I can *do attentively*. And while walking is something I can do attentively, I cannot do *your* walking attentively. Using a *Deictic Term* to refer is something about which one can be care-attentive. And it is something which the reference-maker

---

[1] See White (1964: 8–17).

must do attentively if they are to express their thoughts thereby. For reference-makers have the task of ensuring that the individual thought about is the same as the individual referred to. And, as we have found, deictic utterances are distinctive in the special requirements they place on accomplishing this task. Utterances of this sort refer to the individual made salient, irrespective of which individual the reference-maker is thinking about. So ensuring that what one says matches what one thinks requires aligning one's salience-making actions with the particular individual thought about. This is the way that expressive use depends on care-attention.

§ 86.   As with any *Deictic Term*, one must be care-attentive about one's use of *I*, and scrutiny-attentive to oneself as the referent, to express one's thinking with the expression. But these attentive tasks sit relatively lightly on *I* in the usual case, as we have discovered; the case in which the reference-maker is the utterer and salient as such. This ease of discriminability and expressive use immediately strikes one about *I*, at least when compared with most other *Deictic Terms*. (The attentive task is similarly light for spoken uses of terms like *This Very Speaker*; i.e. terms which share with *I* the fact that the individuals its uses express thoughts about are usually the individuals by whom the thoughts are uttered.) It might recall a similarly unusual ease relating to another facet of *I*'s meaning. For in examining inferential roles, we found that several uses of *I* could be recognized as co-referential without appeal to intra-sentential devices like anaphora or extra-sentential devices like identity-judgement. At the time, it was noted that this is likely to be because one is aware of one's own salience in ways that one is not aware of others. And we are now in a position to augment this suggestion. It is one's referential salience that is at issue; salience in relation to the various uses of *I*. And the awareness required to appreciate that salience enables one to be attentive, just as in expressive use.

In short, both the expressive use and inferential role of *I* depend on care- and scrutiny-attention. We should not confuse these aspects of *I*'s meaning, of course. For one concerns how an object thought about is identified as the one referred to; this is a link between thought and utterance which grounds the expressive use of *I*. While the other concerns how singular terms are known to be co-referential; this is a link between different uses which grounds the inferential role of *I*. But there is considerable common ground between expressive use and inferential role. Both aspects are characterized by what we may call attentive ease; the fact that, in the usual case, it is particularly easy for the reference-maker to carry out the attentive tasks (aligning one's salience-making actions; discriminating the referent; etc.) With regard to both, the question arises: how is it possible that, in the usual case, the attentive tasks are so easy to accomplish? We shall offer one response in what follows, once we have examined another facet of *Deictic Terms* which is similarly dependent on attention: communicative role. Then it will be possible to see that, in all these cases, the same solution suggests itself. There is a form of awareness which enables one to be care-attentive about one's own doings and scrutiny-attentive to oneself, in ways that one cannot be so attentive with others.

To conclude. We have found that the determinate reference of an *I*-use depends on the salience of its referent. And the discriminability of that referent to the reference-maker depends on attention to the circumstances of use, so that the salient individual can be recognized as such. The expressive use of *I* and other *Deictic Terms* is a topic that faces two ways. It looks back, to what determines reference. For uses have to be determinate to be discriminable. It also looks forward, to how such uses communicate thoughts. For uses have to be discriminable to be communicative.

11

Communicative Role

§ 87.   Heloise calls out, 'I must get out of here fast; I can't breathe,' when in the midst of a noisy crowd that is moving too slowly towards a cathedral's exit-door. Not knowing which individual is being referred to, an attendant asks, 'Who would like to get out of here fast?' Heloise replies by raising her hand and saying, 'I would.'

This is a common enough case, for *I* as for other *Deictic Terms*. It reveals central features of *I*'s communicative role, on which we should now focus. This aspect of the meaning of *I* is related to its expressive use, as we have often noted. For discriminability—knowing which individual is the referent—is at the heart of both. In the case described, *ex hypothesi*, merely saying *I* is insufficient for an audience to discriminate the referent. If Heloise had not accompanied her uses of *I* with a demonstration, over and above mere enunciation, the audience's attention would not have been drawn to the one particular item referred to, and the possibility of misidentification would not have been averted.

How significant is the communicative role of a singular term in relation to other aspects of its meaning? In one sense, priority of purpose, its significance is primary. For, ultimately, it is in order to communicate what individuals are thinking that singular terms fulfil their referential function and occur in sentences with expressive use. This is a position with support across the board.[1] In another sense, priority of elucidation, its significance is subordinate. For a singular term must fulfil its referential function and have an expressive use if it is to communicate thoughts. But the converse does not hold. Our task is elucidation, and we have already investigated the referential function and expressive use of *I*. So we are in the happy position of having already elucidated much of what is necessary for its communicative role.

WHAT COMMUNICATIVE ROLE REQUIRES

§ 88.   *I* is a *Deictic Term* in its communicative role, just as in all other aspects of its meaning. If an *I*-use is to occur in sentences which communicate thoughts, the

---

[1] See Wittgenstein (1958: §§ 1–89); Strawson (1950: 11–18); Quine (1960: 5–8; 56); Davidson (1984: *passim*); Searle (1969: 79); Evans (1982: 143–5); McDowell (1998: 136–43).

salient individual in relation to that use must be made discriminable to its audience, by demonstration or some other means.

The cathedral case draws attention to three main points specific to communicative role. First, the reference-maker for a *Deictic Term* needs to be attentive in many ways, the audience in few. In this sense, the audience is fortunate. For it is up to Heloise, not the cathedral attendant, to ensure that the use of a *Deictic Term* refers. And it is Heloise, not the attendant, whose salience-making actions must single out whichever individual corresponds to the particular one thought about. The reference-maker alone is faced with these particular attentive tasks.

In another sense, however, the audience is considerably less fortunate. For the audience needs to know whether the deictic use refers, and which individual it refers to, if it is to understand the sentences in which the terms occur. And the reference-maker is usually in a better position to discriminate reference. So this is the second point: the reference-maker is more fortunate than the audience in various ways. For example, he is usually in receipt of more information relevant to the discriminating task. This information is available to others, but it is particularly prominent and more easily selected for one focused throughout on the referring task. Moreover, the reference-maker has access to information denied to others; information gained through various sorts of bodily awareness proper to himself (we shall investigate proprioception at length below). This is not to deny that an audience is occasionally in a position to correct the reference-maker. Seeing Heloise's demonstration, Abelard would have known which building was referred to when she said, 'This is Notre-Dame,' and carelessly pointed at the royal palace. But such occasions are rare for the reasons just given.

Being dependent on less, and lower-grade, information, it is not surprising that the audience often needs auxiliary means if it is to discriminate deictic reference. This will usually take the form of a demonstration, as in the case of Heloise and the cathedral attendant. This is the third point. An individual may have been made referentially salient without such means. But the audience is likely to be ignorant of any of the number of conditions that make this the case. For the audience may be unaware of various facts that make the individual unique: some (implicit or explicit) domain-restriction; the existence of just one candidate of a certain kind within that domain; the features of surrounding discourse, or of the perceptual field, which make one individual the leading candidate; and so on. Lacking this knowledge, in whole or in part, the audience will need demonstration to know which individual has been referred to.

WHAT ROLES DEMONSTRATION PLAYS

§ 89.   Demonstrations play a crucial part in the communicative role of *Deictic Terms*. This has been the cause of considerable confusion about the nature and purpose of demonstration. For it has made it easy to ignore the fact that demonstrations play different roles elsewhere in the meaning of *Deictic Terms*. So our understanding of other aspects of their meaning has been affected. And the results are particularly marked in the case of *I*. Indeed, confusion about demonstration largely accounts for the failure to recognize *I* as a *Deictic Term*, failure that survives destruction of the three myths. So this is an appropriate place to show how our findings resolve the issues arising.

We have already met with one effect of confusion about demonstration; one that can now be related directly to the communicative role of *Deictic Terms*. Chapter 8 noted that such expressions are commonly misdefined as those whose uses *refer by* demonstration. This distorts our view of terms like *You*, *He/She*, and *This/That*, not just *I*. For the reference of all these terms is determined not by demonstration but by the making-salient of an individual. At the time, we noted that the mistake occurs when the outcome (i.e. referential salience) is taken for the means sometimes needed to achieve it (i.e. demonstration). The one may innocently be substituted for the other in synecdoche. But it is far from innocent to confuse the two in definition. At that point, we had no explanation of why it is so common to make this mistake. Now, perhaps, we do. For, as we have seen, demonstrations play a constant and crucial part in the communicative role of *Deictic Terms*. So it is understandably tempting to suppose that they are criterial of the terms; that they are 'the mark' of the deictic.

Further confusions over demonstration explain failures to perceive the character of *Deictic Terms* in general and of *I* in particular. Some claim that demonstration plays a standard role in all aspects of meaning; others that it plays no role in any aspect of meaning. Both positions have been endorsed by Kaplan at different times. Some claim that demonstration accompanies every deictic use of a term and that it is relevant to that use; others that its accompaniment is merely for emphasis and hence irrelevant. Again, Kaplan has held both positions. Some deny that whatever demonstrations do accompany *I* play the same role as those accompanying other *Deictic Terms* (e.g. Hacker). Others that it is the same role, but an unnecessary one (e.g. Kaplan). Some deny that such demonstrations have the same form in the two cases (e.g. Hacker). Finally, some take Wittgenstein's discussion of pointing to show that demonstrations accompanying *I* are too hard to interpret for us to know what role they might have. Others would be correct to point out that his comments are not directly relevant to present concerns. Wittgenstein's focus is not on pointing *per se* but on pointing as an example of one way of giving the definition of words (ostensive definition). This is certainly not our present concern. We may assume that the definitions of *I*, *He/She*, *This/That*, and so on are known. The question to which pointing is relevant is how these terms single out a particular object on occasions of use.[2]

---

[2] Kaplan (1989: 491; 582–4); Hacker (1993: 224); Wittgenstein (1958: particularly §§ 28–38).

§ 90.   In order to deal with the other objections, it will be helpful first to review in summary form what we now know to be the case about demonstration. By establishing precise differences between the roles required of demonstration in the various aspects of *I*'s meaning, it will be possible to spot and guard against the temptations to confuse those roles.

Demonstrations play a subsidiary role in referential function. Like any singular term, *Deictic Terms* carry out that function by providing positive answers to the 'which?' question. In their case, specifically, this means making an individual salient relative to the use. So it is salience which is the determinant of such terms. Demonstrations will occasionally be necessary to achieve salience, but there are a variety of other means which make this circumstance comparatively rare.

Demonstrations play a more significant role with regard to expressive use. In order to use singular terms to express their thoughts, reference-makers need to know what the positive answer to the 'which?' question is. And in the case of *Deictic Terms*, that means knowing which individual has been made salient. On all occasions where the individual has been made salient by being demonstrated, reference-makers need to know which is the demonstrated individual. On some occasions, the individual has been made salient by other means of which the reference-maker is aware. Then they do not rely on demonstrations. Finally, on some occasions, the individual has been made salient by other means of which the reference-maker is not aware. And then they may have to rely on an auxiliary demonstration. Because particular *Deictic Terms* differ with respect to meaning, they differ in their dependence on demonstration. So this third scenario is standard in the use of *Deictic Terms* like *This F* and *That F*; common for *This* and *That*; unusual for *He/She*; exceptional for *You*; and most rare for *I* (as the five bishops case demonstrated). It is a scenario in which the individual made salient is the individual demonstrated. But it is not by being demonstrated that the individual is salient. It is by being demonstrated that the individual is discriminable to the reference-maker. In short: determinacy does not depend on demonstration, but discriminability for the reference-maker—and hence expressive use—does.

Demonstrations are most influential in the communicative role of *Deictic Terms*. In order to use singular terms to communicate thoughts, the audience needs to be acquainted with the positive answer to the 'which?' question. That means knowing which individual has been made salient if the attempt is being made with the use of a *Deictic Term*. On all occasions where the individual has been made salient by being demonstrated, the audience needs to know which is the demonstrated individual. On most occasions where the reference-maker needs a demonstration to discriminate the referent, the audience will too. And on very many occasions where demonstration is unnecessary for any other purpose, it is necessary if the audience is to discriminate the referent. There is a similar ordering of *Deictic Terms* here, though the need for demonstration is greater in every case. So it is standard for *Deictic Terms* like *This* and *That*; common for *He/She* and *This*

F/That F; and unusual for *You* and *I* (as the cathedral case demonstrated). To describe this scenario more precisely. The individual made salient is the individual demonstrated. But it is not by being demonstrated that it is either salient or made discriminable to the reference-maker. It is by being demonstrated that it is discriminable to the audience. In short: neither determinacy nor discriminability for the reference-maker depend on demonstration, but discriminability for the audience—and hence communicative role—does.

§ 91.   So we now have sufficient resources to resolve the various difficulties associated with demonstration.

First, demonstration does not play a standard role in all aspects of the meaning of *Deictic Terms* in general or of *I* in particular. But it does play a role in each, helping to make an individual salient (referential role), to make the salient individual discriminable as such to the reference-maker (expressive use), and to the audience (communicative role).

Second, demonstration does not accompany every deictic use of a term. But, when it does, its roles are relevant for the reasons just given and hence not merely emphatic. Peter Hacker claims that someone using *Deictic Terms* gestures to avert misidentification and that no gesture produced with a use of *I* serves this purpose.[3] Both claims are false. On the one hand, someone may accompany their use of a *Deictic Term* with a gesture even if they have no communicative purpose in mind, and hence no need to avert misidentification. On the other hand, someone may gesture while using *I* precisely to avert misidentification, even when there is no *other* need for the demonstration. Such is the case with Heloise and the cathedral attendant. She raised her hand precisely to avert the possibility that someone else be (mis)identified as the person who said *I*. She was not *simply* drawing attention to herself. She was trying to have the correct object picked out from among others so as to have it correctly discriminated as the referent of *I*—just as her pointing gesture when saying, 'This is Notre-Dame,' was designed to pick out the correct object as the referent of *This*. Without demonstration, the audience could be in doubt about is, or misidentify, the referent.

Third, the demonstrations accompanying *I* play the same role as those accompanying other terms. As we have noted, there is less call for demonstration to carry out the various aspects of *I*'s meaning. But there is significant variation here between the various *Deictic Terms* even if we ignore *I*.

Fourth, the demonstrations accompanying *I* have the same *general* form as those accompanying other terms: they are all ostensive gestures with a referential function. As we found, demonstrations are only partly conventionalized gestures (unlike iconic movements). So there is no *specific* form for a demonstration accompanying any *Deictic Term* to have or to lack. Heloise raises her hand in the cathedral case. This differs in its specific form from pointing with one's finger. But both differ from other specific forms that have referential, expressive, or

---

[3] Hacker (1993: 224).

communicative roles in relation to deictic usage. For example: pointing with one's foot; nodding one's head in a certain direction; using non-bodily devices like pointing signs; exaggerating the mode of utterance or its medium; manipulating the context. Any demonstration accompanying uses of *I* directs us to the user rather than to some other object. But the same is true of other *Deictic Terms*. Suppose you are one of the speakers at a noisy demonstration, and someone from the crowd asks, 'which speaker has something coherent to say?' You might answer, 'this one,' and raise your hand. Demonstrations accompanying uses of *I* are of the same general kind as those accompanying other *Deictic Terms*.

Finally, accounting for the ways we are able to interpret demonstration is indeed complex, but the difficulties arising are not exclusive to the use of *I*. They are general to the class of *Deictic Terms*. Consider, for example, the stage-setting required to recognize Heloise's hand-raising. Seeing this action as a *gesture* at all is an achievement, let alone being able to pick out the particular item gestured *at* by a bare form of words and accompanying arm movement. But it is no peculiarity of the term *I* that we have to interpret any such demonstrations. For we have also had to learn to interpret the paradigm ostensive use—a pointing finger accompanying uses of *That*—as tracing out in the opposite direction an imaginary shortest line of solid discrete points between two items which would effect direct contiguity (to some approximation whose permissibility-settings in different situations themselves require learning and stage-setting). It is no peculiarity of *I* that the interpretation given will contain features particular to the term. For the same is true of any demonstration accompanying uses of other *Deictic Terms*. Only salient males/females are relevant to demonstrations accompanying *He/She*, for example.

WHY THE ATTENTIVE TASKS CAN BE EASY

§ 92.   The communicative role of *I* depends on care- and scrutiny-attention. The same is true of its expressive use and inferential role, as we found in previous chapters. We have frequently remarked on the phenomenon of attentive ease; the fact it is particularly easy for the reference-maker to carry out the attentive tasks in the usual case of *I*-use (aligning their salience-making actions; discriminating the referent; etc.)

Unfortunately, attentive ease has been the cause of no less confusion than the nature and purpose of demonstration. And again, this confusion has contributed to the general failure to recognize *I* as a *Deictic Term*, a failure that survives destruction of the three myths. In fact, the explanation of attentive ease is quite simple. There are forms of awareness which enable one to be care-attentive about one's own doings and scrutiny-attentive to oneself, in ways that one cannot be so attentive with others. Seeing why will enable us to complete our investigations into *I*, and particularly its inferential role, expressive use, and communicative role.

To count as a solution to the question of attentive ease, a form of awareness would have to explain why the attentive tasks are easier to accomplish in the usual case of *I*-use than in the usual case of other *Deictic Terms* and in unusual cases of *I*-use. So we should start by noting what is comparable and what is not.

In usual cases of *I*-use, the referent is a corporeal object. By this, I mean a material object located in space and time (extended in the former; persisting in the latter) which is either impenetrably solid or force-exerting. 'Material object', as is standard, means an item which does not exist in virtue of being perceived; which cannot be in its entirety located in two places at one time; which possibly moves; which is the nexus of certain causal relations; which is internally causally connected over time, having an inherent tendency to retain its current properties or to change them in various ways; and which, externally, is the possible cause of various kinds of phenomena as a consequence of being interrelated with other objects.[4] Being impenetrably solid is Locke's criterion: 'impenetrability ... of all other, seems the idea most intimately connected with, and essential to body.' Being force-exerting is Leibniz's criterion: 'the essence of a body ... is to be located in the power of acting and resisting alone.'[5] I have made the definition disjunctive to avoid deciding on the issue. And it is really not necessary to do so, given that our subject is usual cases of *I*-use. For whether or not the primary properties of mass, weight, position, size, shape, and motion must be ascribable to an item if it is to count as a *body* (as the Lockean account would suggest), they are certainly necessary if that item is to count as the utterer and perceptibly salient as such.

Moreover, it is *as* a corporeal object that the referent is perceptible in usual cases of *I*-use. The same is true of the usual cases in which other *Deictic Terms* are used. It is usual with *I* and common with other *Deictic Terms* that it is the reference-maker who makes an individual salient, and that the only action necessary to accomplish this is the act of using the term, of uttering it. *I* differs in its usual cases in that the individual making the reference is the individual referred to, and in that the individual expressing the thought is the individual thought about.

§ 93. So we now have an idea of what form of awareness would explain attentive ease: being perceptually aware of oneself as a corporeal object engaging in action, and as the subject of that awareness, the one perceiving as well as being perceived.

Awareness of this sort explains what is common between the use of *I* and of other *Deictic Terms*. For in both cases attentiveness depends on a form of awareness that is perceptual; the object of that awareness is corporeal; using the

---

[4] See Hoffman and Rosenkrantz (1997: 4–5); Campbell (1994: 25–36).
[5] Locke (1689: ii. iv. 1); Leibniz (1686: 82).

term to refer requires engaging in action; and using the term to express thoughts requires identifying the individual thought about with the individual referred to. But it also explains what is different about usual cases of *I*-use; namely, attentive ease. For it is a form of awareness that makes identifying the individual thought about with the individual referred to peculiarly straightforward. It is an awareness of the same individual as its object and its subject; i.e. oneself. And this is just what is required for attentiveness in the usual case: identifying the same individual as the referent and the reference-maker; i.e. oneself.

Moreover, awareness of this sort is constant and ubiquitous for most *I*-users. To take the cases literally and not just immediately to hand: my typing this chapter; your turning the pages of this book. I am pressing my fingertips down onto the keyboard, hitting the keys; you are pressing the sides of your finger against the page, moving it from right to left. It is by touching keys and page that we move them. So focus on the awareness associated with touch. Assuming we are not numb and that our fingers are sensitive, this awareness satisfies all the conditions required: perceptual awareness of oneself as a corporeal object engaging in action and as the subject of that awareness. For this awareness is proprioceptive, and hence awareness of oneself as its subject, not merely its object. And it is perceptual awareness of a corporeal object engaged in action, being formed from the various bodily sensations associated with tactile contact and the application of pressure.

Sensitivity and the absence of numbness are vital to the point, which recalls the Nonsense Question Phenomenon (*Nonsense*) examined in Chapter 3. Compare two situations in which I assert, 'my fingers are pressing down on the keyboard'. In the first case, say my fingers are numb and I am constrained to look only at a closed-circuit television screen. My assertion rests on my seeing a person I take to be me on this screen. Now I may know what *someone's* fingers are doing, but be wrong about whose they are—the figure I see is an actor made up to look like me. In the second case, my fingers are sensitive, I am not restrained, and my assertion rests on the various bodily sensations associated with tactile contact and pressure-exertion. It is the second case we are interested in. Here, it would make no sense to say, 'someone's fingers are pressing down on the keyboard, but is it me?'

We discover the solid and force-exerting properties of the keys and page touched by recognizing that we are not penetrating them. And what gives us access to this information is the simultaneous awareness of our own bodies as impenetrably solid and force-exerting. The point is that the sensations which we experience in touching the keyboard or the pages of a book are intrinsically located in our bodies as spatio-temporally located, force-exerting, and impenetrably solid objects. In having the sensations, therefore, we are aware of ourselves as corporeal objects. This is to draw attention to a point others have remarked on: as O'Shaughnessy says: 'the space and solidity of our bodies provides the access to the space and solidity of other bodies.'[6]

---

[6] O'Shaughnessy (1989: 38).

This claim might be vulnerable to attack if it were merely a matter of what we learn through sensations. But the sense of touch cannot be reduced to a matter of using sensations of contact as a means of access to some perceived item. It is bodily awareness that is the basic means of access. After all, say our fingers are numb. Nevertheless, we would find that they, one part of our bodies, could not be moved through this object (the keyboard; the page), which is another body. Our awareness that this is the case is certainly not given through any sensation of contact (because we are numb), but rather through perceiving our bodies as spatio-temporally located, force-exerting, and impenetrable items. That is, the body of which one is aware is experienced not only as subject, but also as the bearer of properties whose possession by some item makes it a corporeal object.

In short, we are proprioceptively aware of our corporeality in exercising it. And this finding can be turned to immediate account, explaining attentive ease for inferential role, expressive use, and communicative role in the usual cases of *I*-use. For in such cases, the reference-maker is the utterer and salient as such. Being salient as the utterer ensures that the *I*-use refers. So it is straightforward for the reference-maker to satisfy that part of the care-attentive task: making an individual salient. They need only utter the term. And being the utterer means that the reference-maker is exercising their corporeality. So it is also straightforward for the reference-maker to satisfy the scrutiny-attentive task: knowing which individual is made salient. Again, they need only utter the term.

There are numerous distinctive forms of proprioceptive bodily awareness associated with uttering: awareness of one's chest moving, the tingling of one's throat, the touch of tongue on palate, one's mouth filled with air, the resonance in one's head. And in each such way, the one uttering is peculiarly aware of himself as the utterer; perceptually aware of himself as a corporeal object engaging in action and as the subject of that awareness. So if uttering is enough to make one salient in relation to some use of *I*, then it is particularly easy to know one is its referent. For it is particularly easy to know one is uttering. Indeed, it is *peculiarly* easy to know one is its referent. For being proprioceptive, one can know one is uttering in ways that others cannot. (As noted in Chapter 3 above, we are dealing here with cases of knowledge; thus we are setting to one side deviant cases in which a subject A is wired up to another person's body, B, in such a way as to receive information of B in a characteristically proprioceptive way; i.e. cases in which one does *not* know that someone is speaking.)

The relevance of proprioception to accounts of the first person has been noted by a number of authors, of whom Evans is probably the most influential at present.[7] My own account of the phenomenon, its nature and role, differs markedly from his, in both the questions asked and the answers given. So it is worth noting here the major points of contrast. Evans interrogates proprioception to find out about the thoughts expressed by *I*, and so entitles his discussion 'self-

---

[7] Evans (1982: ch. 7).

identification'. Whereas I am appealing to proprioception to explain what puts one in a position to use *I* in inference, in expression, and in communication. The major difference in the answers given derives from the fact that Evans endorses *Independence*. His adherence to this doctrine determines his views on how proprioception functions and what role it plays in first-personal thinking. Whereas I regard *Independence* as a myth and as fundamental a feature of *Purism* as the other two myths.

§ 94.   Proprioceptive awareness accounts not only for attentive ease in discriminability, expressive use, and communicative role. It also explains such ease in the exercise of *I*'s inferential role. For it is a form of awareness that makes identifying several uses of *I* as co-referential equally peculiarly straightforward. It is an awareness of the same individual engaging in the same action. And this is just what is required for attentiveness to co-reference in the usual case: identifying the same individual as the referent of each use; i.e. oneself.

In inferential role, where recognizing several uses of *I* as co-referential is at issue, the particular kinds of attentiveness required may take the form of 'keeping track' of their referent. This notion has become familiar in the literature through the work of Gareth Evans, who described it as an ability 'having perceived an object, to identify later perceptions involving the same object over a period of continuous observation'. But if we ask what makes this possible, Evans is tentative: 'When a subject keeps track ... of an object ... I think we should regard the slightly varying forms of the judgements he is disposed to make as manifestations of a single persisting belief (a continuing acceptance of the same thought).'[8] The notion of 'slightly varying forms' of judgement is rather obscure and underdeveloped. Given a sufficiently long period of observation and the intervention of appropriate circumstances, the subject's original thought will have developed sufficiently to be no longer a variant and become another altogether.

John Campbell has extended the notion on this point, remarking that one might construct an inference about 'that building' while walking towards it in some situation where 'it is obvious in one's perception of it that it is but a single building over the period of observation'. But Campbell explicitly rules out the possibility of regarding *I*-uses as involving 'keeping track'.[9] He argues that

1. 'it is wholly obscure what keeping track of oneself would come to, anyhow.'
2. 'if there really were such a thing as keeping track of oneself through the course of an inference, then it ought to be possible for the inference to go wrong because of a failure to keep track. But there is no such possibility, so long as the first person is in use.'
3. 'one can perfectly well engage in first-personal thinking even though one is not in a position to keep track of oneself as a physical object.'[10]

---

[8] Evans (1982: 175; 236; see also 192–6).   [9] Campbell (1994: 86; 73–153).
[10] Campbell (1994: 90; 91; 90).

Now Campbell evidently supposes that keeping track of an object as the referent of one's use of terms over the course of an inference only makes sense if some 'unnoticed substitution' might replace that object with another.[11] If this were the only way in which reference, and hence the validity of an inference, were vulnerable, then, given the pragmatics of utterance, it would indeed be difficult to show that other *Deictic Terms* offer a model for *I*. But this is not the only way. For the reference of any *Deictic Term*, including *I*, is dependent for its determinacy on the salience of an individual relative to its use. Thus Campbell's three points can be met.

Pace (1), we can make perfect sense of 'keeping track' of oneself: it is doing what is required to ensure that an object, and the same object, is made salient throughout the course of an inference; and it is doing what is required to *know* which individual is salient (and hence referred to) throughout the course of an inference. Consider the five bishops case, in which a single speaker is producing several people's utterances and individual speakers are demonstrated by flashing lights at the time of utterance. I need to keep track of myself, to be aware of my movements and position as a physical thing within a certain changing context, to know that the light which is supposed to flash when it is I speaking is indeed continuing to signify me sufficiently when I produce tokens of *I*. And in the ordinary situation, where enunciation apparently provides sufficient salience, I nevertheless need to keep track of myself, to be aware of my movements, position, and general context, to know that it is indeed sufficient.

Pace (2), it is possible to fail to sustain salience of this kind—and thus fail to keep track of the referent while the first person is in use. This might mean that no individual is made salient (hence no individual is referred to). It certainly means that, if an object is made salient, one will not know which individual it is.

Pace (3), if salience is not sustained, one's uses of *I* will fail to refer—and reference-failure renders invalid the attempt to draw conclusions through inference using *I*.

Consequently, and *pace* Campbell's conclusion, the inferential role of *I* may be regarded as dependent on 'keeping track' of its referent. There is no logical difference here between the first person and other *Deictic Terms*. Employing *any* such term in its inferential role requires attentiveness. And we should understand what is required for uses of *I* in terms of 'keeping track' of its referent.

§ 95.   Some have denied that the particular form of awareness to which we have been appealing is possible—being perceptually aware of oneself as a corporeal object engaging in action, and as the subject of that awareness. Sydney Shoemaker is currently the foremost opponent, though it is not always clear at precisely what strength. Showing why his various arguments fail will serve to fix the position we have arrived at.

---

[11] Campbell (1994: 90; 93).

Shoemaker summarizes the aim of his discussion at one point as 'denying that *self-awareness* involves *any* sort of perception of oneself'.[12] But the position is untenable—and not just because catching sight of oneself in the mirror may count as providing one with perceptual awareness of oneself. For this choice of example gives the false impression that the phenomenon occurs only intermittently and for visual perception alone. In fact, of course, the phenomenon occurs almost continuously for corporeal subjects and involves the use of all five senses. It is possible to be perceptually aware of oneself as a corporeal object in much the same way as others perceive one. And *they* are not aware of one as the subject of their awareness.

Looking at my hand typing this sentence, for example, I am presented to myself in a certain way—I *see* and *hear* the corporeal object that is me much as others do and as I perceive them to be. True, I cannot see *all* of myself in this way. But then I cannot see all of other corporeal subjects when presented with them either. As I speak, I am presented to myself as an audible object much as others are to me. Taking a shower, I smell, taste, and touch myself as a corporeal object just as I might smell, taste, and touch others. I can observe myself in the way I observe others. It is even possible to be surprised that the object one is observing perceptually turns out to be oneself. Think of exploring by touch a solid object that turns out to have been, once one is fully awake, one's own numb arm; or of studying a distorted image of someone in a mirror that turns out to be oneself. Previously, I concentrated on kinds of perceptual awareness of oneself as a corporeal object that leave no room for surprise as to who it is that one is aware of; i.e. proprioception. But that special form of self-awareness only comes into focus when seen against the background of these other and various ways of being aware of oneself.

So we may legitimately be regarded as presented to ourselves 'as objects', thus fulfilling the conditions on perceptual self-awareness. Of course, we are not always overly conscious of this. It may be that too conscious a perceptual awareness of ourselves would impede us—in performing actions, for example. This is one of the few occasions where the common sense of 'self-consciousness' (i.e. akin to anxiety, embarrassment) points up a moral about perceptual self-awareness. Consider a stock example: the potter who is unable to turn the clay if he concentrates on himself, the corporeal object making a pot, rather than on the pot itself. It may be for similar reasons that we are usually not reflectively aware of the sensations universally and routinely present in bodily awareness.

§ 96.   Shoemaker has also denied that introspective self-awareness could count as perceptual awareness of oneself as a corporeal object. He offers eight conditions 'satisfied by ordinary kinds of sense perception' and claims that introspective self-awareness cannot meet them.[13] In fact, as I shall show, the cases I have described do meet these conditions.

---

[12] Shoemaker (1968: 89).
[13] Shoemaker (1986: 1994; 1996: 204). See Cassam (1995: 311–36); Martin (1995: 267–89). All references for claims (1)–(8) are to Shoemaker (1996: 204–6).

1. Sense perception must involve 'the operation of an organ of perception whose disposition is to some extent under the voluntary control of the subject.'

Now the kind of bodily awareness we are experiencing in typing or page-turning involves various receptors on the skin and below its surface, in the joints, internal organs, and muscles over which we have the kind of control characteristic, for example, of vision. Just as it is not entirely up to us what we see when positioned in a certain way, even though we are relatively free in how we position ourselves, so we are relatively free in what we do with our bodies (I am now touching the keyboard; but I could turn myself upside down; wholly immerse myself in water; etc.), even though it is not entirely up to us how we perceive ourselves to be once engaged in whatever activity or posture we have taken up.

2. Sense perception must involve sense-experiences 'that are distinct from the object of perception, and also distinct from the perceptual belief (if any) that is formed'.

I might have felt my fingertips to be a certain way, raw for example, and yet have no rawness. And, knowing the illusion of old, though I cannot help feeling raw, I would not then have believed that I was. More generally, bodily experiences are evidently belief-independent in the required sense. A veteran may feel his phantom leg to be a certain way and yet have no leg (no object of the experience). If I put my very-hot-hand into tepid water, I cannot help its feeling an icy-cold-hand to me, though I believe it is at worst by now a tepid-hand.

3. 'While sense perception provides one with awareness of facts, i.e. awareness *that* so and so is the case, it does this by means of awareness of objects.'

Our awareness that there is pressure on our fingers as we type-turn is explained by our awareness of the objects involved—our fingers, the keys, the page, their solidity, shape, location, impenetrability, etc.

4. 'The perception of objects standardly involves perception of their intrinsic, nonrelational properties. To perceive that this book is to the right of that one I must perceive ... intrinsic properties of the two books, e.g. their colors and shapes.'

Perceiving the shape of the keys at my fingertips, without seeing them, by touch alone, involves my perceiving the shape of my fingers and the hand to which they belong, information that is given through sensory-receptors in my fingers, their joints, and in skin-stretch. The same holds for your fingers on the page.

5. 'Objects of perception are potential objects of attention.'

Our pressured fingers are such objects. Without altering what one perceives, one can shift one's attention from it to the other fingers of one's hand which are lightly curled, compare them, and thereby enhance one's ability to gain differentiated knowledge about one's whole hand.

6. 'Perceptual beliefs are causally produced by the objects or states of affairs perceived, via a causal mechanism that normally produces beliefs that are true.'

If this is true of perception in general, then there is no reason to deny that it is true of the kind of bodily awareness here described.

7. 'The objects and states of affairs which the perception is of, and which it provides knowledge about, exist independently of the perceiving of them, and, with certain exceptions, independently of there being things with the capacity for perceiving them or being aware of them.'

Since Shoemaker explicitly allows that 'it is in principle possible for … human bodies to exist in this way', this condition is fulfilled by bodily awareness.

8. 'Sense perception affords "identification-information" about the object of perception … The provision of such information is involved in the "tracking" of the object over time, and its reidentification from one time to another.'

So tracking an object requires perceptual information. It is difficult to see how this can be a condition on something's counting as perceptual awareness. It would do if the passage were claiming that no awareness of an object, O, counts as perceptual awareness of that object unless the perceiver *does* use it to keep track of O. But this is untenable. We are continually being made perceptually aware of objects that we do not keep track of—because we cannot, need not, or choose not to. The passage might mean that no awareness of an object, O, counts as perceptual awareness of that object unless the perceiver *could* use it to keep track of O if the need arose. But it is compatible with this interpretation to claim that awareness of oneself as subject is both perceptual and quite independent of keeping track. For suppose we think that no awareness could count as of the subject if it involves keeping track of the self.[14] Nevertheless it might be perceptual. It can hardly be counted against a form of awareness that it does not satisfy a need that could not arise. So Shoemaker's various objections fail.

§ 97.   As we have seen, the care-attentive task of making an individual salient is easy to achieve in the usual case of *I*-use. But this is not surprising. It is exactly what we would expect, given our earlier investigations of the 'Nonsense Question Phenomenon' (Chapter 3). We found that one can know something has some property in such a way that it would be otiose to ask which thing has that property. And this phenomenon occurs in cases of self-ascription expressible using *I* (though not exclusively and not always). So it would be otiose on certain occasions to ask 'something is *F*; but is it *I* that am *F*?'

---

[14] See Cassam (1995: 329).

This phenomenon tells us little if anything about the meaning of *I*. For it arises with the use of other singular terms, including *Deictic Terms*. It reflects facts about the ways we can come to know things rather than about the term used to express what we know. And it can be explained by a pragmatic resolution on our parts not to mislead by asking a question when there is no doubt about the answer. So what explains this phenomenon is not a feature of the meaning of *I* itself, but of the forms of awareness on which uses of *I* often depend. Far from showing that *I* is independent of identification in the usual case, they represent the very forms of awareness on which *I* depends for identification in the usual case.

Until now, this picture has been left incomplete. For we had no explanation of these particular ways of coming to know things. More specifically, and maintaining our focus on *I*, we had no account of how a subject can self-ascribe some experience using *I* and be so certain about who it should be ascribed to. But we are now in a position to answer this question. For recall the forms of proprioceptive bodily awareness we have just investigated. It would be otiose in these circumstances to ask, 'something is typing, but is it me?' or 'something is turning the page, but is it me?' This is because one is aware of oneself on these occasions not simply as an object among others but as the subject of that awareness. These forms of awareness are available and drawn on in the usual cases of *I*-use. They help explain why the Nonsense Question Phenomenon arises for that term. This discharges the obligation acquired in Part I: to provide substance for the pragmatic explanation of why uses of *I* express thoughts when there is no likelihood of misidentifying what one has thought about.

§ 98.   A summary of this discussion of attentive ease enables us to represent its wider significance.

When using any *Deictic Term*, the reference-maker must accomplish various tasks. To refer with them means ensuring that an individual is made salient in relation to its use. To express one's thoughts and to communicate them using such terms means ensuring that the individual made salient is the same as the individual thought about. To use them inferentially means ensuring that one knows which individual is the referent. And these are attentive tasks for the reference-maker. They depend on exercising care- and scrutiny-attention. *I* does not differ from other *Deictic Terms* in these respects. Its various uses make the same demands of one's attentiveness.

In the usual case of *I*-use, the reference-maker finds carrying out these tasks very easy. But that is a different matter, and one that may be explained readily enough without appeal to the meaning of *I*. It is rather the special (i.e. proprioceptive) forms of awareness to which the reference-maker has access which explain this peculiarity. For *any* term is similarly affected when the salience of its referents is something of which the reference-maker can be proprioceptively aware. So access to this special information makes the attentive tasks similarly easy with uses of *This Body*, *This Speaker*, and *This F* (where *F* stands for any body part of which one is proprioceptively aware), for example. The appearance of the Nonsense

Question Phenomenon is sufficient evidence of this. Thus I can know that some *body* is tired or hungry or upside down by proprioceptive awareness of fatigue or the homeostatic condition or the workings of the vestibular system. I can know that some *hand* is clenched into a fist or some *head* is hot or some *speaker* is exercising its ability to speak by proprioceptive awareness of muscle tension and skin-stretch or temperature or resonance. And in these cases it will be unnecessary to wonder and otiose to ask; 'But is it *this body* which is tired, hungry, upside down; *this hand* which is clenched; *this head* which is hot; *this speaker* which is exercising its ability to speak?' These phenomena have a common explanation; not in the meaning of *I*, but in the forms of awareness available to users of *I*.

§ 99.   To conclude this part of the essay. The determinate reference of an *I*-use depends on the salience of its referent. And the discriminability of that referent to reference-maker and audience depends on attention to the circumstances of use, so that the salient individual can be recognized as such.

These findings are confirmed by our investigations in Part I, and give further substance to them in return. For we concluded there that one needs to identify oneself as the referent of an *I*-use to express one's thoughts using the term. But it is not as the user that one is referred to. Hence it is not as the user that one must identify oneself. And what we now know is entirely consistent with this earlier finding. We could go no further at that point because we did not know how one *is* referred to by an *I*-use.

The answer to this question has been provided in Part II: it is by being made salient relative to the utterance that one is referred to by an *I*-use. So we have now been able to fill the gaps left by the earlier enquiry. It is as the individual made salient that one must identify oneself in order to express one's thoughts using *I* and to make them communicable. And this depends on attentiveness to the circumstances of use.

Hence *I* is a *Deictic Term* in every aspect of its meaning: logical character; inferential role; referential function; expressive use; and communicative role.

12

Conclusion

§ 100.   Frege was right: *I* does indeed 'give rise to some questions'. Russell was overly optimistic in claiming that *I* must have 'some easily accessible meaning'. For it is not a straightforward expression like a *Pure Indexical*. But we should not swing too far in the opposite direction. Wittgenstein exaggerates in regarding *I*-use as 'one of the most misleading representational techniques in our language'. And Nietzsche was overly pessimistic in his pointedly anti-Cartesian remark: 'We set up a word at the point our ignorance begins, where we can see no further, for example the word *I* ... '[1] For the term belongs to a class of familiar referring expressions, and one that we have been able to elucidate. *I* is a *Deictic Term*, like the other singular personal pronouns, *You* and *He/She*.

This conclusion forces us to renounce at each point the current conception of *I*. But this should not discourage us. For the standard view is a fabrication, constructed out of myths and false doctrines. The purpose of this final chapter is to summarize the central arguments of the book, to list its main conclusions, and to learn what we can about its implications by examining the main routes out of the subject.

SUMMARY

§ 101.   The first part of this book showed that:

1. *I* is a genuine singular referring expression. It is a linguistic counter whose meaning indicates which one particular thing is relevant to the truth-value of the sentence containing it.
2. *I* is a device with varying referents (a 'variant device'). *I* may be used by anyone to refer to themselves; everyone who uses *I* can only refer to himself; context disambiguates which object is referred to by any use, not which term is in use.
3. *I* is not a proper name or descriptive term.
4. *I* is not a *Pure Indexical*; no rule entirely gives its meaning and sufficiently determines its reference in context.

---

[1] Russell (1914: 164); Wittgenstein (1930: 88); Nietzsche (1968: § 482).

5. When used to express thoughts, uses of *I* are not independent of identification of the individual thought about. As with other terms, it would be anti-conventional for the user to ask which individual is identified when there is no likelihood of misidentification.

6. Uses of *I* are secure against reference-failure; but this is not part of the meaning or logical character of the term.

These findings enabled us to discover which questions needed to be resolved if we were to account fully for the meaning of *I*:

(A) What are *Deictic Terms*?

(B) Is *I* a *Deictic Term*?

The second part of the book focused on providing answers to these questions. Dividing the enquiry into five aspects of the meaning of terms, it asked what is definitive of the logical character, inferential role, referential function, expressive use, and communicative role of the deictic use of expressions. And by investigating expressions like *You*, *He/She*, and *This/That*, it found that:

7. Expressions which satisfy the descriptions (*a*)–(*e*) are *Deictic Terms*:

(*a*) *Logical Character*: Deictic uses of a term refer to an individual salient in the extra-sentential context.

(*b*) *Inferential Role*: If sentences containing the deictic use of a term are to entail or be entailed by other sentences, they must refer to an individual salient in the extra-sentential context. The inferential role of deictic uses is irreducible to that of non-deictic uses.

(*c*) *Referential Function*: Deictic uses of a term achieve determinacy of reference by making individuals salient relative to the utterance.

(*d*) *Expressive Use*: Deictic uses of a term are discriminable to some reference-maker, *A*, if and only if the individual referred to is made salient to *A*. So in order to make one's thoughts expressive with such a use, one must identify the individual made salient by that use. This requires attentiveness to the circumstances of use.

(*e*) *Communicative Role*: Deictic uses of a term are discriminable to some audience, *A*, if and only if the individual referred to is made salient to *A*. So in order to make one's thoughts communicable with such a use, one must ensure that others can identify the individual made salient by that use. This requires attentiveness to the circumstances of use.

In all its uses, *I* was found to conform to each of these defining characteristics. Hence Question (B) has been answered in the affirmative and we have been able to add the most significant property to the list of known facts about *I*:

8. *I* is a *Deictic Term*.

§ 102.   Apart from (*7a–7e*), we have found that *I* shares certain other features with *Deictic Terms* like *You, He/She*, and *This (F)/That (F)*. Two are particularly worth recalling because they answer two questions left over from the first part of the book.

The first notable shared feature is

> (*f*) *Security:* In deictic uses of a term where the person uttering is the referent and salient as such, it is sufficient simply to engage in the act of using the term for its referential function to be achieved; uttering noises that count as meaningful uses of the term provides positive answer to the 'which?' question. Hence such uses are secure against reference-failure.

This feature helps answer

(C) Uses of *I* express thoughts where there is no likelihood of misidentifying what one has thought about. This may be explained pragmatically rather than by appeal to the meaning of the term. But what accounts for the phenomenon?

For '*Security*' is something *I* shares with other *Deictic Terms*. There is a subsidiary pragmatic feature which is not shared: it is standard for *I* and very few other such terms that the person uttering is the referent and salient as such. It is the conjunction of these two features that explains the peculiar security of *I* against reference-failure, answering Question (C) and adding to our understanding of (6). The security of *I* against reference-failure is not built into the meaning of the term. It is due to a fortunate conjunction of two features: one that is shared with any *Deictic Term*, and one that is peculiar to *I* and a few other expressions, like *This Very Speaker.*

§ 103.   The second shared feature of note is

> (*g*) *Identification:* In deictic uses of a term where the person uttering is the referent and salient as such, the reference-maker has additional means to achieve the attentive task of identification required for expressive use; it is possible to be proprioceptively aware that the individual made salient is the same as the individual thought about. Hence there is no likelihood of mis-identification in such uses.

This feature helps answer

(D) Uses of *I* are secure against reference-failure. This may be explained pragmatically rather than by appeal to the meaning of the term. But what accounts for the phenomenon?

Again, *I* shares '*Identification*' with other *Deictic Terms*. What is not shared with most is the same subsidiary pragmatic feature: that the person uttering is standardly the one referred to and salient as such. It is the conjunction of these features that explains the peculiar unlikelihood of misidentification in the use of *I*, answering Question (D) and adding to our understanding of (5). The unlikelihood of misidentification when using *I* reflects facts about the ways we can come to know things rather than about the term used to express what we know.

This explains what we have called the *Nonsense Question Phenomenon*. The phenomenon is due to a blend of several features, all of which are shared with other terms. The first feature is shared with any *Deictic Term*. There are attentive tasks on the expressive use of a referring term: the reference-maker needs to identify the individual referred to with the individual thought about. With *Deictic Terms*, that means identifying the individual made salient with the individual thought about. And this task is considerably eased when the salience of that individual is something of which the reference-maker can be proprioceptively aware. For proprioception offers additional and immediate means of identifying the individual referred to by the use. In these cases, misidentification is so unlikely that there would usually be no doubt about the answer to the identification question 'which individual is meant?' The second feature is common to all uses of language: there is a pragmatic resolution on our parts not to mislead by asking a question when there is no doubt about the answer. The third feature is peculiar to *I* and a few other expressions, like *This Very Speaker*: that the cases at issue are standard for these terms.

§ 104.   Seeing that *I* is a *Deictic Term* enables us to distinguish aspects of the meaning of the expression in fine detail. For individuating characteristics are thrown into relief against the common background.

Features (7*a*–7*g*) are *externally* characteristic to the class of *Deictic Terms*. They distinguish the deictic use of expressions from non-deictic uses and from non-*Deictic Terms* like proper names and definite descriptions. So they show what *I* has in common with other singular personal pronouns like *You* and *He/She*, and with deictic uses of *This (F)* and *That (F)*.

We have also discovered features which are *internally* characteristic. They distinguish among the expressions that have deictic uses. So they show what sets terms like *I*, *You*, *He/She*, and *This (F)/That (F)* apart from each other. Noting the following features, which are peculiar to a few such uses or even exclusive to *I* alone, has enabled us to discriminate the meaning of the term in finer detail.

> (*h*) *Kind Salience*: The uttering of a *Deictic Term* is sometimes sufficient
>   to make an individual salient because there is only one item of a
>   particular kind.

This distinguishes among *Deictic Terms* because the relevant kind depends on which such expression is being used: males with uses of *He*; females with *She*; utterers with *I*; addressees with *You*; proximate non-human individuals with *This*.

> (*i*) *Expressive Demonstration*: The uttering of a *Deictic Term* is sometimes not
>   sufficient to make the salient individual discriminable to the reference-
>   maker and so a demonstration is relied on.

This distinguishes among *Deictic Terms* because the phenomenon is most rare for *I*; exceptional for *You*; unusual for *He/She*; common for *This F* and *That F*; and standard for *This* and *That*.

> (*j*) *Communicative Demonstration*: The uttering of a *Deictic Term* is sometimes not sufficient to make the salient individual discriminable to the audience and so a demonstration is relied on.

The phenomenon is unusual for *I* and *You*; common for *He/She* and *This F/That F*; and standard for *This* and *That*.

> (*k*) *Standard Cases*: Some *Deictic Terms* have standard cases where the individual referred to is made salient in the act of uttering.

The standard case for *I* is one in which the person uttering is the one referred to. *He/She*, *This (F)*, and *That (F)* have no such standard cases.

> (*l*) *Obligatory Reference*: Some *Deictic Terms* have obligatory reference: they have no non-deictic uses.

I and *You* belong to this sub-group. Others follow *He/She*, having free reference on occasion, and both deictic and non-deictic uses.

> (*m*) *Mixed Terms*: Some *Deictic Terms* are conjoined with a sortal to create a 'mixed' term.

This describes expressions like *This F* and *That F*. Other such terms (like *This* and *That*) are not conjoined with a sortal but could be. Others again (like *I*, *You*, and *He/She*) are not so conjoined and could not be.

CONTRAST WITH THE LEADING THEORY

§ 105.   Further aspects of our findings come into view when we list the basic points of comparison and contrast with David Kaplan's highly influential theory of variant terms. The differences could not be more fundamental. Kaplan describes his position as 'based on two obvious principles' and we have rejected both.

Kaplan's *Principle 1* states, 'the referent of a *Pure Indexical* depends on the context, and the referent of a [*Deictic Term*] depends on the associated demonstration'.[2] But this attempt to distinguish *Deictic Terms* and *Pure Indexicals* fails. For Kaplan's paradigm *Pure Indexical* is *I*. And we have found that

9. The referent of a *Deictic Term* depends on referential salience, which need not itself be dependent on demonstration. The referent of a use of *I* depends on referential salience.

---

[2] Kaplan (1989: 492).

Relations with ostensive gesture *do* help distinguish *I* from certain *Deictic Terms*, as we have found. Examples include the sentence 'I was *this* tall.' But *pace* Kaplan, these relations distinguish *I* from certain uses of *This F* and *That F* rather than from all other *Deictic Terms*. Moreover, again in contrast to Kaplan's view, they distinguish by gesticulation rather than by demonstration. And finally, they distinguish between referential uses and ascriptive uses; not, as Kaplan claimed, between two different kinds of referential use.

Kaplan's *Principle 2* states that *Deictic Terms* and *Pure Indexicals* are both 'directly referential'. This is to say that their 'semantical *rules* provide *directly* that the referent in all possible circumstances is fixed to be the actual referent'. In the case of *Pure Indexicals*, of which the paradigm is *I*, this means that 'the linguistic rules which govern their use fully determine the referent for each context'.[3] But this attempt to connect *Deictic Terms* with *Pure Indexicals* fails even for the alleged paradigm case. As the demise of *Rule Theory* showed,

> 10. The linguistic rules governing the use of *I* do not fully determine the referent for each context.

Concerning demonstration, Kaplan has held three views, one consistently and two at different points in his career. *Consistent Kaplan* holds that demonstration is the mark of the deictic. What makes the use of a singular variant term count as deictic is that its reference is associated with a demonstration. He has held conflicting views about the *nature* of this association. *Early Kaplan* views *Deictic Terms* as those whose reference is determined by demonstration. *Late Kaplan* views *Deictic Terms* as those whose reference is 'externalized', or made manifest, by demonstration. It is the speaker's intentions which determine reference. Demonstrations themselves lack semantic significance. More precisely, the referent of uses of *Deictic Terms* is the perceived object which the speaker *intends to demonstrate* and on which he *directs his demonstration*. The speaker is free to produce gestures. But they will be 'a mere externalization of this inner intention'; 'an aid to communication, like speaking more slowly and loudly, but ... of no semantic significance'; 'there only to help *convey* an intention', to obtain 'accuracy [in] *communicating* what was said'.[4]

But each of these three positions is false, as we have found. *Pace Consistent Kaplan*,

> 11. What makes the use of a singular variant term count as deictic is that its reference is associated with (because determined by) referential salience. Since that use need not be associated with demonstration, it is not demonstration but referential salience which is the mark of the deictic.

---

[3] Kaplan (1989: 492–3).   [4] Kaplan (1989: 492; 582–4).

Pace Early Kaplan,

12. The reference of some uses of *Deictic Terms* is *not* dependent on demonstration but on utterance-relative uniqueness or on leading candidacy, given either the surrounding discourse or the perceptual environment.

Pace Late Kaplan,

13. The reference of some uses of *Deictic Terms is* dependent on demonstration; it is demonstration which secures their referential salience.

Consider uses of *He*, for example, where the speaker demonstrates one man when there are several present. What is said and done is sufficient to determine which among the things of a given kind the speaker is referring to. There is no *further* question about the speaker's intentions—'to which thing does the speaker *intend* to refer?' Some one thing has already been singled out as the referent. Conversely, if no deictic gesture had been used, no one thing would have been singled out *whatever* the speaker's intentions. Indeed, demonstration sometimes determines reference *in spite of* the speaker's intentions.

The example of Abelard and the birds was used earlier to make this point. Consider another example. My horse *Doorlatch* is in a race. As the horses thunder past for the finish, *Doorlatch* in the lead, I point and say, 'that's my horse!' Unfortunately, in my excitement, I have closed my eyes for an instant and my gesture has not quite kept track of the field. So, as I utter the sentence, my finger actually points to the leading contender, *Two-fingered Salute*. My friend says—and I agree, once the facts are made clear—'No; that [used anaphorically] was not *Doorlatch*.' If Late Kaplan's theory were correct, then *Doorlatch* should be the referent of my use of *That*. It is the perceived object I *intended to demonstrate* and on which I (unsuccessfully) *directed my demonstration*. But evidently this theory must be false. We cannot make sense of my friend's response unless *Two-fingered Salute* is the referent.

§ 106. Setting these basic contrasts with the heart of Kaplan's theory aside, there are good reasons why advocates of his approach should welcome our findings. For the inspiration for his account is the maintenance of a proper distinction between semantic and epistemic issues; the former are independent of the latter. And secondary features of Kaplan's accounts, both Early and Late, undermine the semantic/epistemic distinction. Whereas our findings show how to preserve semantic independence. This is a further positive result, and worth exploring a little.

Consistent Kaplan makes demonstration the mark of the deictic. So one question is immediately pressing: what *is* it about demonstration that justifies ascribing it significance of any sort, let alone of this criterial kind? With the findings of this book, of course, we can appeal to referential salience:

14. We are justified in ascribing (semantic) significance to demonstrations; on occasion, demonstrations secure referential salience, which in turn determines reference.

But Kaplan cannot give this answer. Demonstration is criterial for him rather than referential salience. So the order of justification would have to operate in reverse. And this leaves the significance of demonstrations quite unaccounted for.

The only other role demonstrations have which might justify the significance ascribed them is this: they make the reference of terms discriminable, to the reference-maker or to the audience. Now, as we have found, discriminability is an epistemic issue. It is about whether or not someone *knows* the positive answer to the 'which?' question. Whereas reference-determination is a semantic issue. It is about how terms *provide* this answer. So if we ask *why* demonstration plays a defining role, and Kaplan must appeal to its epistemic function in his answer, then epistemic properties are being made to justify the ascription of semantic features. This is disastrous to Kaplan's scheme because it obliterates the chances of achieving what motivated him: the independence of semantics from epistemic features.

It was precisely discomfort with this prioritizing of the epistemic in *Early Kaplan* that persuaded him to change his position radically, to *Late Kaplan*. But the discomfort is not relieved thereby. For Kaplan retains the view that demonstration is the mark of the deictic. So the significance attributed to demonstration still has to be explained, and appeal to referential salience is still blocked. Since the only alternative is to ground that significance in the epistemic value of demonstration (i.e. in its contribution to discriminability), Kaplan is forced to deny that the significance of demonstration is semantic. Hence he arrived at *Late Kaplan*. But this drastic alteration of his earlier position is radical in exactly the wrong way. On the one hand, *Late Kaplan* denies what we have good reason to assert: it is clear that demonstrations are semantically significant since they secure the referential salience which determines reference. And on the other hand, *Late Kaplan* asserts what we have good reason to deny: it is at the least peculiar (probably just plain contradictory) to claim that *Deictic Terms* count as such in virtue of something that is accorded no semantic significance.

So how can we explain the significance of demonstration while maintaining a proper distinction between the semantic and epistemic features of the terms in question? The solution lies in denying that demonstration is the mark of the deictic. And we are able to do so for reasons that escape being ad hoc. For the denial is precisely what our independent findings, (9)–(14), state anyway. Referential salience is what makes the use of a term deictic. Demonstrations have deep semantic significance. We can explain that significance by appeal to referential salience: demonstrations help secure referential salience for some uses of *Deictic Terms*, which in turn determines their reference. And we can explain all these features without appeal to epistemic properties, to the role of demonstration in effecting discriminability, to what enables someone to *know* the positive answer to the 'which?' question. For in explaining the significance of demonstrations, we have only needed to appeal to reference-determination. And reference-determination is a semantic issue, about how terms *provide* a positive answer to the 'which?' question.

In short, we maintain the independence of semantic features by denying that demonstration is the mark of the deictic. In this way, we preserve the inspiration behind Kaplan's account by rejecting its heart.

WHERE THE FINDINGS LEAD

§ 107.   Every exit is an entrance somewhere else. This is as true of philosophical subjects whose dimensions are abstract as it is of physical rooms in the concreteness of spatial location. Indeed, the traffic in information is two-way. For there is usually as much to be learnt about the region one has just left from the region to which it leads as there is about the space to which one is given access by the space which grants it.

One route out of our present subject is historical. Assumptions and conjectures about the meaning of *I* ground much of the most significant work in philosophy. As a result of our enquiry, we can see which such views are correct, which assumptions are justified, which conjectures stand up to scrutiny. Very few, as it happens. For as we saw, the history of philosophy is riddled with appeal to the three doctrines: *The Guarantee, Independence,* and *Rule Theory.* And these doctrines have turned out to be myths.

Three examples will suffice. Descartes was right to regard *I* as a referring term, but wrong to assume its uses are logically guaranteed against reference-failure. One situation in which it is conceivable that an *I*-use should fail to refer is precisely that in which the meditator finds himself at the end of the doubting process. For in doubting away the existence of all but the barest contents of his present consciousness, the resources for making any item salient are lacking. This is disastrous to Descartes's purposes, of course. For whatever substance and logical form we give to the *Cogito* argument, it must at least have these properties: that the statements representing its premises and conclusion be formed by concatenating *I* with a predicate. So Descartes offers no release from the doubting process unless *I*-uses refer in the meditator's situation. And if there is no means of making the correct item salient, such uses could not refer.

A second example: Hume's notorious denial that we have an idea corresponding to the self. Crucial to his position is the claim that we do not refer to something simple, continued, and individual when we express thoughts about ourselves using *I*. But his argument for this claim depends on an assumption that we now see to be false: that one can express such thoughts without identifying what is being referred to.

Finally, Kant thought that *I* is an expression that can serve as a completely empty term, one without referential or ascriptive significance. This was crucial to his project, since he made the application of such *I*-uses necessary to self-ascription and hence to the possibility of experience. But, as we have found, *I* is in each of its uses a referring expression. There is no expression which might furnish the empty *I*-uses Kant requires.

§ 108.   So the main historical routes out of our present subject turn out to be dead ends. But it is misleading to emphasize this negative result when the constructive opportunities are so much more significant. As Chapter 1 made clear, philosophers have built a great deal on the meaning of *I*. Now that we have the chance of gaining considerable knowledge about that meaning, the prospects of building a good deal more securely on these foundations are good. To support this claim, I shall conclude with some sketches of ways we might move forward from the findings of this book.

Consider first how we should go about elucidating first-personal thinking. Linguistic expression and behaviour give access to, demonstrate, and indicate what is thought. Our ordinary practice is heavily and unavoidably committed to this. When I produce utterances that you understand, my linguistic labours let you know what (that, how, why) I am thinking. And there is considerable theoretical support for this order of elucidation. The semantic information content of singularly referring statements (i.e. whatever makes them semantically evaluable) corresponds to the content of thoughts about some one thing among others in the world. In both cases, it is that content which is asserted, which is assessable as true or false, and whose truth-value depends on that one thing referred to or thought about. Thus the correspondence between singular thought and singular reference is sufficiently deep to justify elucidating the former by the semantic conditions governing the latter.

This conclusion holds independently of whether we think language is *prior* to thought in terms of the elucidation of each; or whether we suppose thought is *dependent* on language in any significant sense (that thought could not exist without language, or that there could not be some particular thought without some particular linguistic entity—where this 'could' might be logical, metaphysical, or even causal); or whether we hold that singular thoughts may be *wholly*—or, indeed, *only*—elucidated by reference to the semantics of the terms expressing them. Nor need we accept a host of alternative explanations about what general relation must exist between language and thought to make it true that the semantics of singular terms elucidates the thoughts they express.

Moving from the general to the particular, we should elucidate first-personal thinking by appeal to what we know about *I*. *I* is a *Deictic Term*, as we have found. So there is excellent reason to treat first-personal thinking as a kind of deictic thinking. This has deep implications. To note just one: deictic thinking has usually been regarded as the best evidence for anti-individualism and externalism about the contents of thought. But, notoriously, finding a cogent epistemology of self-knowledge that is consistent with these positions has eluded theorists. If first-personal thinking, being deictic, itself demands an anti-individualist and externalist construal, then we have a principled reason for supposing that a consistent epistemology must be available in advance of any cogent proposal. For the first-personal thoughts expressing self-knowledge are deictic and thus as the externalist construes them. So we would expect that whatever correctly accounts for self-knowledge must at least be consistent with externalism.

§ 109.   When we consider particular examples of self-knowledge, the significance of regarding *I* as a *Deictic Term* takes on greater specificity. Consider, for example, the kinds of self-knowledge manifest in practical reasoning. Much of what we do depends on judgements and inferences about the future, present, and past that provide us with certain kinds of reason for what we do; reasons that motivate. (I leave it open whether we should regard motivating reasons and normative reasons as two different kinds of reason (e.g. Smith; Parfit), or a single type occurring in two different kinds of context (e.g. Dancy).[5]) There may be facts that provide one with reason to φ, but they will not count as reasons sufficient to motivate one to φ, or to explain why one φ-ed, unless they provide *one's own* reasons for φ-ing. And to provide one's own reasons for φ-ing plausibly requires the self-conscious self-ascription of features of the situation in which one finds oneself.

The following are examples of such motivating judgements: '*I* would not cope with prison, so *I* should not risk arrest'; '*I* hear the Police, so *I* had better run'; '*I* was not prosecuted, so *I* am free to go.' Such judgements are particularly relevant to agency, to explaining why someone is motivated to act in some way and for some reason. Explaining these fundamental aspects of our engagement with the world and with each other requires clarity about *I*, for *I* is *the* device of self-conscious self-ascription. And the fact that *I* is a *Deictic Term* has implications here. For example, just to count as the referent of such a term requires that one be the salient individual. So making judgements using *I*, judging of situations including oneself, counting oneself as having reason to act, requires knowing which individual is salient and identifying that individual as oneself, the one deliberating over these various motives and reasons.

The importance being accorded to the first person here is quite different from that 'magic ... in the pronoun *my*' which Godwin famously saw through.[6] He asked what special force attaches to the first person 'that should justify us in overturning the decisions of impartial truth'. So his target was the supposed rationality of personal concern, a set of interests which are distinct from moral constraints and may oppose them.[7] But the point I am making has nothing to do with partiality. To see why, suppose we deny that believing '*I* am in such-and-such a situation, and φ-ing would resolve things satisfactorily *for me*' gives one a *special*

---

[5] Smith (1994); Parfit (1997); Dancy (2000: in particular, the appendix to ch. 1).
[6] Godwin (1798: 170).   [7] See Crisp (1997: 145).

or *good* or *justifying* reason to φ *at all*. This would nevertheless be perfectly consistent with the conclusion I do wish to draw: that without some such self-conscious self-ascription of features of the situation, one would not be *motivated* to φ at all. Indeed, being motivated to act *impartially* requires self-conscious self-ascription of some sort. No matter how strongly held my impartial principles of action are, they will not motivate me to φ in a certain situation unless I recognize that it is *I* who am in a situation such that *my* φ-ing would benefit others to such a degree that, given what *I* believe (or ought rationally to believe, on the evidence), *I* should φ.

Consider another example of the significance of *I*: its role in the kinds of self-knowledge made manifest in belief-acquisition and -ascription. Much of what we believe is self-ascriptive; it involves thinking of things as standing in relation to ourselves. This is obvious in the case of your believing that you are one foot from this book. But it may be that your having a belief about anything (an object, property, event, state of affairs, etc.) is to think of it as related to you in some particular way. This would follow for a variety of reasons. Because Kant was right: having beliefs involves being able to attach the 'I think' to them. Because my believing of this apple that it is tasty or green is to self-ascribe eating or looking at one thing (this apple) tasty and green. Because my believing that Abelard wrote the *Sic et Non* is to self-ascribe the property of living in one of the possible worlds of which that proposition is true. In each case, accounting for belief requires an account of self-ascription. And seeing that *I* is a *Deictic Term* will be of fundamental importance here, for *I* is *the* device of self-ascription.

In short, elucidating the referential role and expressive use of *I* is necessary if we are to gain an adequate account of self-knowledge, and of the many abilities and capacities which depend directly on self-knowledge, such as acting for reasons. So we have gained something by that elucidation: learning that *I* is a *Deictic Term*. We will gain more with the next step: exploring what that fact implies about the thoughts and knowledge *I* expresses. These are instances of a general expectation. *I* is a slender capital, but one that will support much once knowledge of its foundations is secured. That preliminary task being accomplished, we should look to the superstructure.

APPENDIX 1

Analytic Table of Contents

§ 10. On the standard view (*Purism*), the meaning of *I* is given by the simple rule that sufficiently determines its reference (*Rule Theory*). *Rule Theory, The Guarantee,* and *Independence* are three mutually supportive doctrines.

2   Questions of Reference

§ 11. What sufficiently determines the reference of *I*-uses? *Rule Theory* answers: its definition ('simple rule') in context.

What is Rule Theory?

§ 12. Special terms are introduced: 'Referent'; 'Content'; 'Determinant'; 'Context'; 'Definition'; 'Demonstration'.

§ 13. *Rule Theory* is precisely formulated using the special terms. Differences between the present arguments and earlier criticisms of *Rule Theory.*

What is the simple rule?

§ 14. Current literature offers a budget with significant internal differences.

What does the simple rule mean?

§ 15. The 'simple rule' is ambiguous, its domain is unspecified, and its reference is not unique.

What does the simple rule determine?

§ 16. 'User' and 'producer' are insufficiently determinate; cases in which they conflict.

§ 17. Problems arise in making 'user' and 'producer' determinate.

§ 18. Problems arise in appealing to underlying or background rules to make the 'simple rule' determinate.

What is the context?

§ 19. Disagreement over whether context is a set of features of the occasion of use or of the occasion in which the user intends the use to be interpreted. The *Answering Machine Paradox.*

§ 20. Problems with using context to make the 'simple rule' determinate.

What role does the simple rule have?

§ 21. The 'simple rule' is only problematic if it is given the role *Rule Theory* insists on. It is helpful in identity-statements, but only if it is not mistaken for the determinant.

§ 22. The 'simple rule' helps determine what is meant by 'user/producer' on different occasions by appeal to the reference of *I*; it does not do as advertised (i.e. determine what is meant by *I* on different occasions by appeal to the reference of 'user/producer').

3   Questions of Expression

§ 23. What characterizes the use of *I* to express thoughts? *Independence* answers: the fact that, in its central uses, one need not identify what is being referred to.

What does The Guarantee *explain?*

§ 38. Since arguments for *The Guarantee* depend on *Rule Theory*, they cannot explain security.

Is The Guarantee *supported?*

§ 39. Professed advocates support not *The Guarantee* (i.e. a semantic explanation) but an epistemological or pragmatic explanation of security.

§ 40. Why Strawson's argument fails to give a semantic explanation of security.

Why has The Guarantee *seemed convincing?*

§ 41. Any pragmatic explanation of security based on *Rule Theory* will fail through indeterminacy; hence *Purism* is forced to accept a semantic explanation (*The Guarantee*) and thus threaten the default claim.

§ 42. If *Purism* is renounced, security can be explained pragmatically and consistently with the default claim. *I* is a *Deictic Term*; this is the fact which accounts for its logical character.

5 Interim Conclusion

Summary

§ 43. *I* is a singular term and a variant device; it is not a proper name, descriptive term, or *Pure Indexical*. The three doctrines are false.

Purism

§ 44. A craving for simplicity explains the almost-universal support for *Purism*, though it is a contradictory position founded on false doctrines.

An alternative conception

§ 45. *Purism* is false for reasons that create a presumption in favour of a sharply diverging conception: that *I* is a *Deictic Term*. So we now need to ask what a *Deictic Term* is, and whether *I* counts as one. This requires investigation into the logical character, inferential role, referential function, and expressive use of such terms.

PART II: THE MEANING OF *I*

6 Logical Character

§ 46. Some one-off devices have obligatory anaphoric reference (e.g. *The Former; The Latter*); some are free (e.g. *He/She*); some have obligatory deictic reference. *I* falls into this third category (together with *You*).

How I *behaves in substitution instances*

§ 47. Substitution instances reveal the obligatory deictic reference of *I*.

§ 61. There is no more to referential function than answering this question; i.e. achieving *determinacy* of reference. In particular, it need not ensure that anyone *knows* what that answer is; i.e. achieving *discriminability* of reference.

What demonstration is

§ 62. Different singular terms fulfil their referential function in different ways; *Deictic Terms* provide no answer prior to their use.

§ 63. If *Deictic Terms* fulfilled their referential function by demonstration, that would account for their differences from other terms. Demonstration is a certain kind of ostensive gesture, distinguished by its referential function from gesticulation, dumb show, and iconic form.

Why demonstration is not the determinant

§ 64. *Deictic Terms* can fulfil their referential function without appeal to demonstration; e.g. by utterance-relative uniqueness.

§ 65. Leading candidacy, given the surrounding discourse or perceptual environment, is another alternative to demonstration.

§ 66. So demonstration is not the determinant of *Deictic Terms*.

9   Referential Function (II)

What is distinctive about Deictic Terms

§ 67. What is distinctive about *Deictic Terms* must be the generic concept to which demonstration, utterance-relative uniqueness, and (intra- or extra-discursive) leading candidature belong as species.

§ 68. It is distinctive of *Deictic Terms* that they fulfil their referential role by action.

§ 69. Specifically, it is the action of making an individual salient. This is the generic concept. Salience is the determinant of *Deictic Terms*.

What referential salience is

§ 70. Referential salience—making an individual stand out in relation to the use of a referring term—is a broad-spectrum concept. It is not a matter of degree.

§ 71. Nor is it relative to observation. This gives application of the concept sufficient determinacy to count as the determinant of a specific class of singular terms; i.e. *Deictic Terms*.

How the reference of I *is determined*

§ 72. *I* fulfils its referential role by action.

§ 73. Uttering, writing, playing back recordings are the species but not the generic concept.

§ 74. The action of making an individual salient is the generic concept.

§ 75. Salience is sufficient to determine the reference of *I*; it is the determinant of the term. Hence *I* refers in the deictic way. This provides substance for the pragmatic explanation of why uses of *I* are secure against reference-failure.

What communicative role requires

§ 88. The discriminability of an *I*-use is that of a *Deictic Term*; it requires attention to the circumstances of use and will often depend on demonstration.

What roles demonstration plays

§ 89. Confusion about the roles demonstrations play is the major source of confusion about *Deictic Terms* generally and *I* in particular.

§ 90. Summary review of the roles demonstrations play in referential function, expressive use, and communicative role.

§ 91. There is no standard role for demonstration; it does not accompany every deictic use; it plays the same roles for *I* as for other *Deictic Terms*; it has the same general form for *I* as for other *Deictic Terms*; interpreting it is no more complex for *I* than for other *Deictic Terms*.

Why the attentive tasks can be easy

§ 92. In the usual case of *I*-use, where the attentive tasks are easy, the referent is not only a corporeal object and easily perceptible as such, but is the reference-maker and the individual thought about. So ease would be explained if one could be perceptually aware of oneself as a corporeal object engaging in action and as the subject of that awareness.

§ 93. This form of awareness is common. We are proprioceptively aware of our corporeality in exercising it. It eases the attentive task (for discriminability, expressive use, and communicative role) whenever the reference-maker is proprioceptively aware of the salience of a deictic referent.

§ 94. Proprioceptive awareness also makes identifying several uses of *I* as co-referential peculiarly straightforward. So it also explains attentive ease in the exercise of *I*'s inferential role. Keeping track.

§ 95. We are commonly perceptually aware of ourselves as corporeal objects engaging in action and as the subject of that awareness.

§ 96. Introspective self-awareness can count as perceptual awareness of oneself as a corporeal object.

§ 97. This provides substance for the pragmatic explanation of why uses of *I* can express thoughts when there is no likelihood of misidentifying what one has thought about.

§ 98. Attentive ease is not restricted to *I*; it occurs whenever the reference-maker is proprioceptively aware of the salience of a deictic referent. So it occurs also with some uses of *This Body, This Speaker, This F* (where F denotes a body part of which one is proprioceptively aware).

§ 99. It is as the individual made salient that one must identify oneself in order to express one's thoughts using *I* and make them communicable; hence *I* is a *Deictic Term* in its communicative role.

12 Conclusion

§ 100. Our findings force us to renounce at each point earlier conceptions of *I*, and in particular that which currently prevails.

Appendix 2

Recurrent Terms of Art

General

Referent   What a referring expression refers to on an occasion of use.

Content   What any use of a referring expression contributes to the meaning of the whole sentence in which it occurs.

Determinant Whatever determines (fixes) the reference of the uses of a referring term; it may include:

Context   the possible occasions of use of a referring expression.

Definition   the linguistic meaning of a referring expression.

Demonstration an ostensive gesture with a referential function.

Part I

(PI1)   If *R* is a singular referring expression whose referents are dependent on context, whose meaning is a rule-like definition, and whose definition-in-context is a determinant, then *R* is an *Indexical Term*.

(PI2)   If *R* is an Indexical Term whose definition-in-context is sufficient determinant, then *R* is a *Pure Indexical*.

(PI3)   If *R* is an Indexical Term whose definition-in-context is not sufficient determinant and which requires demonstration as a determinant, then *R* is an *Impure Indexical* (*Deictic Term*).

Rule Theory *I* is a *Pure Indexical*; its meaning is a 'simple rule' (e.g. 'any use of I refers to whoever uses it').

Independence *I* can be used to express thoughts about an individual (oneself) without having to identify what is being referred to.

The Guarantee All uses of *I* are logically guaranteed against failure to refer; security is a semantic truth.

Purism   The composite of *Rule Theory*, *Independence*, and *The Guarantee*.

PART II

Determinacy of reference	The use of a singular term has determinate reference (i.e. it refers) if and only if it provides a positive answer to the 'which?' question (i.e. 'which individual is being spoken of, written about, etc?').
Discriminability of reference	The use of a singular term is discriminable to some individual, A, if and only if A knows the answer to the 'which?' question.
Referential function	The use of a singular term fulfils its referential function if and only if its reference is determinate.
Referential salience	An individual, a, is referentially salient if and only if a is made to stand out by, and in relation to, the use of a referring term.
Anaphora	One singular term a is anaphorically dependent on another such term b (its source) if and only if a refers to whatever b refers to in a systematic way and with this implication: a's contribution to the truth-conditions of the whole sentence in which a occurs is not evaluable from a's immediate sentential context alone, but depends on evaluation of the context in which b occurs.
Deictic terms	A class of variant expressions with deictic uses. For deictic uses of such terms to refer, their referents must be referentially salient in the extra-sentential context. The inferential role of such uses is irreducible. It is by virtue of singling out objects made salient in the extra-sentential context that they contribute systematically to what entails what. Such terms fulfil their referential function by making an individual referentially salient. Their discriminability, expressive use, and communicative role depend on identifying the individual made referentially salient, which in turn requires attentiveness to the circumstances of use.

References

ALMOG, J., PERRY, J., and WETTSTEIN, H. (eds.) (1989), *Themes from Kaplan* (Oxford: Oxford University Press).

ANSCOMBE, G. E. M. (1975), 'The First Person', reprinted in Cassam (1994: 140–59).

ARISTOTLE (1985), *Nichomachean Ethics*, tr. T. Irwin (Indianapolis: Hackett Publishing Co.).

BACH, K. (1987), *Thought and Reference*, reprinted with postscript (Oxford: Oxford University Press, 1994).

—— (1992), 'Intentions and Demonstrations', *Analysis*, 52: 7–11.

BARWISE, J., and PERRY, J. (1981), 'Situations and Attitudes', *Journal of Philosophy*, 78: 668–91.

BECKETT, S. (1952), *L'Innomable*, trans. S. Beckett (London: John Calder Publications, 1959).

BERKELEY, G. (1734a), *Three Dialogues between Hylas and Philonous*, ed. J. Dancy (Oxford: Oxford University Press, 1998).

—— (1734b), *A Treatise Concerning the Principles of Human Knowledge*, ed. J. Dancy (Oxford: Oxford University Press, 1988).

BERMÚDEZ, J. L. (1998), *The Paradox of Self-Consciousness* (Cambridge, Mass.: MIT Press).

—— MARCEL, A., and EILAN, N. (eds.) (1995), *The Body and the Self* (Cambridge, Mass.: MIT Press).

BRANDOM, R. (1994), *Making it Explicit* (London: Harvard University Press).

—— (1997), 'Precis of *Making it Explicit*', *Philosophy and Phenomenological Research*, 153–6.

BRAUN, D. (1996), 'Demonstratives and their Linguistic Meanings', *Noûs*, 30: 145–73.

BREWER, M. W. (1992), 'Self-Location and Agency', *Mind*, 101: 17–34.

—— (1995), 'Learning from Experience', *Mind and Language*, 10: 181–93.

BRINCK, I. (1997), *The Indexical 'I'* (Dordrecht: Kluwer).

BROOK, A. (1994), *Kant and the Mind* (Cambridge: Cambridge University Press).

BROWN, P. (1978), *The Making of Late Antiquity* (London: Harvard University Press).

BÜHLER, K. (1982), 'The Deictic Field of Language and Deictic Words', in R. J. Jarvella and W. Klein (eds.), *Speech, Place and Action: Studies in Deixis and Related Topics* (Chichester: John Wiley), 9–30.

BURGE, T. (1992), 'Philosophy of Language and Mind: 1950–1990', *Philosophical Review*, 101: 3–51.

CAMPBELL, J. (1994), *Past, Space and Self* (Cambridge, Mass.: MIT Press).

CARUAP, R. (1937), *The Logical Syntax of Language*, tr. A. Smeaton (London: Kegan Paul).

CASSAM, Q. (1993), 'Parfit on Persons', *Proceedings of the Aristotelian Society*, 93: 17–37.

—— (ed.) (1994), *Self-Knowledge* (Oxford: Oxford University Press).

—— (1995), 'Introspection and Bodily Self-Ascription', in Bermúdez, Marcel, and Eilan (1995: 311–36).

—— (1997), *Self and World* (Oxford: Oxford University Press).

CASTAÑEDA, H.-N. (1966), ' "He": A Study in the Logic of Self-Consciousness', *Ratio*, 8: 130–57.

—— (1968), 'On the Phenomeno-Logic of the I', reprinted in Cassam (1994: 160–6).

—— (1999), *The Phenomeno-Logic of I* (Indianapolis: Indiana University Press).

CHARLES, D., and LENNON, K. (eds.) (1992), *Reduction, Explanation and Realism* (Oxford: Oxford University Press).

COHEN, L. J. (1992), *An Essay on Belief and Acceptance* (Oxford: Oxford University Press).

CORAZZA, E. (2002), '*She* and *He*: Politically Correct Pronouns', *Philosophical Studies*, 111: 173–96.

—— FISH, W., and CORVETT, J. (2002), 'Who is I?', *Philosophical Studies*, 107: 1–21.

CORNISH, F. (1999), *Anaphora, Discourse, and Understanding* (Oxford: Oxford University Press).

CRIMMINS, M. (1995), 'Contextuality, Reflexivity, Iteration and Logic', in J. Tomberlin (ed.), *Philosophical Perspectives*, 9 (Atascadero, Calif.: Ridgeview), 381–99.

CRISP, R. (1997), *Mill on Utilitarianism* (London: Routledge).

DANCY, J. (2000), *Practical Reality* (Oxford: Oxford University Press).

DAVIDSON, D. (1984), *Inquiries into Truth and Interpretation*, (Oxford: Oxford University Press).

DESCARTES, R. (1984), *The Philosophical Writings of Descartes* (vols. i–iii), trans. J. Cottingham, R. Stoothoff, D. Murdoch, and (vol. iii) A. Kenny (Cambridge: Cambridge University Press, 1984–91).

DEVITT, M. (1989), 'Against Direct Reference', *Midwest Studies in Philosophy*, 14: 206–40.

DIAMOND, C., and TEICHMAN, J. (eds.) (1979), *Intention and Intentionality* (Brighton: Harvester Press).

DONNELLAN, K. (1966), 'Reference and Definite Descriptions', *Philosophical Review*, 75: 281–304.

DUMMETT, M. (1981), *Frege: Philosophy of Language*, 2nd edn. (London: Duckworth).

EILAN, N., McCARTHY, R. A., and BREWER, M. W. (eds.) (1993), *Spatial Representation: Problems in Philosophy and Psychology* (Oxford: Blackwell).

EVANS, G. (1982), *The Varieties of Reference*, ed. J. H. McDowell (Oxford: Oxford University Press).

—— (1985), *Collected Papers*, ed. A. Phillips (Oxford: Oxford University Press).

FEIGL, H., and SCRIVEN, M. (eds.) (1956), *Minnesota Studies in the Philosophy of Science*, vol. i (Minneapolis: University of Minnesota Press).

FREGE, G. (1891), 'Function and Concept', trans. P. T. Geach, in Geach and Black (1980: 21–41).

—— (1892*a*), 'On Concept and Object', trans. P. T. Geach, in Geach and Black (1980: 42–55).

—— (1892*b*), 'On Sense and Meaning', trans. Max Black, in Geach and Black (1980: 56–78).

—— (1918), 'The Thought: A Logical Inquiry', trans. A. and M. Quinton, in Strawson (1967: 17–38).

GARCIA-CARPINTERO, M. (1998), 'Indexicals as Token-Reflexives', *Mind*, 107: 529–63.

GAYNESFORD, R. M. DE (1996*a*), 'How Wrong Can One Be?', *Proceedings of the Aristotelian Society*, 96: 387–94.

—— (1996*b*), 'Critical Notice of John McDowell, *Mind and World*', *Australasian Journal of Philosophy*, 74: 495–509.

GAYNESFORD, R. M. DE (1997*a*), 'First-Personal Thinking' (doctoral thesis).

—— (1997*b*), 'Critical Notice of J. L. Bermudez, A Marcel, and N. Eilan (eds.), *The Body and the Self*, *Ratio*, 10: 91–6.

—— (1998), 'On Referring to Oneself', *Theoria*, 70 (2004), 121–61.

—— (2001), 'Object Dependence in Language and Thought', *Language and Communication*, 21: 183–207.

—— (2002), 'Corporeal Objects and the Interdependence of Action and Perception', *Ratio*, 15: 335–53.

GAYNESFORD, R. M. DE (2003*a*), 'Kant and Strawson on the First Person', in Hans-Johann Glock (ed.), *Strawson and Kant* (Oxford: Oxford University Press), 155–67.

—— (2003*b*), 'Is *I* Guaranteed to Refer?', *Pacific Philosophical Quarterly*, 138–56.

GEACH, P. T. (1957), 'On Beliefs about Oneself', *Analysis*, 18: 23–4.

—— (1972), *Logic Matters* (Oxford: Blackwell).

—— and BLACK, M. (eds.) (1980), *Translations from the Philosophical Writings of Gottlob Frege*, 3rd edn. (Oxford: Blackwell).

GLOCK, H.-J., and HACKER, P. (1996), 'Reference and the First Person Pronoun', *Language and Communication*, 18: 95–105.

GODWIN, W. (1798), *An Enquiry Concerning Political Justice, and its Influence on General Virtue and Happiness* (Harmondsworth: Penguin, 1976).

GOLDIN-MEADOW, S., and MYLANDER, C. (1984), 'Gestural Communication in Deaf Children: The Effects and Non-Effects of Parental Input on Early Language Development', *Monographs of the Society for Research in Child Development*, 49 (serial no. 207).

GRICE, P. (1961), 'The Causal Theory of Perception', in J. Dancy (ed.), *Perceptual Knowledge* (Oxford: Oxford University Press, 1988), 66–78.

—— (1989), *Studies in the Way of Words* (London: Harvard University Press).

HACKER, P. M. S. (1993), *Wittgenstein: Meaning and Mind* (Oxford: Blackwell, 1990; rev. (paperback) edn., vol. i, 1993).

HAMMETT, D. (2002), *The Maltese Falcon* (London: Orion Books).

HEAL, J. (1996), 'Critical Notice of John Campbell (1994)', *Philosophical Books*, 37: 14–21.

HEIM, I., and KRATZER, A. (1998), *Semantics in Generative Grammar* (Oxford: Blackwell).

HOFFMAN, J., and ROSENKRANTZ, G. (1997), *Substance* (London: Routledge).

HUME, D. (1739), *A Treatise of Human Nature*, ed. L. A. Selby-Bigge and P. H. Nidditch (Oxford: Oxford University Press, 1978).

JAMES, W. (1891), *The Principles of Psychology*, reprinted (Cambridge, Mass.: Harvard University Press, 1981).

KANT, I. (1787), *Critique of Pure Reason*, trans. Norman Kemp Smith, 2nd impression (London: Macmillan, 1933).

KAPLAN, D. (1989), 'Demonstratives' and 'Afterthoughts', in Almog, Perry, and Wettstein (1989: 481–614).

KATZ, J. J. (1990), 'Descartes' *Cogito*', in Yourgrau (1990: 154–81).

KENNY, A. (1989), *The Metaphysics of Mind* (Oxford: Oxford University Press).

KLAGGE, J., and NORDMANN, A. (eds.) (1993), *Ludwig Wittgenstein: Philosophical Occasions 1912–51* (Indianapolis: Hackett).

KRIPKE, S. (1972), *Naming and Necessity*, enlarged edn. (Oxford: Blackwell, 1980).

LARSON, R., and SEGAL, G. (1995), *Knowledge of Meaning* (Cambridge, Mass.: MIT Press).

LASNIK, H. (1976), 'Remarks on Coreference', *Linguistic Analysis*, 2: 1–22.

LEIBNIZ, G. W. (1686), *Philosophical Writings*, ed. G. H. R. Parkinson (London: Dent, 1973).

LEWIS, D. (1983), *Philosophical Papers* (Oxford: Oxford University Press).

—— (1998), *Papers in Philosophical Logic* (Cambridge: Cambridge University Press).

LICHTENBERG, G. C. (1796), *Schriften und Briefe*, vol. ii, ed. W. Promies (Munich: Carl Hanser Verlag, 1971).

LOCKE, J. (1689), *An Essay concerning Human Understanding*, ed. P. H. Nidditch (Oxford: Oxford University Press, 1975).

LYONS, J. (1977), *Semantics II* (Cambridge: Cambridge University Press).

McDOWELL, J. H. (1986), 'Singular Thought and the Extent of Inner Space', in Pettit and McDowell (1986: 137–68).

—— (1990), 'Peacocke and Evans on Demonstrative Content', *Mind*, 99: 255–66.

—— (1944), *Mind and World* (London: Harvard University Press).

—— (1996), 'Reductionism and the First Person' in his *Mind, Value, and Reality* (London: Harvard University Press, 1998) 359–82.

—— (1997), Response to Brandom's *Making it Explicit*, *Philosophy and Phenomenological Research*, 157–62.

—— (1998), 'Referring to Oneself', in L. E. Hahn (ed.) The philosophy of P. F. Strawson (Chicago: open court), 129–45.

McNEILL, D. (ed.) (2000), *Language and Gesture* (Cambridge: Cambridge University Press).

McTAGGART, J. (1927), *The Nature of Existence* (Cambridge: Cambridge University Press).

MADELL, G. (1981), *The Identity of the Self* (Edinburgh: Edinburgh University Press).

MALCOLM, N. (1979), 'Whether *I* is a Referring Expression', in Diamond and Teichman (1979: 15–24).

MARTIN, M. G. F. (1995), 'Bodily Awareness', in J. L. Bermúdez, A. Marcel, and N. Eilan (eds.), *The Body and the Self* (Cambridge, Mass.: MIT Press), 267–89.

MARTIN, R. B. (1980), *Tennyson: The Unquiet Heart* (Oxford: Oxford University Press).

MELLOR, D. H. (1988), 'I and Now', *Proceedings of the Aristotelian Society*, 89: 79–94.

MILL, J. S. (1843), *A System of Logic* (London: Longmans, Green and Co Ltd., 1967).

MILLIKAN, R. G. (1993), *White Queen Psychology and Other Essays for Alice* (Cambridge, Mass.: MIT Press).

MORTON, A. (1999), 'Where Demonstratives Meet Vagueness', *Proceedings of the Aristotelian Society*, 1–18.

NIETZSCHE, F. (1968), *The Will to Power*, trans. W. Kaufman and R. J. Hollingdale (New York: Vintage Books).

NOZICK, R. (1981), *Philosophical Explanations* (Cambridge, Mass.: Harvard University Press).

NUNBERG, G. (1993), 'Indexicality and Deixis', *Linguistics and Philosophy*, 16: 1–43.

O'BRIEN, L. (1994), 'Anscombe and the Self-Reference Rule', *Analysis*, 54: 277–81.

—— (1995*a*), 'The Problem of Self-Identification', *Proceedings of the Aristotelian Society*, 95: 235–51.

—— (1995*b*), 'Evans on Self-Identification', *Noûs*, 29: 232–47.

O'SHAUGHNESSY, B. (1989), 'The Sense of Touch', *Australasian Journal of Philosophy*, 67: 37–58.

PARFIT, D. (1984), *Reasons and Persons* (Oxford: Oxford University Press, reprinted with corrections 1991).

—— (1997), 'Reasons and Motivation', *Proceedings of the Aristotelian Society,* 71: 99–130.

PEACOCKE, C. (1983), *Sense and Content* (Oxford: Oxford University Press).

PEARS, D. (1988), *The False Prison*, vols. i–ii (Oxford: Oxford University Press).

PELCZAR, M., and RAINSBURY, J. (1998), 'The Indexical Character of Names', *Synthese,* 114: 293–317.

PERRY, J. (1977), 'Frege on Demonstratives', reprinted in Yourgrau (1990: 50–70).

—— (1979), 'The Problem of the Essential Indexical', reprinted in Cassam (1994: 167–83).

—— (1997), 'Indexicals and Demonstratives', in Wright and Hale (1997: 586–612).

—— (2001), *Reference and Reflexivity* (Stanford, Calif.: CSLI Publications).

PERRY, J. (2002), *Identity, Personal Identity and the Self* (Indianapolis: Hackett Publishing Company).

PETTIT, P., and McDOWELL, J. (eds.) (1986), *Subject, Thought and Context* (Oxford: Oxford University Press).

PLATO (1973), *Theaetetus*, trans. J. H. McDowell (Oxford: Oxford University Press).

PREDELLI, S. (1998a), 'I am not here now', *Analysis,* 107–15.

—— (1998b), 'Utterance, Interpretation and the Logic of Indexicals', *Mind and Language,* 13: 400–14.

PROUST, M. (1913), *In Search of Lost Time*, vol. i, trans. C. K. Scott Moncreiff and T. Kilmartin, rev. D. J. Enright (London: Chatto & Windus).

PUTNAM, H. (1975), 'The Meaning of "Meaning" ', in his *Mind, Language and Reality* (Cambridge: Cambridge University Press), 215–71.

QUINE, W. V. O. (1953), *From a Logical Point of View* (London: Harvard University Press).

—— (1960), *Word and Object* (Cambridge, Mass.: MIT Press).

QUIRK, R., GREENBAUM, S., LEECH, G., and SVARTVIK, J. (1972), *A Grammar of Contemporary English* (London: Longman Group Ltd.).

RADFORD, A. (1997), *Syntactic Theory and the Structure of English: A Minimalist Approach* (Cambridge: Cambridge University Press).

RECANATI, F. (1993), *Direct Reference: From Language to Thought* (Oxford: Blackwell).

REICHENBACH, H. (1947), *Elements of Symbolic Logic* (London: Collier-Macmillan, 1966).

REIMER, M. (1991), 'Do Demonstrations have Semantic Significance?', *Analysis,* 51: 177–83.

RICHARD, M. (1993), 'Attitudes in Context', *Linguistics and Philosophy,* 16: 123–48.

ROBERTS, G. W. (ed.) (1979), *Bertrand Russell Memorial Volume* (London: George Allen & Unwin).

ROVANE, C. (1987), 'The Epistemology of First-Person Reference', *Journal of Philosophy,* 84: 147–67.

—— (1993), 'Self-Reference: The Radicalization of Locke', *Journal of Philosophy,* 90: 73–97.

—— (1998), *The Bounds of Agency* (Princeton: Princeton University Press).

RUSSELL, B. (1905), 'On Denoting', in Russell (1956: 41–56).

—— (1910), 'Knowledge by Acquaintance and Knowledge by Description', in Russell (1917: 209–32).

—— (1912), *The Problems of Philosophy* (Oxford: Oxford University Press).

—— (1914), 'On the Nature of Acquaintance', in Russell (1956: 125–74).

—— (1917), *Mysticism and Logic* (London: Longman, Green and Co.).

—— (1918), 'The Philosophy of Logical Atomism', in Russell (1956: 175–281).

—— (1956), *Logic and Knowledge*, ed. R. C. Marsh (London: G. Allen & Unwin Ltd.).

RYLE, G. (1951), 'Thinking and Language', *Proceedings of the Aristotelian Society*, 25: 65–82.

SEARLE, J. (1969), *Speech Acts* (Cambridge: Cambridge University Press).

SELLARS, W. (1953), 'Inference and Meaning', *Mind*, 62: 313–48.

—— (1954), 'Some Reflections on Language Games', in his *Science, Perception and Reality* (California: Ridgeview, 1991), 321–58.

—— (1956), 'Empiricism and the Philosophy of Mind', in Feigl and Scriven (1956: 253–329).

SHOEMAKER, S. (1963), *Self-Knowledge and Self-Identity* (London: Cornell University Press).

—— (1968), 'Self-Reference and Self-Awareness', reprinted in Cassam (1994: 80–93).

—— (1970), 'Persons and their Pasts', *American Philosophical Quarterly*, 7: 269–85.

—— (1986), 'Introspection and the Self', reprinted in Cassam (1994: 118–39).

—— (1994), 'Self-Knowledge and "Inner Sense" ', *Philosophy and Phenomenological Research*, 54: 249–314.

—— (1996), *The First-Person Perspective and Other Essays* (Cambridge: Cambridge University Press).

SIDELLE, A. (1991), 'The Answering Machine Paradox', *Canadian Journal of Philosophy*, 81: 525–39.

SMITH, M. (1994), *The Moral Problem* (Oxford: Blackwell).

SOAMES, S. (1989), 'Critical Notice of Gareth Evans, *Collected Papers*', *Journal of Philosophy*, 89: 141–56.

—— (2002), *Beyond Rigidity* (Oxford: Oxford University Press).

SPERBER, D., and WILSON, D. (1995), *Relevance*, 2nd edn. (Oxford: Blackwell).

STALNAKER, R. (1999), *Context and Content* (Oxford: Oxford University Press).

STRAWSON, P. F. (1950), 'On Referring', reprinted in his *Logico-Linguistic Papers* (London: Methuen and Co. Ltd., 1971), 1–27.

—— (1959), *Individuals* (London: Methuen and Co. Ltd.).

—— (1966), *The Bounds of Sense* (London: Methuen and Co. Ltd.).

—— (ed.) (1967), *Philosophical Logic* (Oxford: Oxford University Press).

—— (1994), 'The First Person—and Others', in Cassam (1994: 210–15).

—— (1998), 'Reply to John McDowell', in L. E. Hahn (ed.), *The Philosophy of P. F. Strawson* (Chicago: Open Court), 146–50.

VALLÉE, R. (1996), 'Who are we?', *Canadian Journal of Philosophy*, 26: 211–30.

VESEY, G. (1979), 'Self-Acquaintance and the Meaning of *I*', in Roberts (1979: 339–47).

WHITE, A. R. (1964), *Attention* (Oxford: Blackwell).

WILLIAMS, B. (1978), *Descartes* (Harmondsworth: Penguin).

WITTGENSTEIN, L. (1916), *Notebooks 1914–16*, ed. G. H. von Wright and G. E. M. Anscombe, trans. G. E. M. Anscombe (Oxford: Blackwell, 1961).

—— (1921), *Tractatus Logico-Philosophicus*, trans. D. F. Pears and B. F. McGuinness (London: Routledge & Kegan Paul, 1961).

—— (1930), *Philosophical Remarks*, ed. R. Rhees, trans. R. Hargreaves and R. White (Oxford: Blackwell).

WITTGENSTEIN, L. (1933), 'Wittgenstein's Lectures in 1930–33', G. E. Moore, in Klagge and Nordmann (1993: 46–114).

—— (1936), 'Notes for Lectures on "Private Experience" and "Sense Data" ', in Klagge and Nordman (1993: 202–88).

—— (1958), *Philosophical Investigations*, trans. G. E. M. Anscombe (Oxford: Blackwell).

—— (1969), *The Blue and Brown Books*, 2nd edn. (Oxford: Blackwell).

—— (1993), 'Wittgenstein's Lectures in 1930–33', G. E. Moore, in J. Klagge and A. Nordmann (eds.), *Ludwig Wittgenstein: Philosophical Occasions 1912–51* (Indianapolis: Hackett), 46–114.

WOODS, M. (1968), 'Reference and Self-Identification', *Journal of Philosophy*, 65: 568–78.

WRIGHT, C., and HALE, B. (eds.) (1997), *A Companion to the Philosophy of Language* (Oxford: Blackwell).

YOURGRAU, P. (ed.) (1990), *Demonstratives* (Oxford: Oxford University Press).

Index